W9-CBW-067

Data Base: Structured Techniques for Design, Performance, and Management

Data Base: Structured Techniques for Design, Performance, and Management

with Case Studies

S. Atre

IBM Corporation
Formerly IBM Systems Research Institute
Lecturer in Computer Science
Polytechnic Institute of New York
Adjunct Associate Professor
Iona College, New Rochelle, New York

A Wiley-Interscience Publication
JOHN WILEY & SONS
New York · Chichester · Brisbane · Toronto · Singapore

This publication is designed to provide accurate and
authoritative information in regard to the subject
matter covered. It is sold with the understanding that
the publisher is not engaged in rendering legal, accounting,
or other professional service. If legal advice or other
expert assistance is required, the services of a competent
professional person should be sought. *From a Declaration
of Principles jointly adopted by a Committee of the
American Bar Association and a Committee of Publishers.*

Library of Congress Cataloging in Publication Data

Atre, S

    Data Base: Structured Techniques for Design,
        Performance, and Management

    (Business data processing ISSN 0193-9734)
    "A Wiley-Interscience publication."
    Includes index.
    1. Data base management. 2. Data base management
—Case studies. I. Title.

QA76.9.D3A9   001.64   80-14808
ISBN 0-471-05267-1

Printed in the United States of America

10 9 8 7 6 5

To Tante Lisel

Preface

We are reaching the stage where the problems that we must solve are going to become insoluble without computers. I do not fear computers. I fear the lack of them.

Isaac Asimov

The computer revolution promises to simplify, ease, and otherwise enhance life in ways undreamed of even by the Utopians. In organizations of all kinds, the computer stores and retrieves vast amounts of information. The volume of data processed in all types of industries, medical services, financial institutions, and governmental agencies is expanding geometrically, and it is very difficult to imagine how these organizations would function without computers. Organizations of various natures are called "enterprises."

The repository of information, called a "data base," is the foundation of the entire computer system for an enterprise. Thus the design and the performance of the data base are perhaps two of the most important areas in information processing.

Although several articles and books have been published that give scholarly treatment to this area, or give survey information regarding existing data base management systems and data models, few offer specific answers to these questions:

1. What are the responsibilities of the people involved?
2. How can a data base that will satisfy performance criteria be designed?
3. What problems may arise in different phases?

This book is intended to fill the need for this and related information. It demonstrates the principles for designing a data base that will achieve the functions and performance needed to satisfy the requirements of the information processing environment. It addresses the roles of the data base administrators, systems programmers, systems analysts, application programmers, information processing managers, data processing managers, and data base users. The material is simple without becoming simplistic and shows a step-by-step approach to data base design. The chapters are organized so that data base designers can follow their sequence during the process of designing a data base. The methodology is independent of any software package; it does not concentrate on any one manufacturer's data base management system.

This book can be used effectively by practitioners in business as well as in government, and also as a single-semester course in a business or technical school where students are interested in the "how to" as well as the "why" of information processing approaches.

A case study approach has been adopted. A case study for designing a data base for a banking environment is carried through from the very beginning to the end in Appendix A. In Appendix B a case study of a university environment is presented in its entirety. The step-by-step approach to designing a data base and the application of this approach to the two case studies are major features of the book.

The material presented was developed in the courses that I have taught for a number of years at IBM's Systems Research Institute. A version of the manuscript was used as a text in a course with the same title, "Data Base: Structured Techniques for Design, Performance, and Management." Portions were presented at various professional seminars, including local chapter meetings of the Association for Computing Machinery (ACM) and the Data Processing Management Association (DPMA). Questions and suggestions from students and colleagues helped to make the material more timely and digestible, while the overall enthusiastic response at these lectures led to the decision to present the material as a book.

The book is divided into three parts, each consisting of a number of chapters. Part I, "Data Base Administration," deals with installing and maintaining a data base. The first chapter sets the stage by discussing the issues that will be treated later. Chapter 2 describes the function of the data base administrator (DBA) and the roles that the DBA and his/her staff play in the information processing system. The third chapter, titled "Data Dictionary," discusses a valuable tool for collecting information about the data base environment.

Part II, "Data Base Design (Conceptual Model and Logical Model)," demonstrates the conceptual and logical data base design process. The fourth chapter creates the basis of any data base management system—the data models. A brief treatment is given of three popular approaches—the relational, hierarchical, and network data models. Chapter 5 describes the design process for developing a conceptual model. Chapter 6 gives the design process for a logical model. Both chapters demonstrate the techniques in detail, with specific examples.

Part III, "Data Base Performance," describes the equally important aspects of the performance of information processing with the data base. The main emphasis is on how to design for good performance, that is, how to optimize the design. Chapter 7 reviews data access techniques, which are key issues of performance. The eighth chapter presents some implementations of these access methods. Chapter 9 discusses the data base design of a physical model with the estimation of space and time. Chapter 10 treats specific performance problems in the design phase, implementation phase, and operations phase.

Appendix A demonstrates a case study of a banking environment. Appendix B contains a case study of a university environment. Finally, Appendix C gives the basic concepts of probability theory and mathematical statistics used in Chapter 9.

And now only the pleasant task of acknowledging my students, friends, and colleagues remains. I am grateful to the numerous students who patiently read the manuscript and made many constructive comments. I also want to thank Charles Bontempo, Robert Bower, Gary D. Bowers, Robert G. Brown, George T. Fadok, Joan Foster, Ron Gale, George Hubbard, Judy King, Barry Kingsbury, Frank Post, Jay Schmoll, Cora Tangney, and everyone else who helped along the way.

S. ATRE

New York, New York
July 1980

Contents

Data Base: Structured Techniques for Design, Performance, and Management

Data

One of the foundations of an enterprise is the information needed for its survival and prosperity. This chapter indicates where this information comes from and how data processing requirements for using the information caused data base systems to evolve. One of the desirable characteristics of a successful data base is flexibility. Flexibility makes a data base less sensitive to changes in information processing requirements. This chapter discusses the issues regarding flexibility and gives a preview of the steps involved in designing a data base to provide adequate performance.

1.1 SOURCES OF DATA

The processing of information has been one of the basic tasks in any civilization. Because of economic and population growth, there are ever increasing needs to administer large quantities of interrelated data for commercial and administrative purposes. The interrelated data taken together is called a *system*. Any system that will create important simplifications in human affairs is likely to need a very complex model of the real world, in addition to other conventional forms of knowledge.

The heart of any information system is its stored data. For an enterprise, the data usually crosses the boundaries of different divisions. For example, management decisions often need information from across the enterprise. For decisions on manufacturing processes, it is necessary to have inventory information, as well as orders received, sales strategy, and so forth. This means that the data spanning the enterprise should be stored in an easily and readily accessible form.

In the early days of electronic data processing, data was stored on paper tapes and punched cards. Hardware equipment could read the tapes and cards. Application programs were written to process the data and transform it into reports. Compilers were used to translate the application programs from source language into machine instructions. To coordinate the electronic data processing, operating systems evolved. As the years passed, the operating systems, compilers, equipment, and procedures used to operate the electronic data processing system became increasingly sophisticated.

The basic goals, however, remained the same. Today the data processing system may be an old fashioned one with a clerk entering the data manually in a binder, or it may be a modern one with the fastest computers and the most sophisticated hardware and software available. The basic goal is always to provide the correct information at the right time, to the right person, at the right place, and at the right cost. The enterprise may be a bank, a manufacturing plant, a utility company, a university, a hospital, a supermarket, a department store, or an agricultural farm, to name just a few.

To understand electronic data processing, it is necessary to know some of the terms used to describe data and its representation.

1.1.1 Enterprise

An *enterprise* is any kind of organization such as a bank, a university, a manufacturing plant, or a hospital.

A problem arises here in distinguishing between a total enterprise (e.g., a big corporation such as an automobile manufacturer, computer manufacturer, chemical concern, or steel manufacturer) and an organizational unit of a big corporation. The organizational unit may represent an enterprise in its own right (e.g., a body manufacturing division of a big automobile manufacturer, or a data processing division of a computer manufacturer). In a situation like this, the divisions themselves may be called enterprises and regarded as such.

A number of enterprises may require information about one or more of the following functions: personnel, payroll, inventories, purchase orders, accounts receivable, sales reports, laboratory tests, course enrollments, financial transactions, medical history reports. The information concerning these items is about a person, place, thing, event, or concept.

1.1.2 Entity

An *entity* is a person, place, thing, event, or concept about which information is recorded.

In a banking environment examples of entities are CUSTOMERS, BANK ACCOUNTS, and MORTGAGE LOANS. In a warehouse the entities are SUPPLIERS, PARTS, SHIPMENTS, and the like.

1.1.3 Attributes (or Data Elements)

Every entity has some basic *attributes* that characterize it. A house can be described by its size, color, age, and surroundings. A customer of a bank may be described by such attributes as name, address, and possibly a customer identification number. A bank account can be represented by an account type, an account number, and an account balance. Customer identification number, customer name, and customer address are three attributes describing the entity "CUSTOMER" of a bank (see Figure 1.1). An attribute is often called a data element, a data field, a field, a data item, or an elementary item.

1.1.4 Data Value

A *data value* is the actual data or information contained in each data element. The data element "customer name" can take values like "Prof. Higgins" and "Mark Twain." The values taken by the data elements can be quantitative, qualitative, or descriptive, depending on how the data elements describe an entity. Figure 1.1 shows the

Entity	Attributes (or Data Elements)	Values (Data)
CUSTOMER	Customer identification number ⟶	123456789
	Customer name ⟶	Prof. Higgins
	Customer address ⟶	55 Snow Street New York, N.Y.
ACCOUNT	Account type ⟶	Checking
	Account number ⟶	634250
	Account balance ⟶	20.53
SUPPLIER	Supplier name ⟶	William Shakespeare
	Supplier number ⟶	S1
	Supplier address ⟶	100 Book Street New York, N.Y.

Figure 1.1 The information about an enterprise can be represented with the help of a number of entities, and an individual entity can be represented by a number of data elements. The values taken by the data elements are referred to as data.

difference between entities, data elements, and values taken by the data elements.

The information about an enterprise can be represented with the help of a number of entities, and an individual entity can be represented by a number of data elements. The values taken by the data elements are referred to as data. One set of values taken by the data elements of an entity is called an entity occurrence. The entities are interconnected by certain relationships. An inherent model of the entities with the data elements representing them, together with the relationships interconnecting the entities, is called a *conceptual model*. The conceptual model gives an overall view of the flow of the data in the enterprise.

The discussion of "data" is frequently confused by a failure to distinguish between the entity, the data element, and the value taken by the data element. In referring to a customer there is an entity CUSTOMER, there are some data elements that represent the customer (e.g., the customer identification number, the customer name, and the customer address), and there are values taken by the data elements, such as "123456789," "Prof. Higgins," and "55 Snow Street, New York, N.Y." It is important to distinguish between the *entity*, the *data element*, and the *value* taken by the data element.

1.1.5 Key Data Element

Some data elements have the property that, knowing the value taken by a particular data element of an entity, we can identify the values taken by other data elements of the same entity. By knowing the customer identification number "123456789," we can determine that the person in question is "Prof. Higgins" and that Professor Higgins has a "checking" account at the bank. These data elements, from which we can infer other data elements, are called *key data elements*. Key data elements can also be called entity identifiers.

It is possible that there are two or more data elements which can uniquely identify an entity. In that case we call those data elements "candidates" for becoming key data elements. Someone (the user or designer) decides which one of the candidates is to be used to access the entity. The designation of key data elements should be done very carefully because the right selection may help one to design the conceptual model correctly.

1.1.6 Data Record

A *data record* is a collection of values taken by related data elements. In Figure 1.2, the data elements are customer name, customer identification number, account type, . . . , remarks. One of the data records is "Prof. Higgins 123456789 Checking . . . Notify Customer Tel. 555-1234." The values taken by the data elements are for the entities CUSTOMER, ACCOUNT, and TRANSACTION. These values form the data records. The data records are stored on some medium. The medium can be a human brain, a piece of paper, a memory of a computer, or an auxiliary storage device of a computer such as a tape, disk, or drum, to name just a few examples.

1.1.7 Data File

The data records form a *data file:* a data file is thus a collection of data records. In Figure 1.2, "Branch Manager's Report (Exception)" is an example of a data file in printed form. It contains data records that are identical, that is, are of the same type. A data file of this type, where all the records are alike (i.e., are made up of the

Entity CUSTOMER | **Entity ACCOUNT** | **Entity TRANSACTION**

Branch Number: 1234
Branch Name: Downtown Branch
Branch Address: 1 First Street, New York, N.Y. 10001
Manager's Name: ABC
Report for: January 10, 1980

Date: January 11, 1980

Customer Name	Customer Identification Number	Account Type	Account Number	Amount Involved	Date of Transaction	Time of Transaction	Transaction Code	Reason Code	Action Code	Remarks
Prof. Higgins	123456789	Checking	653210	268.50	1/10/80	10:15:20	Check withdraw	Checking over-drawn	Auto-matic loan	Notify customer Tel. 555-1234
Zalaf, Amir	345678901	Savings	12345—1	10,000.00	1/10/80	15:02:10	Check deposit	Savings exceeds 100,000 limit	No deposit	Send back check and inform customer

A Data Element

A "Value" of the Data Element

A Data Record

A Data File

• Values taken by the data elements form a data record.

same number of data elements), is called a "flat" file. A data file may also consist of heterogeneous types of data records, that is, it may contain records of different types. A data file is also called a file or a data set.

1.2 DATA FILE ENVIRONMENT

Sources of data are the basic necessities of information processing in an enterprise. Some examples of enterprises and their sources of data are listed below.

Environment	Sources of Data
Brokerage firms	Stock activities, historical trends of the stock market
Manufacturing companies	Inventories
Airlines	Flights, crews, passengers, reservations, maintenance, inventory
Police precincts	Criminal patterns, types of crime
Hospitals	Patient medical records, bed utilization, billing, inventory of supplies
Insurance companies	Policyholder vitae, claims, premiums
Universities	Student records, courses offered, degree requirements, course schedulings
Banks	Checking accounts, savings accounts, installment loans, mortgage loans

The conventional data processing approach is to develop a program or a number of programs for each different application, for example, banking applications such as checking and savings accounts, installment loans, and mortgage loans. This results, most probably, in one or more data files for every application. This type of development is reflected in Figure 1.3.

Each application of the enterprise, such as checking, savings, installment loan, and mortgage loan, has its own "view of data." In the early days of data processing, every application programmer had to write the data file handling routines to add, delete, replace, and retrieve data from the data files associated with the programs. A big improvement was the advent of generalized routines.

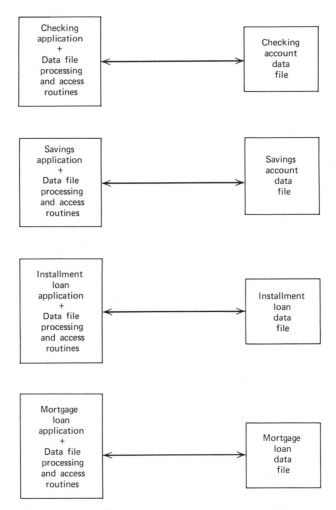

Figure 1.3 "Popular Bank." One-to-one correspondence between an application, its data file processing, its access routines, and a data file. In the early days of data processing, every application programmer had to write the data file handling routines to add, delete, replace, and retrieve data from the data files associated with the programs.

1.2.1 Advantages of Generalized Routines

The generalized routines provided predefined "access methods." These "methods" freed the application programmer from having to code, test, and "debug" methods specific to a particular application. The common access methods are thus generalized routines that add,

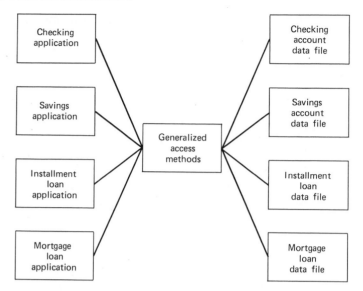

Figure 1.4 "Popular Bank." Generalized access methods can be used in place of individual data file handling routines. Every application programmer did not have to write the data file handling routines. But most generalized access methods do not allow other applications with different views of the common data to share and access that data. All users are constrained to a single view of the data.

delete, replace, and retrieve data from the auxiliary storage such as tape, disk, and drum. These access methods then become integral parts of the "operating systems."

Figure 1.4 shows that a checking application can be written to create or access a checking account data file using generalized access methods. However, most generalized access methods do not allow other applications with different views of the common data to share and access that data. All users are constrained to a single view of the data. Different views may be provided using various sorting techniques.

The access methods, or the generalized access routines, provide varying degrees of physical data storage independence, since some changes in physical storage can be reflected in the access methods without having to rewrite the application programs. In a later section we will see how the application programs can be detached further from the physical characteristics of data storage devices. First, however, we shall examine some drawbacks of the conventional data file environment.

1.2.2   Drawbacks of the Conventional Data File Environment

Consider the banking environment illustrated in Figure 1.5. Information processing has to deal with the following problems when working in an environment with a number of data files, such as the one illustrated.

Data Redundancy. It is unavoidable that some data elements such as name, address, and customer identification number are used in a number of applications. Since data is required by multiple applications, it often is recorded in multiple data files. In most cases, the data is stored repeatedly. This situation, called "data redundancy," leads to many problems concerning the integrity of data. Data redundancy requires multiple input, updating, and reporting procedures.

Data Integrity Problems. One reason for inadequate data integrity is data redundancy. It is inevitable that some inconsistency will result from storing the same information in more than one place. Figure 1.5 shows that the address of the same customer is stored in four different data sets: checking account data file, savings account data file, installment loan data file, and mortgage loan data file. If

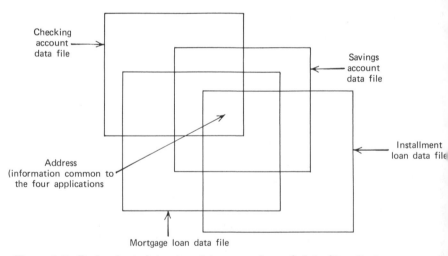

Figure 1.5 Redundant data stored in a number of data files. Savings account data file has redundant data stored with checking account data file, mortgage loan data file, and installment loan data file. All data files in this example have redundant data between one another. Address is common between all the four data files.

the customer moves, the address change has to be reflected in four different places. It is highly probable that on some occasions the change may not be made in all four places, and as a result the enterprise will have different information in different places about the same entity occurrence.

Lack of data integrity can also result from poor validity checking of data when making changes. Attempts to integrate data before the advent of data base technology were more difficult because of:

- Insufficient security provided to the stored data.
- Inadequate recovery procedures in case of a failure.
- Difficulty in managing long records.
- Inflexibility to changes.
- High programming and maintenance costs.
- Difficulty in managing procedures of computer operations (human negligence and error).

Limited Data Sharing. Since in our banking environment the applications checking, savings, installment loan, and mortgage loan represent one organization, there is some relationship between the data elements of different data files. When the data files are implemented as separate units, however, it is difficult if not impossible to relate the data elements across the applications. For an enterprise to function as one unit of organization, it is desirable to share data between different data files.

Data Availability Constraints. In today's fast moving environments, data must be available at the right time to an authorized person. When data are scattered in a number of data files, the availability of the combined data from these files is somewhat constrained.

Difficulty in Management Control. As a result of data redundancy in the data files, it is difficult to implement new guidelines across the whole enterprise. For example, as a result of the Privacy Act of 1974, the social security number may not be used as an identification number in governmental agencies. Where the social security number has been used, it will be time-consuming to implement the change through all the data files.

To solve these kinds of problems, data base systems were developed.

1.3 DATA BASE ENVIRONMENT

1.3.1 What Is a Data Base?

A *data base* is a collection of related data about an enterprise with multiple uses. In a data base the data definitions and the relations between the data are separated from the procedural statements of a program. The question to be asked here is, "What is the major distinction between a data base and a data file?" A data base may have more than one use, and the multiple uses may satisfy multiple "views" of the data stored. A data file may have more than one use, but only one "view" of the stored data can be satisfied. Multiple views of a data file can be satisfied only after the data have been sorted. In a data base environment, multiple uses may be the result of multiple users; for example, in a banking environment the information about customers may have several users, such as checking, savings, installment loan, and mortgage loan. Thus data sharing is a major objective of an enterprise data base system.

Figure 1.4 shows that generalized access methods were developed to create and access the data files separately from the application programs. Some extension of the common access methods is needed to handle the data base separately from the application programs. This extension is called a "data base management system."

1.3.2 Data Base Management System (DBMS)

A system is needed that will integrate the data files into a data base and that can provide different views to different users. The software, the hardware, the firmware, and the procedures that manage the data base comprise a *data base management system* (DBMS). A data base management system makes it possible to access integrated data that crosses operational, functional, or organizational boundaries within an enterprise. See Figure 1.6.

1.3.3 Drawbacks of Data Integration

Integration of data about an enterprise into a central place may pose some disadvantages. Because the data from individual data files is integrated in a central place in a data base, the sense of ownership and, as a result, the responsibility for data are easily lost. As a result, inaccurate data may not be detected. This can cause serious problems unless extensive data integrity and data validity measures are imple-

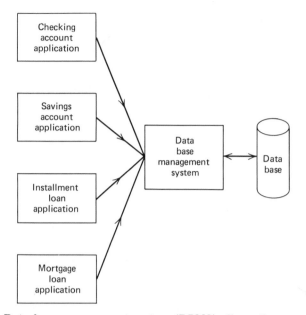

Figure 1.6 Data base management system (DBMS) allows the use of data that crosses operational, functional, or organizational boundaries. DBMS enables the data base users to satisfy multiple "views" of the data stored.

mented. The data base can also become a target of security breaches unless stringent security disciplines are maintained. Moreover, a data base can increase political and organizational struggles within the organization because it serves the needs of multiple users, some of whom may have legitimate conflicts of interest and may have different requirements. An integrated data base may also threaten privacy. Traditionally, privacy has been defined as the right of an individual to be "left alone." In an integrated data base environment, it becomes easier to collect information about people and organizations and then expose the information to some unauthorized person or organization. Therefore, if the data base management system does not ensure adequate integrity, security, and privacy and if the data base is not designed properly, the data base environment may result in new problems.

To avoid these potential drawbacks we may say that a data base management system (DBMS) should satisfy the following objectives:

• Different functions of an enterprise can be served effectively by the same DBMS.

- The amount of redundancy in stored data can be minimized.
- Consistent information can be supplied for the decision-making process.
- Security controls can be applied.
- Application programs can be developed, maintained, and enhanced faster and more economically, with fewer skilled personnel.
- Physical reorganization of the stored data is easy.
- Centralized control of the data base is possible.
- Easier procedures for computer operations can be established.

How should the collected information about the entities of the enterprise be organized, and what relationships should be provided to interconnect the information about the various entities? How can the enterprise's data base be made less sensitive to the expansion and reorganization of the business? How should the security, integrity, and validity measures be implemented and controlled? How should the recovery and backup procedures be provided, that is, how should the data base be designed, implemented, and maintained efficiently?

To answer these questions, an in-depth knowledge of the enterprise's environment, as well as technical expertise, is required. It is necessary to establish a central function that can provide an efficient data structure of the entities and their relationships to a community of users. This data structure is efficient for the community of users rather than for any one particular user. The central function is called a data base administration function.

1.4 DATA BASE ADMINISTRATOR

In a data base environment, multiple users are involved. A function that can review different requirements and resolve conflicts of interest is absolutely necessary. To coordinate and carry out all the steps in designing, implementing, and maintaining an integrated data base, an ongoing administrative function must be established.

Thus data base administration is a function made up of people responsible for protecting a valuable resource—data. In the conventional data processing environment, an application programmer "possesses" a data file. Users "lock" their data, keeping others from using it and forcing them to collect the same data. The data base era has removed the sense of individual "property." The person in charge of the data base administration function is called a *data base administrator* (DBA). The data base administrator is *not* the "possessor" of data but the "protector" of it. For a sophisticated enterprise, the information generation and decision processes become complicated as the spectrum of the functions expands. Since direct data control is "taken away" from the application programmer, he/she loses the feeling of personal contact and responsibility for it. This loss of personal contact forces the enterprise to develop procedures to assure that data integrity is not compromised. This goal should be coordinated through the data base administration function.

The data base administration is a function providing services to the users of the data base. An analogy could be drawn between the data base administrator (DBA) and the comptroller of the enterprise. The comptroller protects the resource of the enterprise called "money," and the DBA protects the resource called "data." In many organizations, the DBA function is considered merely that of a highly technical person. This identification defeats the purpose of a DBA. The DBA function should be high enough in the hierarchy of the organization to have authority over, as well as responsibility for, the data structures and their access. The person in charge of the DBA function must also have an understanding of how the enterprise works and how it uses data. Although it is desirable for the DBA to be technically competent, an understanding of the enterprise and the ability and responsibility to interact with people and to submit alternatives to standard procedures are more important. Otherwise, the DBA function is much less effective.

Although it is beneficial to have an authoritative DBA function, the placement of the data base administrator may vary from organization to organization. The first major factor in determining this placement is the importance of the data base for survival of the organization. The second factor is the sophistication of the organization both in data processing and in the nature of its business. In today's data base environment the DBA function most often remains in the DP department and most often within an application area of this department.

The DBA has to coordinate the functions of collecting information about data and designing, implementing, and maintaining the data base and its security. The DBA's mission does not terminate at the implementation of the data base. Integration of new functions into the data base makes the DBA more necessary than ever. One of the major functions of the DBA is to pay attention to the future as well as to the present information requirements of the enterprise. To fulfill this function, the data base design should be as flexible or data independent as possible.

The DBA function is clearly important in multiuser data base system operations. We should not, however, rule out the possibility that some of these functions will some day be automated. Also, we should not forget the future importance of "personal" data bases over which the user has total control. Even with a single user, it is possible to take different "views" of the data or to make nonprocedural requests. But in the data base environment of today and of the near future, the data base administrator will play a major role.

The data base administration function is discussed in more detail in Chapter 2.

1.5 DATA INDEPENDENCE

1.5.1 What Is Data Independence?

In the conventional data set environment, the application programmer has to know answers to the following questions before manipulating the data:

What is its format?
Where is it located?
How is it accessed?

Changes in any of these three items may affect the application program and result in other changes, since the details of these three points may be locked into the application code. Let us assume that the details about data regarding where, how, and what are coded in the application program. In that case any changes to where, how, and what to the data have to be reflected in the application code, and the application programs must be recompiled and maintained. It is highly probable that as the needs of the enterprise change, the format of the data may change. The data set has to be expanded by the addition of new data elements representing new entities.

With enhancements in computer architecture and improved efficiency in software and hardware, the methods of accessing and the means of storing the data are likely to change. The access methods and the storage means are built into the application logic. As a result, programmers must spend an increasing percentage of their time in program maintenance and updating. This is both a source of error and a diversion of resources. The users (application programmers and terminal users) of the data base should be oriented toward the information content of the data and should not be concerned with details of representation and location. The ability to use the data base without knowing the representation details is called *data independence*.

Data independence is crucial from the economic viewpoint. An enterprise may spend thousands of dollars for implementing very simple changes, such as increasing a field length or adding a new field. An ideal data base design should provide, to some degree, for changes of this nature without affecting the application programs. But one thing which should not be forgotten is that the extent of data independence provided depends on the data base design, as well as on the data base management system.

Data independence provides, at a central location, a solution to the problems mentioned above. The individual application programmer no longer must change the application programs to accommodate changes in access method or location or format of the data. Unfortunately, data base management system packages available today do not appear to achieve full data independence. Since a data base design depends on the DBMS package, it seems difficult to achieve total data independence, even with the best data base design.

The central location for reflecting changes in the method of storing, the ways of accessing, the format of the data elements, and the relationships between the data elements representing the entities of the enterprise should be anchored in the data base management system. The issue here is when, where, why, and who should specify the changes to the DBMS. And who should control these changes? These responsibilities should be given to the data base administrator.

In summary, the reasons for data independence are as follows:*

"1. To allow the DBA to make changes in the content, location, representation and organization of a data base without causing reprogramming of application programs which use the data base.

2. To allow the supplier of data processing equipment and software to introduce new technologies without causing reprogramming of the customer's application.

3. To facilitate data sharing by allowing the same data to appear to be organized differently for different application programs.

*From R. W. Engels, "A Tutorial on Data Base Organization" (see complete reference at the end of this chapter).

4. To simplify application program development and, in particular, to facilitate the development of programs for interactive data base processing.

5. To provide the centralization of control needed by the data base administrator to insure the security and integrity of the data base."

1.5.2 Two Stages of Data Independence

The data base design process starts with the conceptual requirements of a number of users. (See Figure 1.7.) The conceptual requirements can also be specified for some applications that will not be implemented in the near future. These requirements of individual users are integrated into a single "community" view, called a *conceptual model*. The conceptual model represents the entities and their relationships. It gives us the ability to view all the data entities and their relationships to each other with no concern about their physical storage. Thus the conceptual model is the inherent model of the enterprise.

The conceptual model that the community needs for the near future is then translated into a data model compatible with the chosen data base management system. It is possible that the relationships between entities as reflected in the conceptual model are not implementable with the chosen package of the DBMS. In such situations, modifications to the conceptual model should reflect these constraints. The version of the conceptual model that can be presented to the DBMS is called a *logical model*. The users are presented with subsets of this logical model. These subsets, called *external models* (also referred to as subschemas in the literature), are the views of the users. The external models are the views that the users "get" based on the logical model. The conceptual requirements are the views that the users "wanted" initially and based on which the *conceptual* model was developed.

The logical model is mapped to physical storage such as disk, tape, or drum. The *physical model*, which takes into consideration the distribution of data, access methods, and indexing techniques, is called an *internal model*.*

The external models should not be affected by physical storage changes or by access method changes to the data base. This is the

---

*The terminology such as "internal model," "conceptual model," and "external model" is from American National Standards Institute (ANSI/X3/Sparc) Data Base Management System's Study Group.

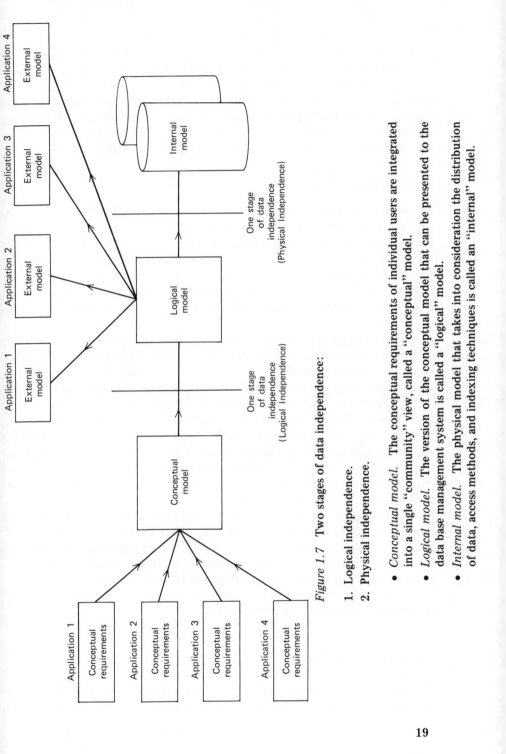

Figure 1.7 Two stages of data independence:

1. Logical independence.
2. Physical independence.

- *Conceptual model.* The conceptual requirements of individual users are integrated into a single "community" view, called a "conceptual" model.

- *Logical model.* The version of the conceptual model that can be presented to the data base management system is called a "logical" model.

- *Internal model.* The physical model that takes into consideration the distribution of data, access methods, and indexing techniques is called an "internal" model.

19

first stage of data independence. On the other hand, if the conceptual model is designed so that it reflects future expansion needs, changes to the conceptual model should not affect the existing external models either. This is the second stage of data independence. Figure 1.7 shows the two stages of data independence. One thing we have to remember here is that the logical model is forced to match the DBMS. Therefore it will change if the DBMS changes.

1.5.3   How to Achieve Data Independence

From an application programming viewpoint, data independence is not a programming technique but a programming discipline. For example, to avoid recompilation for any changes, it is advisable not to define constants in a program. A better technique is to pass the values as parameters to the program. The DBA is responsible for tracking as much information as possible about the enterprise, the entities, the data elements, and the relationships between the data elements.

All the information about the present needs of the enterprise and adequate information about intended needs should be reflected in the conceptual model in the design phase. Of course, all the possible uses of the data base cannot be anticipated, but for most enterprises the basic data, that is, the entities and the relationships between them, is relatively stable. What changes is the information needs, that is, the ways in which the data is used to produce information. Another aspect of data independence is that the internal representation of the data may differ from the form in which the application program wishes to use it. Unfortunately, few DBMS can totally provide that kind of independence.

The degree of data independence provided depends on the thoroughness of the data base design phase. A thorough analysis of the enterprise's entities and their relationships minimizes the impact on other programs of changes in the data requirements of one program. This is what data independence is really all about.

One of the management tools supporting the development of a data base design is a data dictionary.

1.6 DATA DICTIONARY

A *data dictionary* is a central repository of information about the entities: the data elements representing the entities, the relationships between the entities, their origins, meanings, uses, and representation formats.

In any enterprise, installation of a data base does not happen overnight. The data base expands as applications are developed and integrated. New data elements are introduced, and data elements used for the data base design may have to be modified. A facility that provides uniform and central information about all the data resources is called a "data dictionary" (DD).

The benefits of using a data dictionary are related to the effective collection, specification, and management of the total data resources of an enterprise. A data dictionary should help a data base user in:

- Communicating with the other users.
- Controlling the data elements in a simple and effective manner, that is, introducing new elements into the systems, or changing the descriptions of the elements.
- Reducing data redundancy and inconsistency.
- Determining the impact of changes to data elements on the total data base.
- Centralizing the control of the data elements as an aid in data base design and in expanding the design.

In addition, an ideal data dictionary contains information about other entities. It stores information about the groups of data elements, about the data bases, and about the cross references between the groups of data elements and the data bases. It also indicates which programs use which data bases, and it keeps information regarding the authorization and the security codes.

A detailed discussion of the data dictionary system is given in Chapter 3.

Let us study the steps in the data base design that should deliver a data-independent design and satisfy the performance requirements.

1.7 DATA BASE DESIGN AND PERFORMANCE—PREVIEW

The design starts with the end users' views of the organization, called the conceptual requirements. An end user is a decision maker who uses information obtained by accessing the data base. The end users also provide data to be stored in the data base.

In considering the end users' requirements, the following trade-offs have to be taken into account:

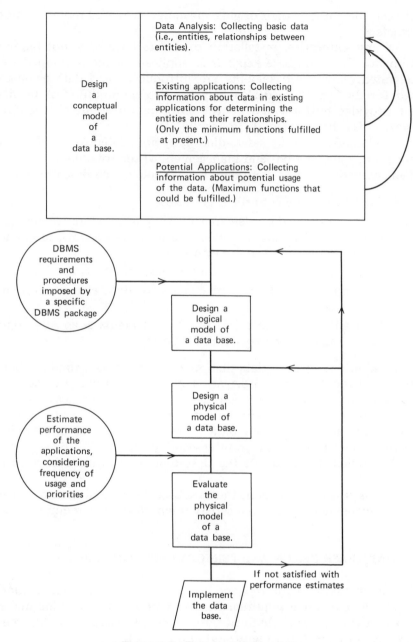

Figure 1.8 **Data base design steps.**

- It should satisfy today's needs for information.
- It should not only satisfy today's needs but also satisfy them in reasonable time, that is, it should satisfy the performance requirements.
- It should satisfy the anticipated as well as the unanticipated requirements of the end users.
- It should be easily expandable with the reorganization and expansion of the enterprise.
- It should be easy to modify in changing software and hardware environments.
- Once correct data is stored in the data base, it should stay correct.
- Before inserting any data in the data base, the data should be checked for validity.
- Only authorized people should have access to the data stored in the data base.

Figure 1.8 shows the steps to be taken in designing a data base, considering the above trade-offs.

REFERENCES

1. *An Introduction to Data Base Systems*, 2nd ed., C. J. Date, The Systems Programming Series, Addison-Wesley, 1977.
2. "A Tutorial on Data Base Organization," R. W. Engels, *Annual Review in Automatic Programming*, Vol. 7, Part 1, edited by Halpern and McGee, Elmsford, N.Y., Pergamon Press (July 1972).

Data Base Administration

Converting the information processing of an enterprise to a data base technology or expanding an existing data base requires a tremendous investment. Therefore this process must be carefully planned and managed. The quantity of data to be converted to a data base and the applications are becoming more complex day by day. As a result, it is absolutely necessary that central control be established for decision making and monitoring through all the phases of the life cycle of the data base system.

CHAPTER 2

Data Base Administration

2.1 DATA BASE ADMINISTRATION FUNCTION

In today's world, the quantity of data stored for an enterprise increases in an almost geometric progression. The management decision-making process depends on the quality and quantity of information. The information that can be extracted from the data base is one of the most valuable resources of the enterprise. The data base must be properly designed, processed, and maintained to provide the right information at the right time to the authorized people. These responsibilities belong to the data base administrator (DBA) and his/her staff. The data base administration function is made up of people and procedures. The expression "DBA" will be used interchangeably to mean both the person and the function.

The DBA function assists the enterprise in managing and controlling the data resource. This function is more that of a manager than that of a technician. As we shall see, the existence and function of the DBA is a commitment to data as a resource; as such, it often begins with the introduction of a DBMS (data base management system), but there is a distinction between DBMS and DBA. In most environments, the DBMS is a vendor supplied package and the DBA is a function. The DBA maintains the overall view of the enterprise which we call a "conceptual" model. This view is the data model of the organization. As we saw in Chapter 1, the one purpose of a data base is to provide information to different users in different functional areas of the organization. This often means that no one department feels responsible, however, and common ground is the last to be tended. The inevitable result is to make the job of the DBA that of a coordinator. In many installations, management commits itself to a data base environment by going the technical route, that is, by deciding on the data base management system package first, rather than going the management route by establishing an administration function and investigating the viability of the data base approach.

The scope of the DBA's position varies from enterprise to enterprise. In enterprises where the DBA function was assigned to a highly technical nonmanagement person (such as a systems programmer) instead of a person with middle management experience, the attempt to convert from a data file environment to a data base environment often failed, or did not achieve all the desired results. The following example illustrates this point.

In a large company, the DBA reported to the technical services manager and the technical services manager reported to the data processing manager. One of the initial meetings for designing a data base was attended by these two managers, along with the DBA, the application development managers, and the user community managers. The first half of the meeting was spent in trying to resolve some departmental conflicts. During the second half of the meeting nobody paid any attention to the DBA's suggestions because he was on a lower level than the other managers attending the meeting. The whole effort was placed in jeopardy because the DBA lacked the authority to resolve differences between conflicting interests and reach a compromise.

If the DBA is placed high enough in the organization chart, she/ he will have the necessary authority to insist that the proper strategies be implemented. Conversely, appointing a new senior manager out of the blue is unlikely to promote a spirit of fellowship and goodwill. The DBA will have to foster cooperation by proving the worth of the function; thus this issue is related to that of choosing the first data base application. The importance of the DBA is established relatively faster in an on-line than in a batch environment because of the visibility of the on-line applications.

2.1.1 Data Base Administrator's (DBA's) Responsibilities

The first important task of the data base administrator is to resolve differences between various functions of the organization to develop a conceptual and then a logical structure of the data base model for the enterprise. He/she has to be the negotiator between the different departments, not just to get agreement between them, but also to get the "right" agreement about the entities of the enterprise. This may also require developing procedures and guidelines for data handling in addition to data definition and ownership. The implication is that the DBA function must know exactly how the business runs and what the policies of the high level management and the future direction of the enterprise are. In the initial phase of designing the data base, the DBA will concentrate on:

- Defining the data elements and the entities of the enterprise.
- Determining the different names that will be used to refer to the same elements.
- Defining the relationships between the data elements.
- Establishing the textual description of data elements.
- Knowing the departments or the users who will be responsible for keeping the data accurate (e.g., updating, data integrity).
- Determining the usage of the data elements for control and planning purposes, that is, determining who is authorized to do what.

Collecting all this information from different departments, and, at the same time, settling any differences that arise, makes the job of a DBA that of a diplomat.

As already mentioned, the sense of "ownership" of data does not exist in a data base environment. This occasionally makes the job of the DBA extremely difficult. He/she may have to persuade some departments to "give away" their property for general use, or may find it necessary to control the access to sensitive information.

This idea of "sharing" may not only antagonize some departments but also may make them hostile to the whole data base development project. The DBA has to be in a position to persuade some, convince some, comfort some, and, if nothing else works, coerce some. This means that the DBA has to know how to use power and influence as needed, and implies that a DBA should not be hired as a completely new individual who does not know the intricacies of the politics within the organization. On the other hand, the DBA should not be someone within the enterprise who has managed to turn a number of people into enemies.

In short, the selection of a DBA should be taken very seriously by corporate management. The selection criteria for a DBA's position should be the same as or similar to those used for filling other management positions within the enterprise. Management qualities are necessary, because the DBA should place as much (or more) weight on the long term needs of the enterprise as on the short term goals. This responsibility becomes extremely complex because a data base implies the integration of data across functional boundaries.

Implementation of guidelines can be successful only if everyone related to the data base is aware of, and is responsible for, the standards established by the DBA. The application programmers' community, the operations staff and the systems people must understand the procedures necessary for doing their jobs efficiently. This means that the DBA has to establish effective two-way communication with all groups that have any involvement with the data base. (See Figure 2.1.)

The following sections give guidelines for the information flow along each of these paths.

2.1.2 DBA and Management

Management is defined as those individuals to whom the DBA reports either directly or indirectly. The DBA desperately needs management's support and approval for managing the data base, and in return the DBA has to establish credibility with management. To design a data base that can accommodate future changes in the mode of operation of the enterprise, ideally the DBA should be supplied

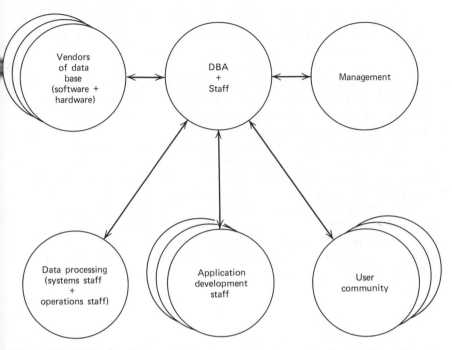

Figure 2.1 DBA function and the two-way communication paths with all groups that have any involvement with the data base.

with the necessary information about future plans by management. The communication should take place as follows.

Management ⟶ *DBA*

- Top priorities of the enterprise, if not directly through the organization then at least through newsletters, minutes, and other types of communication.
- Management's commitments with respect to time for the development of the new data base or for the expansion of it.
- Budgetary limitations for the project (including people, software, hardware).
- Commitment made to other parties (e.g., information availability, performance requirements).
- Future plans, for example, any changes that might affect the data base environment.
- Possibilities for restructuring the organization.

A part of the information that should be provided by the management to the DBA may be confidential. If the DBA is at a substantially lower level as compared to the top executives, it would be inappropriate to pass such information to her/him. But if the data base is considered as an extremely vital resource for the enterprise, the DBA will be placed at least at the management level, and then passing confidential information of this type from the top executives to the DBA will be appropriate.

In turn, the DBA should communicate with management about the data, the data base design, its implementation, and its operation. Pertinent information about the added value to the enterprise resulting from the data base and any existing limitations must be communicated to the management by the DBA and staff. He/she has to be informed by the project managers about the status of every project in the data base environment in order to forward the information to the senior management. The information should include the following.

DBA ⟶ Management

- Time estimate for the development in the initial phase.
- Staff requirements (for the DBA's staff).
- Project status reports in data base design and implementation and any application development. (These reports should be coming to the management from application development departments. But the DBA needs to be aware of them and be prepared to analyze and report on the effects of any deviations in an application's schedule as it relates to the DBA function.)
- Budget agreement or an alternative proposal.
- Description of query facilities for the occasional users, especially management.
- Description of security and control of access to sensitive information.
- Space requirements (size and location, especially for any new hardware acquisitions for the data base).

2.1.3 DBA and User Community

The data base will be designed for the users. The DBA's task is to design and maintain it in a proper fashion. The users should have full confidence in communicating with the DBA; they should have the feeling that they are talking to an impartial authority who is going to help them to be more productive. To reflect all the needs of the users that have to be satisfied by the data base, the following flow of information to the DBA has to take place.

User Community ⟶ *DBA*

- Data requirements of the applications.
- Priorities of various applications in the data base environment.
- Ownership of data.
- Data elements for every application and their relationships.
- Relationships between different applications of the enterprise.
- Information about the quality assurance plan for the contents of the data elements.
- Data archiving requirements.
- Documentation.
- Data access restrictions (privacy and security).
- Possible future applications.
- Frequency of use and response requirements.

In a banking environment, for example, information regarding the interest paid to depositors has to be saved for at least 4 years as required by the Internal Revenue Service. Information regarding the frequency of access to this interest information should be provided to assist the DBA in deciding how to store this information in the data base.

It may be a future requirement to notify customers of all inquiries concerning their accounts. The data base should be designed so that this possible future application can be added at a future date without much difficulty. It is difficult, if not impossible, to try to anticipate all possibilities, however, and the DBA must make trade-offs with current performance.

The DBA has to tell the users how the data base will fulfill their needs, and the limitations as well. The following exchange of information is necessary between the DBA and the user community.

DBA ——➤ *User Community*

- Guidelines for changing any information regarding the entities, the data elements, and the relationships between them in the data dictionary.
- Procedures for making such changes.
- Implementation and/or recommendations for:
  - Security controls.
  - Privacy controls.
  - Auditability controls.
- Any changes, modifications, or compromises made in a specific user's requirements and the reasons for them.
- Status of development of the data base design, implementation, and operations.
- Education and training suggestions.
- Any available tools that could make the user community more productive.
- Procedures regarding the data element synonyms.
- Cross-reference list of applications and data elements.
- Plan for phase-in of new data base systems.
- Performance objectives and their status, that is, whether they are met.
- Procedures for purging and archiving data.

2.1.4   DBA and Application Development Staff

The DBA communicates with all the application development departments concerning the data base environment. She/he has an overall view of the application development and therefore, can communicate with the individual application development departments effectively in the following areas.

DBA ——➤ *Application Development Staff*

- Schedules for the application development, showing the database-affected portions.

- Information about the data base required for application development (e.g., external model definitions such as data elements, symbolic names, contents, formats).
- Security controls as specified by the user departments.
- Privacy controls as specified by the user departments.
- Auditability controls as specified by the management.
- Education and training suggestions.
- Cross-reference list of applications and data elements.
- Archival storage requirements.
- Rules and procedures for assuring the accuracy and the integrity of the data.
- Specifications for the data base maintenance program.
- Interface rules for applications (external models).
- Aids available and the ways to use them.
- Effective use of DBMS interface (remembering that powerful software is by definition easy to abuse).

The application development staff, by the same token, has to inform the DBA and the staff in the following areas.

Application Development Staff ⟶ DBA

- Concurrence on the schedule for application development or alternative proposals. The application development staff should set the schedule, and the DBA should concur.
- Requirements of the application development staff.
- Procedures for implementing the security, privacy, and access controls.
- Updating procedures.
- Storage of historical data and updates.
- Recovery procedures.
- Methods for implementing the auditability controls.
- On-line and off-line data storage.
- Education and training requirements.
- Test plan, including any subset/test data bases.
  - Who should create the test data bases, the DBA's staff or the application development staff?

- Who should maintain the test data bases?
- Who should verify proper operation vis-à-vis the data bases?
- Project status of the data base applications.

2.1.5 DBA and Systems Staff

The data base will be physically established, preserved, and accessed in an environment provided by computer operations, together with systems programming. The DBA and her/his staff must inform the systems staff on the following issues. This is especially important during the process of designing the physical structure of the data base.

DBA ⟶ Systems Staff

- Additional software and hardware, if any, required to support the data base.
- Performance constraints (e.g., response time) that affect the system.
- Security, privacy, and access control implementation plans.
- Any work that is expected to be performed by the systems staff in order to implement the data base.
- Changes in schedules and procedures.
- Off-site storage of historical data.
- Reliability, availability, and serviceability characteristics.
- Backup, recovery, and restart procedures.

The following information should be transferred by the systems staff to the DBA.

Systems Staff ⟶ DBA

- Incompatibility with any existing or planned software and hardware.
- Alternatives for handling any problems.
- Schedules for implementation of required hardware and software.
- Additional capacity requirements.

2.1.6   DBA and Operations Staff

The information to be supplied to the operations staff must be put together by the DBA, the application development management, and the user community management. It may look as follows.

DBA ⟶ *Operations Staff*

- Availability requirements for the data base (e.g., the data base should be accessible between 7:00 A.M. and 10:00 P.M.).
- Priorities of the applications as set by the users for batch jobs.
- Data base security procedures.
- Error recovery requirements for the data base.
- Archival requirements.
- Routine procedures to run the data base management system.
- Schedules and procedures for cutover of new applications in concurrence with the users.
- Enabling/disabling of certain applications (if applicable) as suggested by the users.
- Applications control: the proper execution of the programs and delegation of responsibility for running abnormally ended programs.

To have an effectively operating data base, the operations staff needs to inform the DBA of the following areas.

Operations Staff ⟶ *DBA*

- Procedures for updating the data base and hours of operation on daily basis, set by the DBA and concurred to by the operations staff.
- Implementation of recovery and restart procedures of the data base as set by the DBA.
- Security, privacy, and authorization mechanisms in place as suggested by the DBA, who in turn concurred with the users.
- Control mechanisms for scheduling as suggested by the DBA.
- Reports of problems and errors encountered in the data base systems.
- Reporting mechanisms for deviations from performance goals of the data base applications.

- Procedures for keeping a log of all activities against the data base that were written up by the DBA and his/her staff.
- Recommendations for changes to the data processing systems (cost savings, performance improvements, increased flexibility and reliability, etc.)
- Procedures for accessing and maintaining archived information.

2.1.7 DBA and Software Vendors

The software vendors may be supplying the enterprise software packages in other data processing areas besides the DBMS. The DBA, however, may be communicating with the software vendors only regarding the data base software and related packages.

DBA ⟶ *Software Vendors*

- Education and training needs of the DBA staff, the users, and the operations staff.
- The extent of security and authorization mechanisms needed.
- Performance bottlenecks in the data base area.

To gain credibility at the customer's location, the software vendors should supply the following information to the DBA.

Software Vendors ⟶ *DBA*

- The best techniques for using the software packages.
- Ways to "think ahead" for expansion purposes.
- Hardware requirements.
- Documentation for the DBMS.
- Program service support and maintenance.
- Potential application areas.
- Implications of the enterprise's future plans on the current or planned software/hardware (e.g., potential problems, bottlenecks).
- Education provided.
- References to other, preferably similar, users.

- Ancillary packages (e.g., data dictionary, aids, applications, data communications interfaces, monitors).
- Hardware configurations supported.

2.1.8 DBA and Hardware Vendors

In most enterprises the systems staff (also called the "technical services staff") communicates with the hardware vendor. The data base environment will use the hardware resources substantially. As a result, the DBA should be talking to the hardware vendors regarding the hardware requirements for the data base. This interface will be more or less direct as data base applications are more or less a part of the systems load.

Hardware Vendors ⟶ *DBA*

- Capabilities of the hardware.
- Procedures for using the hardware effectively.
- Expansion possibilities.
- Any incompatibilities with the existing hardware.
- Reliability factors.
- Servicing requirements.
- Software requirements when appropriate.
- Configurations needed to satisfy the enterprise's goals or needs.
- Training of personnel.
- Maintenance plan (e.g., preventive maintenance).

To prevent any bottlenecks due to insufficient hardware, it will be beneficial if the DBA and his/her staff can supply the hardware vendors with the following information.

DBA ⟶ *Hardware Vendors*

- Tentative future changes in the handling of information processing, including capacity and performance requirements.
- Equipment failures and any performance bottlenecks.

2.2 DATA BASE SYSTEM'S LIFE CYCLE

The main phases of the data base system's life cycle are as follows:

1. Design of the data base.
2. Physical creation of the data base.
3. Conversion of the existing data sets and applications to match the newly created data base.
4. Integration of the converted applications into the new data base.
5. Operations phase.
6. Growth, change, and maintenance phase.

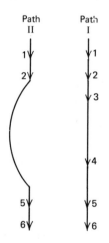

Path I will be taken if the existing data sets are to be converted to the newly created data base.

Path II will be taken if the existing data sets are not to be converted to the newly created data base.

(See Figures 2.2 and 2.3.)

This section explains the DBA's role during the six phases of the data base system's life cycle.

Before any data base is designed, it is necessary for an enterprise to take an inventory of all areas in which data exists, whether or not these areas are to be included in the total data base system. This is probably one of the important steps in data base system design. The DBA must review the resources available and understand the data, its sources, dependencies, and relationships with other systems, so as to develop a picture of the total data resource of the enterprise

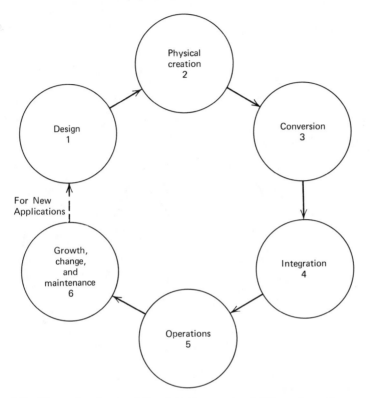

Figure 2.2 The main phases of the data base system's life cycle without overlap.

and the way this information flows among the various systems, and to create a written system design plan.

By performing a review of all systems, conflicts of data ownership, redundant data sources, and ambiguous or inconsistent data groupings can be identified early so that the system design will not have to be compromised at some later time. From this study, which should have detailed information of the systems and operating procedures, a plan can be developed that will allow for an orderly conversion to a data base environment. Depending on the complexity of the enterprise's system relationships, number of data entities, resource availabilities, and management commitment, this plan may extend over a 5-year period or longer.

The system design plan will serve as a guide to assure that the data base system is developing in an orderly fashion. Because this plan will set the direction that the enterprise is to take, it must be complete and address *all* systems. The format should be similar to

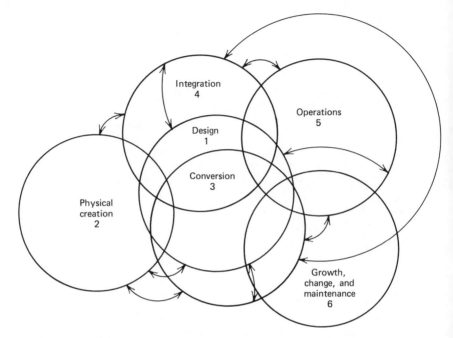

Figure 2.3 The main phases of the data base system's life cycle with overlap (real world).

- Phase 1: Design.
- Phase 2: Physical creation.
- Phase 3: Conversion.
- Phase 4: Integration.
- Phase 5: Operations.
- Phase 6: Growth, change, and maintenance.

that of any long range plan, detailed for the first year, outlined by quarters for the next 2 to 3 years, and thereafter summarized by years. The plan should also be subject to review and revision on a periodic basis and be used by management and users to check the conversion progress. It should be a dynamic document, not just a one-time effort.

This first step is not to be taken lightly, because it will serve as the foundation for all future development. From this plan a logical approach may be taken toward determining which areas are to be converted first, and in what order this effort will proceed. These selections should not be made for "visual" effect. Most importantly, this primary step will allow for user involvement in (and, it is hoped, commitment to) the data base design process and will promote a feeling that the user is not just a helpless bystander but an active participant working with the DBA.

2.2.1 Design of the Data Base (Phase 1 from Figures 2.2 and 2.3)

The data base structure is a model of the enterprise and should represent it accurately and support its needs. The design process must have the support of all the functional areas of the enterprise. These functional areas need to describe and define the data elements from management's and users' viewpoints. The DBA then has to resolve any discrepancies and ambiguities in the data definitions. The design of the data base will be only as good as the definitions of the data elements and their relationships. In fact, the design process is a definition of the organization in terms of its important entities and intrinsic relations.

In an educational environment, the important entities are the students and the instructors. Some other important entities are courses taught, enrollments, classroom scheduling, money received as tuition fees, money spent, and special projects. These entities have to be defined in the initial design phase, and the DBA must be involved in the determination of these entities and their relationships.

A data dictionary (DD) is necessary to do this job effectively. A detailed discussion of the data dictionary will be given in Chapter 3.

In the real world, it is not advisable to implement a data base at once for all the applications necessary for running the organization—in fact, it may be impossible. However, the impact of the applications that cannot be implemented immediately must be considered, and a long range plan should be established. It is definitely better to proceed in smaller steps. The key aim in any project implementation is that the first part of the project be successfully finished to demonstrate the potential of the data base approach, as well as the ability of the DBA to convert all the functions of the enterprise to a data base environment. The first applications chosen should be quite visible but need not be the most vital ones. At the same time, they should not be the least important ones. The step-by-step implementation of all the functions makes the design phase extremely important.

The design should be easily expandable. Few enterprises can afford to start all over again if a design proves too rigid. Since the data base will constantly need to change and grow, easy restructuring of it is mandatory as new data types and new applications are added.

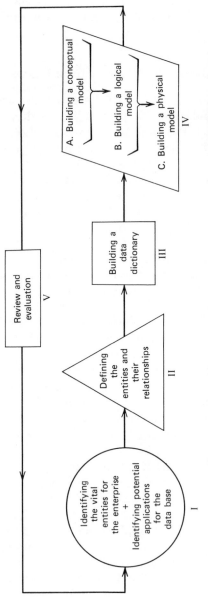

Figure 2.4 Design steps of the data base project. These steps are for accomplishing phase 1 from Figures 2.2 and 2.3.

Some data base management systems provide a restructuring tool. With others, the user must write her/his own (usually called a load/unload procedure). The DBA must be mindful that two of the main reasons for abandoning the conventional "data set era" and implementing data base technology are to reduce maintenance costs and to provide additional capabilities.

Figure 2.4 reflects the design steps. The major role of the DBA in the logical design steps is to concentrate on "why" certain relationships between the entities exist and not on "how to" implement them.

2.2.2 Physical Creation of the Data Base
(Phase 2 from Figures 2.2 and 2.3)

After the physical structure of the data base(s) has been adjusted to meet performance requirements, the next step is to present the skeletal structure(s) of the physical data base(s) to the DBMS. These skeletons are sometimes placed in a data base description library. Also, the logical views of the users (also called "external models") can be placed in similar libraries.

Before loading and exercising the complete full scale data base, it is advisable that an experimental prototype of the data base be implemented or a model built. The prototype can give a reasonable estimate of the performance of the complete data base and can also be used for prediction purposes when expanding the volume or the functions. In no event should production runs be started immediately on the complete data base without any testing. This analysis phase can be overlapped with the conversion phase and with the integration phase. (See Figure 2.3.) It is feasible to go back to the design phase from this prototype phase if the performance requirements are not fulfilled.

After the prototype has been tested for satisfactory performance, the data base can be loaded. It must be remembered, however, that predicting performance with a prototype is very difficult and that it is very hard to tell when the job is done. In most cases, although a prototype is desirable, the model cannot reflect performance in an on-line environment satisfactorily. The reason is that no generalizable mathematical procedure exists to help someone judge whether the model is correct. Specifically, it is hard to do an adequate load test where there are 50 or 100 asynchronous transactions accessing the data base. Nor is it easy to replicate the quantity of information in the data base. Many things run fine on 1000 records but "blow up" on 100,000. It should be kept in mind that the performance of a data base is also dependent on the size of the data base. Some applications from the conversion phase (phase 3) and from the integration phase (phase 4) (see Figures 2.2, 2.3, and 2.5) can be run against the complete data base. The performance is verified on the basis of design requirements on the complete data base. If the results are unsatisfactory, the data base design must be modified. If the results are satisfactory, the security, privacy, and authorization controls are checked against the complete physical data base. If these controls pass the test, a green light can be given to the full scale phase (phase 3) of conversion. (See Figures 2.2, 2.3, and 2.5.)

2.2.3   Conversion of the Existing Data Sets and Applications to Match the Newly Created Data Base (Phase 3 from Figures 2.2 and 2.3)

In many environments, the data base evolves from the existing information processing system. Existing data sets are converted to the data base. In the example discussed in Section 2.2.1, the educational institution might have data sets for courses taught, enrollment, and student information.

Figure 2.6 shows the decision paths taken in this phase.

2.2.4   Integration of the Converted Applications and the New Applications into the New Data Base (Phase 4 from Figures 2.2 and 2.3)

This phase may be heavily overlapped with phase 3. Ease of expansion of the physical structure is absolutely necessary in this phase. It means supporting application development by proper management of the data base rather than scheduling application development. Application development is not the DBA's responsibility. For example, in a banking environment, integrating a new type of credit card system should be possible. If the data base is not designed with this in mind, chances are very high that a return to the design phase will be required. This could be demoralizing for the DBA's staff and disastrous for the application development staff.

2.2.5   Operations Phase (Phase 5 from Figures 2.2 and 2.3)

In this phase all applications that are supposed to run using the data base are run full scale. Privacy, security, and access control proce-

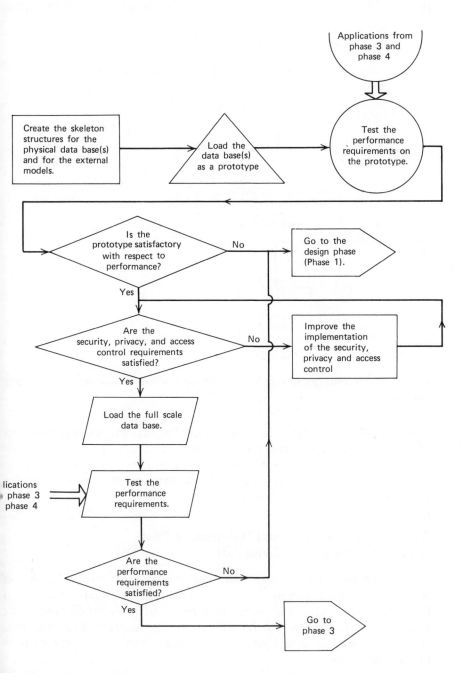

Figure 2.5 **Phases of the physical creation (phase 2) of the data base(s) from Figures 2.2 and 2.3.**

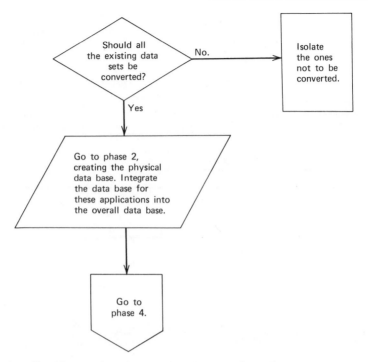

Figure 2.6 Decision paths taken in the phase 3 of conversion from Figures 2.2
and 2.3.

dures must be in place. Recovery and backup procedures must be
established, and performance criteria met. There is heavy involvement on the part of the operations expert and the systems expert.

A detailed discussion of the DBA's staff and the responsibilities
of the various members is given in Section 2.3.

2.2.6 Growth, Change, and Maintenance Phase
(Phase 6 from Figures 2.2 and 2.3)

This is the last phase in the data base system's life cycle. In almost
every environment, change is a way of life. The change can be in
business practices, it can occur as a result of business expansion or
business reduction, it can be due to reorganization. For example,
if an environment is unionized, the change can be a result of new
union contracts.

Coping with changes is the maintenance phase. In most situations, maintenance work is not necessarily very challenging. If the

data base design is relatively flexible, the maintenance phase, most probably, is not the most difficult one to live with.

It is possible that the data base will need to be redesigned if changes are massive. But in most environments, it is a luxury to redesign a functioning data base. And in some environments, it is nearly impossible. Most often the approach taken, for practical reasons, is that of patchwork. The staff member with the major involvement in this phase is the applications expert.

2.3 DBA, DBA'S STAFF, AND THEIR RESPONSIBILITIES

To pursue the interests of the enterprise, it is necessary that the DBA be provided with an efficient staff. As the data base becomes operational and everyone starts depending on it, the DBA function will gain importance. Establishing a data base and running it is an ongoing process, not a one-time event. The upper level management of the enterprise must be convinced that the DBA function is valuable throughout the design phase, the implementation phase, and the operations phase.

The resources provided for the DBA function should not reflect undercommitment. The organization cannot be expected to provide a satisfactory data base system and to meet schedules without adequate support. Before discussing the DBA's staff, let us look again at the DBA's placement in an organization.

2.3.1 DBA's Placement in Organization

The placement of the DBA in an organization depends on:

- The nature of the enterprise.
- The importance of the existing applications that the data base will serve.
- The importance of the applications to be implemented in the future that the data base will serve.
- The management style of the enterprise.
- The maturity of the enterprise in regard to data processing.
- The personality of the DBA.

Within each enterprise, the data processing function has its own unique nature, as defined by its purpose for existence. Certain basic interfaces and functional relationships with the data processing department, however, are common to all installations.

The data processing environment tries to serve the needs of the enterprise in terms of information. Most installations have an application development group that interacts with the users from various areas, such as finance, manufacturing, marketing, and personnel. The group develops and maintains application programs in such programming languages as COBOL, PL/1, ASSEMBLER, and FORTRAN for information processing for the user community. Another group is data processing systems and operations, which tends the hardware equipment, schedules and runs the applications on it, maintains the tape library, takes care of physical security, and keeps up to date the operating system and other software necessary for running the applications. For the applications group the major source of data for running the applications may be the data base, and for the operations group the major maintenance activity may involve the hardware and software related to the data base. The DBA's function is to develop a data base design that represents the entities and their relationships within the enterprise, and to maintain and expand these relationships as the enterprise grows.

In the initial phase of feasibility study, research, and initial implementation the DBA may be reporting to the director of information processing. The applications and systems operations group may be at the same level as the DBA, as in Figure 2.7. Ideally, the DBA should be at the same level in the organization as the user departments for whom the data base is being developed and implemented.

The influence of the DBA increases as the data base starts to play a major role in the existence and the normal running of the enterprise. The importance of the DBA depends on the maturity of the enterprise in the data processing area, the enterprise's confidence in

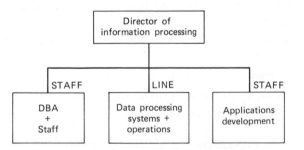

Figure 2.7 The DBA's placement in data processing. The DBA is independent of the data processing function and the applications development staff.

the data base as a major resource for its continued existence, and the ability of the DBA and his/her staff to satisfy the user needs.

The placement of the DBA will vary among enterprises. The organizational level of the DBA should be based on her/his relative value and importance, which may vary among organizations, rather than on an artificial need to save face.

An organization where the DBA function has not been very successful is shown in Figure 2.7a. In this organization, as in many others, the service function is blamed for any delays in delivering proper service. The data processing department, in turn, blames the application programmers for not maintaining the programs properly. There is "finger pointing" between line and staff departments. The "line" departments perform the day-to-day functions, like running production jobs and providing a test environment for applications. The "staff" departments are the developers of applications. The fact that the DBA reports to the data processing manager means that the DBA is part of the line function. Because of the tense relationships between the line and the staff, the application programmers do not cooperate well with the line, and vice versa. The achievements of the DBA are also dependent on the quality of the people reporting to him/her.

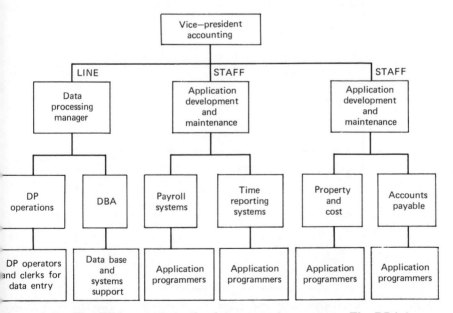

Figure 2.7a The DBA reports to the data processing manager. The DBA is on the line side, and the application programmers are on the staff side.

2.3.2 DBA's Staff

In the preliminary stages, the staff may consist of two or three people who are capable of planning, organizing, and communicating with the upper level management and the user community. These skill requirements should be considered when staffing this function. More people can be added as the design progresses.

The size of the DBA's staff will depend on the size of the enterprise, the complexity of the applications to be run with the data base, the complexity of the DBMS chosen and its ability to generate the relationships required by the logical views, the level of the users' sophistication, and the phase of the data base project. The staff should be made up of individuals who are able to define, organize, structure, and protect the data base and to communicate with people from various areas of the enterprise.

The DBA's function involves communication with such groups as management, non-DP users, DP programmers, and DP systems/operations. Ideally there should be at least one person on the DBA's staff who can communicate effectively with a group or a combination of groups. Figure 2.8 shows the functions of the DBA and her/

Function	Major Interface
DBA	Management DP programmers DP operations Non—DP users
Operations expert	DP operations
Systems expert	DP systems
Applications expert	DP programmers Non—DP users
Librarian	DP programmers Non—DP users
Query languages expert	DP programmers Non—DP users DP systems
Auditor	Non—DP users DP operations DP programmers

Figure 2.8 The DBA's staff and their major interfaces. The DBA's function involves communication with a number of different groups, such as management, non-DP users, DP programmers, DP systems/operations.

his staff and their major interfaces. Figure 2.9 shows the DBA's staff at its full capacity and the responsibilities of its members. The staffing suggestion illustrated is, of course, for a relatively large environment where 100 or more application programmers are employed. If there is a relatively small application group, the DBA group will also be realtively small.

2.3.3 Responsibilities of the Individual Staff Members

The members have various duties in different stages of the data base development. We distinguish between the following six phases, as in Figure 2.2

1. Design phase.
2. Physical creation of the data base.
3. Conversion of the existing data sets and applications to match the newly created data base.
4. Integration of the converted applications and of the new applications into the data base.
5. Operations phase.
6. Growth, change, and maintenance phase.

Operations Expert. The operations expert is responsible for establishing effective communication between the DBA function and the operations staff of the data processing function.

1. Design Phase

• Evaluate the impact on performance of several physical structure alternatives.
• If applications need operator intervention, develop operator interfaces that are easy to learn and to use.
• Evaluate the credibility of backup, recovery, security, and privacy procedures.

2, 3, 4. Physical Creation, Conversion, and Integration Phases

• Supervise the necessary operational preparations (e.g., checking the quality of auxiliary storage for the data base).
• Organize the implementation of the DBMS (e.g., defining the libraries, establishing the data sets).
• Assist the operations manager in the implementation plan.

DBA						
Operations expert	Systems expert	Applications expert	Librarian	Query language expert	Auditor

Operations expert

2 Persons

Experts in communicating with the operations staff, possibly previous operations staff members

Systems expert

4 Persons

1 Person: software expertise major and hardware expertise minor.

1 person: hardware expertise major and software expertise minor.

2 Persons: experts in DBMS.

Applications expert

4 Persons

2 Persons: experts in applications (possibly previous systems analysts from the application group)

2 Persons: experts in programming applications (possibly previous application programmers from application group)

Librarian

2 Persons

Experts in maintaining data dictionary, security definitions, previous experience in user community necessary, articulate in native language

Query language expert

2 Persons

Experts in formatting the screens for on-line transactions, in implementing security, and in authorizations for on-line transactions; experts in query languages, previous experience in user community necessary, articulate in native language

Auditor

1 Person

Expert in locating deficiencies in usage of data-base, in regard to security, privacy, and charging mechanism, on the part of DP operations and application programmers; expertise in accounting, preferably from the user community with some application programming background.

Figure 2.9 The DBA's staff at full capacity and their responsibilities. The size of the DBA's staff will depend on:

1. The size of the enterprise.
2. The complexity of the applications to
3. The complexity of the DBMS chosen.
4. The level of the user's sophistication.

- Reserve time slots for the operations people, and arrange to have "good" operators from the operations department for the loading of the data base.
- Establish the procedures for starting up the DBMS every morning.
- Prepare the procedures for logging the data base operations.
- Set up the procedures for recovery, backup, security, and authorization. Set up procedures also for information requirements for troubleshooting and analysis of unexpected errors.
- Provide for the operators' training, investigate their training programs, and make recommendations to the data processing manager.

5. Operations Phase
This phase is made up of day-to-day chores.

- Check that the daily starting, logging, running, and stopping of any operations on the data base are done properly by the operators.
- Supervise all restarts and recoveries after failure.
- Supervise all reorganizations of indices and data bases.
- Check that all loggings of the transactions and any activities against the data bases are done.
- Establish a plan for periodic dumps of the data base, including initiating and supervising them. Control the physical transfer of copies of the data base on auxiliary storage to locations other than the data center.
- Monitor the recording of all malfunctions of the hardware, and initiate the regular preventive maintenance done by the operations staff.
- Obtain the data base performance reports on a daily, weekly, and monthly basis, and track down any performance problems. Inform the systems experts about the problems. Use performance measurement tools.
- Continually evaluate and exercise backup/recovery plans.
- Evaluate the data base quality (e.g., consistency of data, of pointers, etc.).

6. Growth, Change, and Maintenance Phase

- Evaluate the impact on performance of growth and changes to the data base.

- Check that backup and recovery procedures are intact before introducing any major changes.

Systems Expert.   In a large data base environment, this is usually a group of experts who are knowledgeable in data base system languages and procedures. The DBA and the applications experts supply the system experts with the logical structure of the data base. The systems experts then have the following responsibilities in the various phases.

1. Design Phase

- Use the logical structure for simulation with the applications profiles and develop the physical structure.
- Apply the performance criteria against the physical structure and make changes accordingly.
- Choose the right access methods and the suitable physical organization to satisfy the performance criteria and any future expansion requirements.
- Design the software and the hardware configuration necessary for the data base.
- Design the recovery, backup, and restart procedures with the operations staff.
- Select or create efficient randomizing modules for accessing the data base.
- Design the security, privacy, and authorization routines.
- Make the DBA aware of all existing software and hardware constraints.

2, 3, 4. Physical Creation, Conversion, and Integration Phases

- Install the DBMS package.
- Coordinate the implementation of the applications with the applications experts.
- Implement with the operations experts the procedures for checking the security, privacy, and access control violations.
- Set up the procedures with the operations experts for performance measurement and evaluation.
- Help the applications experts with any dumps of the data base system as a result of abnormal terminations.

5. Operations Phase

• Tune the system as required because of performance problems.

• Periodically check the auxiliary space utilization, and try to make it as efficient as possible.

• Try to project the workload, based on the past and present workloads, and make the DBA aware of any anticipated performance problems.

• Help the application development people with any dumps of the data base system as a result of abnormal terminations.

• Analyze problems, dumps, traces, and so on. Often problems cannot be isolated to one application, or are not application problems at all.

6. Growth, Change, and Maintenance Phase

• Design the software and hardware configurations necessary for growth of the data base.

• Coordinate the implementation of the "changed" applications with the application experts.

Applications Expert. This group consists of experts in data base design and of experts in data base programming techniques. Its responsibilities are as follows.

1. Design Phase

• Define the data elements and their relationships.

• Develop the logical structure of the data base with the user community.

• Attempt to incorporate the long term goals of the enterprise in the logical structure of the data base.

• Determine the data element synonyms with the help of the user community.

• Provide the systems experts with information about usage frequency and changes to the data elements. These numbers affect the physical design and the performance of the data base.

• Supply the data element information and their relationships (i.e., which programs use which data elements) to the librarian, who will insert the information into the data dictionary.

- Control the entry of the new data elements into the data dictionary. The application programmer cannot perform insertions into or deletions from entries in the data dictionary.

2, 3, 4. Physical Creation, Conversion, and Integration Phases

- Assist the application development staff in the conversion and the integration phases.
- Assist the systems experts and the operations experts in checking the implementation of procedures for security, privacy, and auditability.
- Assist the librarians in the expansion of the data dictionary/ directory system.

5. Operations Phase

- Check whether the applications are following the security, privacy, and access control restrictions.
- Check whether the applications are storing historical data properly.
- Supervise the proper sequence of running the applications.

6. Growth, Change, and Maintenance Phase

- Evaluate the results of changes to the existing applications, and the interaction between the applications.
- Supply the data element information and their relationships (i.e., which programs use which data elements) to the librarian, who inserts the information into the data dictionary.
- Control the entry of new or changed data elements into the data dictionary.
- Assist the application development staff in the "changing" phase.

Librarian. One of the major responsibilities of a librarian is to establish the communication mechanisms for the data base administrator. Figure 2.1 shows the necessary communication paths in the data base environment. It is the librarian's function to set up the meetings between the DBA and the different functions from Figure 2.1. This part of the librarian's responsibility is similar to the "public relations" function. The other responsibilities are as follows.

1. Design Phase

- Keep a record of the changes in the data dictionary/directory system.
- Document and distribute the results of design and of meetings to those who need the information.

2, 3, 4, 5, 6. Physical Creation, Conversion, Integration, Operations, and Growth, Change, and Maintenance Phases

- Control the data dictionary/directory system's libraries.
- Keep a record of any security, privacy, and/or authorization violations.
- Keep records for the auditability mechanisms.
- Document and distribute the results of these phases and of meetings to those who need the information.

Query Languages Expert. Since most data bases are used on-line, it is desirable to have a query facility for accessing the data base. A high level query language is better than a procedural one for unanticipated requests. For the occasional user, the chances of making mistakes in setting the query are higher with a procedural than with a high level query language. Also, a high level query language will be able to satisfy ad hoc queries from management. To support the function effectively, the DBA staff should include a query language expert.

The responsibilities in the various phases are as follows.

1. Design Phase

- Determine the authorization levels for different types of queries.
- Establish the formats for the queries.
- Design, in conjunction with the systems experts, queries with adequate performance.
- Assist people with unanticipated queries. The ability to handle such queries is a prime benefit of a DBMS.

2, 3, 4, 5, 6.   Physical Creation, Conversion, Integration,
Operations, and Growth, Change, and Maintenance Phases

- Track the performance of queries.
- Make the DBA aware of queries that cannot be satisfied by the data base, and suggest alternative queries that retrieve the required information from the data base.
- Assist the user in query development and maintenance.

Auditor. In a number of environments, it is possible for the application programmers to circumvent the implemented security restrictions. More often than we think, they succeed in doing so. An auditor should be able to pinpoint possible places where security breaches may take place, as well as the ones that have already occurred. Hardware as well as software security has to be considered.

Security and privacy issues go hand in hand. If security is at stake, privacy violations may follow immediately.

REFERENCES

1. *The Database Administrator*, John K. Lyon, A Wiley-Interscience Publication, a division of John Wiley & Sons, New York.
2. *The Data Base Administrator*, Prepared by the members of the Data Base Administration Project of the Information Management Group, of the Information Systems Division, of the GUIDE International Corporation, November 3, 1972.
3. "On some Metrics for Databases, or What Is a Very Large Database?" Rob Gerritsen, Howard Morgan, and Michael Zisman, *ACM SIGMOD RÉCORD*, Vol. 9, No. 1 (June 1977).

Data Dictionary

3.1 WHAT IS A DATA DICTIONARY?

In a data base environment, one of the major objectives is the sharing of common data by multiple users. Another major objective is providing correct data to these users. To realize the objectives of correct data, minimum redundancy, and control of data usage, a centralized control mechanism is mandatory. A data dictionary is a prime candidate to establish and to maintain these controls. An additional advantage is that systems established using a data dictionary tend to be more effective and less expensive to develop.

But the decision to acquire and to implement a data dictionary should not be taken lightly. One aspect that should not be overlooked is that effective use of a data dictionary will probably require some organizational and procedural changes. Acquiring a data dictionary is a commitment, just as acquiring a data base management system is a commitment. Later in the chapter, we shall investigate the cost/benefit considerations. Let us first see where the data dictionary fits in the design process.

The first step in designing a data base is to collect information about the enterprise, that is, about the usage, relationships, and meaning of data. As the design process progresses, it is necessary to store information about the conceptual, logical, internal, and external models at a central location. A tool that enables one to control and manage the information about the data in the design, implementation, operation and expansion phases of a data base is called a *data dictionary*.

In the beginning stage of collecting information regarding data, naming conventions for the data elements must be established, conflicts between different departments regarding the meanings, the sources, and the naming conventions resolved, descriptions of the data elements agreed upon, and synonyms of the data elements recognized. This process inevitably involves many iterations and many political struggles. Every department or other part of the organization considers its mission to be the most important one, and its perspective of the organization the right one. This results in conflicts regarding the collection of information about data. In these situations the data base administrator has to play the role of a tie breaker. To keep track of and to record information about data effectively, it is desirable for everyone involved with the data base to use an automated data dictionary.

The data dictionary stores such information about data as its origin, description, relationship to other data, usage, responsibility, and format. It is a data base itself, which stores "data about data." The data dictionary is a guide and contains "road maps" to the data base instead of "raw data."

3.1.1 Basic Objectives of a Data Dictionary

One of the basic objectives of a data dictionary is to allow management of the documentation about data. Since the data base serves a number of users, it is vital that every user understands precisely what the data is and what it means.

There are many aspects about data that a data base designer has to know. In the early stages of the design, the very first thing that should be recorded about each item of the data is the English (or the native language) definition. These definitions or descriptions should be such that every person who is going to use the data understands exactly what each definition means and agrees with it.

There should be an understandable definition or description of every piece of data. If three different departments are using the same piece of data in three different contexts, however, it is not at all easy for the three departments to agree on one definition or one description of the shared item. Problems of this nature have to be resolved by the data base administration function. Finding solutions to problems of this type will serve as evidence that political disputes can be much more complicated to solve than technical issues in the data base environment.

At this stage, when an attempt is being made to arrive at a textual description of every piece of data, no attention need be given to the actual physical representation. The designer does not have to determine whether the data is going to be stored as packed or in character form or in some other format.

It is advisable to begin to collect the information about data in a data dictionary on the day the project starts. As soon as the project is under way, the designer begins asking each user questions, such as what kind of system the user wants, what information the user wants to get from the system, and what type of input can be provided. As soon as the user and the designer start talking about the user's needs, they are going to use data element names; in a banking enterprise examples may be "account number," "balance," and "interest." The data base designer and the user have to be confident that when they use a term they mean precisely the same thing; otherwise the designer may build a system that is not what the user wanted. This points out another basic objective of a data dictionary, that is, helping to establish effective communication between the designer and users and among the users themselves.

Let us consider an example. In a banking environment, one of the key data elements is "balance." What is the balance of a specific account? For most nonbankers, there is an obvious definition of what a balance means. But if an account master file for a commercial accounting system is studied, it is possible that in one account's record there are approximately 25 fields with the word "balance" in their title. It is extremely important, therefore, that when the designer talks to the user it is made very clear which balance the designer is referring to: the "opening balance this morning," the "closing balance last night," the "book balance," the "available balance," and so on. The "closing balance last night" is not necessarily identical with the "opening balance this morning." The "book balance" goes up as soon as the customer makes a deposit, but if the deposit was made with a check, the "available balance" rises only after the check has cleared. There are many more diverse "balance" fields. The data dictionary can be used to store the information about all the data elements in a central location to establish effective communication between all parties concerned.

In most enterprises, management does not have control over the data resource because there is no corporate view of data. To gain control over the data resource, information about data has to be collected at a central place. Management then can begin to impose controls over the use of the data resource.

Thus the two basic objectives of a data dictionary are management and control of data as a resource at a central location through the phases of design, implementation, and operations, as well as establishment of effective communication between all those who are interested in the data base.

In the case of a distributed data base environment, the data bases or portions of data bases may be physically stored in different locations on different computers, and connected via data communication facilities. It is possible that some installations may store and access data only at the local places, whereas other installations may store and access local as well as remote data.

Let us take an example of a nationwide life insurance company. The insurance agents in the New York City area will request information about clients in the New York City area much more frequently than about clients in the San Francisco area, and vice versa. It may be advisable to store the data about New York City clients for on-line retrieval at some local places on the East Coast. If an agent from the East Coast needs information about a client on the West Coast, it can be retrieved in batch from the data base stored on the West Coast, and vice versa.

A data dictionary installed at every location may be provided with the information about all the physical locations where the data is stored, access control, and security and privacy constraints. With the help of this information, the data dictionary may decide "intelligently" whether to satisfy a request from the local data base, or whether the user is authorized to access the remote data, in which case the request is sent to the remote location.

In this book when we talk about a data dictionary it will be in the context of a DBMS. Some people argue that the data dictionary may also be put on paper, either handwritten or typewritten. But the problem with a manual data dictionary is that it will be difficult to satisfy the designer, who is going to need the definition of a data element sorted in a number of different ways. The same data element may be used by a number of different users in different contexts. In the beginning stage there will be a list of the data elements in some semirelated form. As the designer proceeds through the design phase, however, the data elements will be used in a number of different places. They will appear on the input formats and on the output formats in relationships to one another. In each place the data elements will appear in a different context. To accomplish all this will be a tedious job, and soon the listings will be difficult to manage. An automated version will be easier to control and to manage.

In order for a data dictionary to be accepted and used in a data processing environment, it needs to have a central input. Information put into this one source can be used through all the design phases and can be copied by programmers into their programs for data structures. If a manual or a nonintegrated dictionary is used, the information therein becomes inconsistent (over time) with what is actually in the system. A data dictionary may be referred to as a "meta data base" which stores information about the data base.

3.1.2 Data Base Management System and Data Dictionary

A data dictionary can also be used in a non-data-base environment. A data dictionary is a central place of information about data description, such as meaning, relationships to other data, and responsibility for keeping the data up to date and recording the origin of the data. In a data base environment, the information stored in a data dictionary is about the data stored in a data base, and in a non-data-base environment the information stored in a data dictionary is about the data stored in data files. It is also possible to use a data dictionary for DBMS and non-DBMS applications simultaneously.

It is necessary to install software to create and manage a data dictionary data base. The software is also called a data dictionary. The data dictionary package may be integrated within a data base management system or may be free-standing. As far as today's marketplace is concerned, there are very few data base management systems in which the data dictionary package is an integral part. Most of the data dictionary packages available today are free-standing. An integrated data dictionary is a part of the DBMS package, whereas a free-standing data dictionary is a separate package in addition to the DBMS package.

In the case of an integrated data dictionary, the data descriptions exist only once in the system and the descriptions are stored in the data dictionary. In a free-standing data dictionary an option exists whether the appropriate data descriptions will be retrieved from the data dictionary or supplied otherwise. In the case of an integrated data dictionary, there is no option, it is necessary to check for currency of data descriptions prior to execution of a program. A free-standing data dictionary may or may not require a check for currency of data descriptions before a program is executed.

Both approaches, a free-standing data dictionary package and an integrated data dictionary package, offer advantages and disadvantages.

Advantages of an Integrated Data Dictionary System

- Data descriptions are not stored redundantly with a data dictionary package and with a data base management system package. This reduces the occurrence of errors due to failure to update both places.
- The data dictionary has access to the data in the data base. One potential use of the data dictionary may be in the area of data access tracking, to provide valuable statistics for improving performance.
- A data dictionary can serve as a much more powerful control tool when integrated with the DBMS, because the data base designer and the users will have to enforce the data dictionary as a tool for documentation and control of the data.

Advantages of a Free-Standing Data Dictionary

- There is less risk involved of commitment to a data base management system in implementing a free-standing data dictionary than an integrated data dictionary. Also, the implementation of a free-standing dictionary is easier, because the dictionary does not have to adhere to the implementation idiosyncrasies of a DBMS.
- An integrated data dictionary needs all the data descriptions required for a data base at one time, whereas the data descriptions can be provided in stages to a free-standing data dictionary. In today's data processing environment not all data files are converted to a data base at one time. A data base exists together with some conventional data files. A data dictionary package that can keep track of data in the data base as an integrated data dictionary, and of data in the data files as a free-standing data dictionary, would be desirable.

There is a recent trend among suppliers of software packages toward having the dictionary as the keystone for all of the related software packages, including a data base management system, a query language processor, and a Teleprocessing monitor.

Whether a data dictionary is free-standing or integrated, we would like to know about its interfaces in an ideal data base environment. The data dictionary packages available in the marketplace today do not necessarily provide all of the interfaces, as illustrated in the next section.

3.1.3 Data Dictionary and Its Interfaces

We will consider a data dictionary's interfaces in an environment with a single data base management system, as in Figure 3.1.

In the beginning stage of the data base designing process, the data base administration function will be interacting with the data dictionary. With the help of a report generator (which probably is an integral part of the data dictionary package), the management and the users will be provided with reports tailored to the individual user's needs.

The reports may contain information regarding the following:

- The data elements and the entities.
- The relationships between the data elements and between the entities.
- Responsibilities of the users for correctness of the data.
- Frequency of usage and textual descriptions of the data elements.
- Access control information.
- Audit reports.
- Predefined summary reports.
- User-designed ad hoc reports
- Cross-reference reports.
- Change reports.
- Error reports.

A data dictionary may also generate data descriptions for high level languages in the form of appropriate language dialects to the program libraries and to the compilers. Information about cross-reference relationships between the data elements and application programs can be stored in the data dictionary. The cross-reference list will enable any authorized person to inform any application

Figure 3.1 Data dictionary's interfaces in an ideal data base environment. There are two types of interfaces:

1. The interface with the people involved, for example, data base administrator, systems programmer, systems analyst, application programmer, management, end user, and auditor.
2. The interface with the software, for example, data base management system, compilers, operating system, and report generators.

programmer or department about an intended modification before it takes place, get concurrence if appropriate, and then implement the change. The change may involve content, format, or relationship to other data elements.

Ideally, the interface between the data base management system and the data dictionary should be such that the DBMS directories are readable by the data dictionary system in order to provide data on the current state of the DBMS. The data types in the data base should be updated after the data dictionary system makes note of the changes, and the data should be updated only when it is found acceptable to the DBMS. Thus the data dictionary, the DBMS, and the data base should form a closed loop.

The data dictionary can be used as an effective tool by the data base administration function in the design, implementation, and operations phases of the data base. It is the responsibility of the DBA to protect the data dictionary by enforcing standards, security, and privacy constraints.

The auditing function has gained more importance in the last few years in the electronic data processing environment. In an environment where the data base is shared, auditing becomes mandatory. A data dictionary is the ideal place for finding answers to questions like "where used," "who used," and "when used" with regard to the data elements and entities. It is also the ideal place to provide information for a cost/efficiency study of the organization's system, as well as to satisfy particular privacy and confidentiality requirements.

These interfaces show that there are two types of uses of a data dictionary. One type of use is by people in their functions as data base administrator, systems programmer, systems analyst, application programmer, management, end user, and auditor. The other type of use is by software in such areas as data base management system, compilers, operating system, and report generators.

These two types of interfaces enhance the management and control of the data base environment as a result of effective communication between the parties involved.

3.1.4 An Ideal Data Dictionary: Its Requirements and Organization

The following is a list of desirable requirements of a data dictionary data base for describing the data. It does not imply that any single data dictionary package available today supports all these requirements.

Conceptual Model. Information about data needed in the designing process of the conceptual model includes entities, data elements or attributes representing the entities, and relationships between the data elements. Also, information about which departments and which users currently use or intend to use which data elements, and how frequently the data elements are used, together with textual descriptions with meanings and purposes, should be stored in the data dictionary. The data elements, entities, and relationships should have appropriate labels, versions, status (proposed, concurred, approved, effective), textual descriptions, synonyms (other data dictionary entities with the same meaning but with different labels), memberships (entities of which a particular data element is a member of by which it is being referenced), and data element groupings with the key data elements.

Logical Model. The following information about the logical model of the data base should be stored in the data dictionary: the data element groupings with the key data elements (these groupings may be the subsets of the groupings specified in the conceptual model), the underlying data model, the relationships of the groupings based on the data model, the external models supported by the logical model (i.e., the different logical paths for information processing), the logical transactions, the programs, and the modules. The inter-dependencies of the transactions, the programs, and the modules should also be stored. The cross-reference information between the transactions, the programs, the modules, and the departments or the functions that are served by them should be included. Other necessary information is the programming language and the program type (batch, teleprocessing) for the programs and transactions.

Internal Model. The physical layout information about the data elements, for example, length (characters); mode (bit string, character string, packed decimal, simple floating point); precision (for numeric elements); justification (right, left); picture (for display purposes only); edit rules (constant, range of values); derivation algorithm (for calculated elements); sequence (the sequential position that a particular data element occupies in the membership); security (security code for read, update); medium (card, disk, tape, video); devices where the data base(s) are stored; and access control information should be stored in the data dictionary.

An ideal data dictionary should be an integral part of the entire data base environment. The data base administrator should be responsible for the input to the data dictionary. Being the central part of the data base environment, a data dictionary has to be saved in backup copies to avoid disastrous effects due to a system malfunction or any unintentional destruction of the production version of the data dictionary. The data base administration function bears the full responsibility of protecting the vital part of the data base environment—the data dictionary.

An ideal data dictionary package should also support the following features.

Retrieval and Reporting Facilities. Any communication and documentation tool can be effective if it provides easy retrieval and reporting facilities. The facilities should support formal as well as ad hoc requests. Reports may include the following items:

- Element lists in alphabetical or any other desired sequence.
- Cross-reference listings between the data elements, groups of the data elements, programs using them, and departments or people responsible for keeping the contents valid.
- Data descriptions for host language programs, and logical views of external models supporting the application programs.

The data dictionary should also contain sufficient information to provide some indication of any effect on programs or transactions as a result of a change to the data model. The provision of cost estimates for implementing the proposed change is a very desirable feature.

Capturing of Data as Input to Data Dictionary. Ideally the data dictionary should be used as a tool by the data base administrator, application programmers, users, management, and any software interacting with the data base. The data stored in the data dictionary should be entered by the people with some people-oriented input language, or by the software from program definitions as in COBOL and PL/1, from the data base management system definitions and from the program procedure statements.

Access Control Information. The data dictionary may contain information regarding access control, specifying who may have access to what part of the data base and in what way. The information can be used as follows:

- Before compiling any programs or printing any reports, it can be checked whether there are any contradictions between the specifications for data retrieval given by the requestor and the specifications provided by the data base administrator.
- To pinpoint any misuse of the data for a part of the data base shared by multiple users, a stringent set of security restrictions has to be implemented.

If the data dictionary is to be used for access control, it must itself be subject to access control. The number of people eligible to make any modifications to the data dictionary must be restricted. Privacy restrictions on the contents of the data dictionary should be implemented.

Support of Utilities. Since the data dictionary is the central part of the data base environment, it should be able to support the various utilities of editing, updating, and restructuring of the data bases, report generators, and so on.

Generation of Program and Data Description Code. Storing the information about the data elements, about their physical layouts, about their relationships to the other data elements, and about the logical and the internal model should enable a data dictionary to generate the data description code, as well as some standard program modules such as access or input/output modules.

Consistency. The information contents of the data dictionary should be complete, correctly formatted, and properly cross-referenced. To satisfy these requirements, any input to the data dictionary should be checked for consistency. The checking should also be based on the mapping information between the conceptual, logical, external, and internal models stored in the data dictionary.

Ideal Data Dictionary System

1. The data dictionary should support the conceptual, logical, internal, and external models.
2. The data dictionary should be integrated with the data base management system.
3. The data dictionary should support various versions of the documentation (e.g., the test versions, the production version).
4. The data dictionary should support the efficient transfer of information to the data base management system. Ideally, the binding between the external models and the internal model should be done at the execution time, when the data dictionary should take the information from the production version and create the data base description and program description dynamically.
5. A data dictionary system should initiate the reorganization of the production version of the data base as a result of changes to the data base description. Similarly, any changes to the program

descriptions should be reflected automatically in the program description library with the help of the data dictionary. This will happen when the data dictionary system is an integral part of the DBMS.

3.2 IMPLEMENTATION STRATEGIES FOR A DATA DICTIONARY

Two types of data dictionary packages are available today. One type of package is independent and supports a varied number of data base management systems. The second type of package has to be implemented on a data base management system. For both types of packages, the data dictionary itself is implemented as a data base(s). Accordingly, the design of a data dictionary is subject to the same criteria as is that of any data base. The first study to be carried out concerns cost/benefit considerations. The second question that remains to be answered is how and when a data dictionary can be phased into the operations of the enterprise.

3.2.1 Cost/Benefit Considerations

As stated earlier, the data dictionary is not an integral part of a data base management system in most of the packages available today. As a result, the decision about buying a data dictionary package has to be made independently of the DBMS. The acquisition has to be cost justified for the benefits to be expected. Let us first consider the expenses that will be incurred as a result of using a data dictionary system. The issue here is not whether to have a data dictionary, but, first, whether to have a data base administration function and, second, whether to provide the data base administrator with a tool for control. From this perspective, we would like to compare a data base environment with and without a data dictionary. We shall not consider the conventional data set (data file) environment with or without a data dictionary.

The cost of an object or of a project can be measured in terms of the resources required. Costs can usually be expressed in terms of dollars: the package acquisition, personnel, creation and maintenance of the data dictionary data base, equipment costs, and so forth. Usually it is more difficult to measure benefits. A benefit is a consequence of an action that protects, aids, improves, or promotes the well-being of an individual or organization. Benefits may be expressed in terms of savings, cost avoidance, improved performance, and hidden opportunities. It is important in any cost/benefit analysis to list the probable effects of the proposed project, positive as well as negative.

It is still an art to put dollar tags on information as far as benefits, costs, and savings are concerned. One school of thought holds that cost/benefit calculations simply do not work for most companies that are considering the acquisition of highly sophisticated software products like data dictionaries and data base management systems. The cost/benefit analysis is not done in the real world for the very practical reason that any relationship between the calculations and the resulting real world environment is purely coincidental. Since, therefore, this type of cost/benefit analysis is still an art, the following points are based more on intuition than on scientific research.

Costs

Personnel. The costs of the personnel to install a data dictionary system, to create the data dictionary data base, and to maintain it have to be considered. These expenses will vary, depending on the size and complexity of the enterprise, the size of the data base, the number of applications supported by the data dictionary, and the sophistication level of the personnel themselves. It should not be forgotten that there is a learning curve associated with the usage of a data dictionary system, just as with any other system. The costs will be considerably higher if the enterprise is running its business in a totally decentralized way. In this kind of environment, the change in organizational procedure will result in higher expenditure.

Creation of data dictionary data base. This will be the main expense. The cost to create the data dictionary data base will depend on the following items:

1. The number of data elements to be recognized and to be entered with their textual descriptions and their attributes.
2. Locating and documenting the relationships between the data elements, between the entities, and between the applications, using the data elements, the entities, and the relationships between them.

The expenses for these two items depend in turn, on the ease of availability of the data to be entered in the data dictionary data base at the time of the initial creation of the data dictionary. For the existing data base or data file applications, the accumulation of the data elements with their attributes and descriptions will be relatively easy if the documentation is at the disposal of the data base administration staff. For the development of a new set of applications, only a part of the costs has to be considered because documentation of a similar nature should be done anyway.

Maintenance of a data dictionary data base. Although maintenance expenses will be only a fraction of the cost of the original creation of the data dictionary data base, they have to be considered for a dynamic environment. The cost of maintaining a data dictionary data base will be equal, in the worst situation, to the expenses without a data dictionary.

Equipment. The data dictionary, to be effective, should be stored on a random access storage for easy retrieval. Usually the costs for the random access storage, central processing unit time, and memory usage are small as compared to the personnel costs.

Let us now consider the benefits to be expected from the use of a data dictionary.

Benefits. The benefits will vary from one enterprise to another. The savings with a data dictionary system will be higher for a data base environment with a larger number of data elements and relationships. The savings will also seem to be higher in an environment with a relatively high number of changes, that is, a dynamic data base environment will benefit more from a data dictionary than a totally static one. A "dynamic" environment does not mean that the data structure is in a state of flux. Then the enterprise should not have a data base. Any data base of real size cannot be restructured on a constant basis without incurring considerable expenses. The benefits from a data dictionary also seem to increase as the sharing of data elements and between programs increases.

Data base design, development, creation, and maintenance. The use of the data dictionary improves communications between the designers and the users and among the users themselves. This results in fewer iterations in the design phase. The development costs are less because of better documentation of specifications and clearer understanding by all involved. Ideally, the data base creation should proceed at a faster pace because of the faster data base design. Also, the maintenance of the data base should be less expensive with the help of a data dictionary than in a nondictionary environment because of better documentation, faster analysis of the effects of proposed changes, and better communication between the maintenance personnel and the people requesting the changes.

"Intangibles." There are also a number of "intangible" benefits as a result of using a data dictionary:

1. The ease of referencing a data base as a result of using a data dictionary, like the ease of referencing a book by using the index, cannot be expressed in terms of dollars.
2. A data dictionary makes possible more complete and systematic keeping of information about data.
3. It is easier to implement standards for data element names, descriptions, usage, and so on, at a central location than in scattered places.
4. A data dictionary enables one to implement changes to the data base faster because of the cross-referencing capability.
5. A data dictionary improves the ability to create records of information accessed and the persons accessing it.
6. It is also easier for the auditors to audit the data base and its use because information about the data base and about its use is centrally located.

In a data base environment with a data dictionary system, the initial costs of implementation (i.e., populating the data dictionary with the information about the data elements, their interrelationships, their usage, etc.) are higher relative to those for a data base environment without a data dictionary system. But the expenses for changes with the data dictionary system taper off with time, whereas without the data dictionary these expenses may continue to increase. Expenses in a data base environment without a data dictionary may also increase with time because of scattered documentation and loss of opportunity.

3.2.2   When to Implement a Data Dictionary

The choice of a reasonable time frame for the phasing in of the data dictionary is important because a wrong choice may jeopardize the entire data base project. At the same time, however, it should not be forgotten that there exists no single best "cookbook" recipe for every single enterprise. The implementation plan of the data dictionary depends on the environment of the enterprise, like anything else in data processing.

It may be ambitious to install a data dictionary for the data base of the entire enterprise, just as it is ambitious to install one data base for the entire enterprise. Data dictionary systems have a learning curve associated with them. The project of installing a data dictionary for the whole enterprise should not be undertaken before a high point on the curve is reached.

One of the following possibilities should be chosen for the first application with the data dictionary package.

A Conventional Application System. If an application system that does not affect the other application systems to a large extent and that is also moderate in size can be found, it may be considered as a possible candidate. At the same time this application system should also have some visibility and importance to the running of the enterprise. Moreover, it should be a dynamic one with changes, because the data dictionary can then demonstrate its potential benefits and effectiveness in the changing environment.

A Set of Existing Data Base Management System Applications. The running data base management system applications seem to have high visibility in an enterprise and also tend to be dynamic. If it is intended to expand the given set of applications, introduction of a data dictionary system may be the right time to show the strengths of the data dictionary in the areas of communications between users, documentation, and the storage of information about a number of applications at a centrally located place.

A New Set of Application(s). If an enterprise is planning on expanding its applications or converting its existing conventional applications to a data base environment, the new applications would be an excellent choice. The programmers, the analysts, and the users will not necessarily like the idea of documenting the applications that are already running. However, for the new application systems to be developed, the work has not been done before, and documenting the applications for the first time is an incentive that should not be undermined.

The main point in selecting when and what to implement with a data dictionary is the advantage that will ensue to the people as managers, users, analysts, programmers, clerks, operators, and so.

A DBMS may provide support for an on-line system with high visibility to management. Typically a dictionary has no such visibility but is important as an internal control tool. Therefore one way of looking at the timing consideration and choosing which application to implement first is to regard the decision as a trade-off in the classic hare/tortoise tradition, with the dictionary being the tortoise.

In the process of answering the questions "when" and "what" about the data dictionary, the objectives about its use must be set. One criterion of major importance is management commitment, and if it is not given, the whole management information system is in trouble. The design team has to research available products, keeping the following aspects in mind: ease of use, ease of changes, servicing by vendor, capability, expansion possibilities, and expenses. The design team also has to research the specific needs of the enterprise and match them to the features of the various products available. The plan for the data collection has to be determined, and the people who are going to use the data dictionary must be trained. Then the collection and reviewing of data can initiate the building and the analyzing of the data dictionary.

The best time to start using a data dictionary is in the requirements definition phase. The user is there and eager to help the designer understand the system. A psychological point mentioned before is that no one has spent time doing data gathering in his/her own way. The use of a data dictionary in the requirements definition will provide a solid baseline for project control and standards, as well as a common denominator for communications.

To get the biggest payback as a result of using a data dictionary, it should be implemented in the requirements definition phase for a new application system, for a major redesign of an existing application system, or for a merger of two or more application systems.

3.2.3   Data Definition Guidelines

If the data dictionary is to be an effective communications tool, there should be a common understanding among the users about its building blocks. The following are the basic parts of the data dictionary data base(s):

- *Data Element.*   An attribute describing an entity. Every data element has a unique name or label. The name or label should be descriptive and should consist of key words or abbreviations taken from authorized lists.

- *Group Data Element.* A grouping of logically related data elements. For a group data element, all subelements (elementary and group data elements) must be explicitly identified. For basic elements, all group data element memberships must be explicitly identified.

- *Derived Data Element.* A data element that originates as a result of a formula or calculation. For all derived data elements, the formula or calculation must be identified, along with all the data elements used in the derivation. These data elements should also be defined in the dictionary.

- *Synonyms or Aliases.* A data element with a different designator but the same meaning as another data element. The description of a synonym must identify the designators of other data elements with which this one is synonymous.

- *Homonyms.* Two data elements with the same designator but different meanings. By entering the data element designators in the dictionary, the synonym and homonym problems should be identified by the dictionary and the problems resolved by the data base design team.

- *Conceptual Model Description.* The model describes the entities of the enterprise, the relationships between the entities, and the information flow.

- *Logical Model Description.* The model is possibly a subset of the conceptual model and is mapped to the data base management system package to be used.

- *External Model(s) Description.* The external models describe the views of the application programs, that is, the ways in which the relationships between the entities are looked at by different applications.

- *Internal Model Description.* The internal model is the physical mapping of the data base. It describes the relationships between the entities, access methods to be used, blocking factors, and other physical mapping details.

In addition to the building block descriptions given above, the following description of the relationships between them should be provided:

- *Text.* The text provides information enabling the dictionary user to decide whether a data element is applicable or potentially applicable to his/her needs. This description should be

understandable by all potential users of the dictionary bu
specific enough to distinguish a particular data element from
similar ones. The following rules should be observed:

1. Use words that are specific and nonambiguous.
   - Avoid phrases such as:
     Some employees
     Certain products
   - Instead of the above, use, for example:
     Retired employees
     Paper products
2. Abbreviate only where necessary because of space limitations. Be
   consistent with abbreviations.
3. Avoid language that has a limited audience (i.e., data processing
   accounting, employee relations, etc.).
4. State units of measure (thousands of dollars, meters, centimeters
   etc.) or frequencies of occurrence (per year, per shift, etc.) fo
   quantities, averages, and the like specifically where applicable.
5. Indicate the source of data. The text should also specify the
   document(s) where the data is used, as well as the program(s
   and the user department(s) requiring the data.

REFERENCES

1. "Data Dictionary/Directories," P. P. Uhrowczik, *IBM Systems Journal*, Vol
   12, No. 4 (1973).
2. "Cost-Benefit Analysis in Information Systems Development and Operation,"
   J. L. King and E. L. Schrems, *ACM Computing Surveys*, Vol. 10, No. 1
   (March 1978).
3. *Data Dictionary Systems.*, H. C. Lefkovits, Q.E.D. Information Sciences
   Inc., Wellesley, Massachusetts, 1977.
4. *Technical Profile of Seven Data Element Dictionary/Directory Systems*
   National Bureau of Standards, Special Publication 500-3, U.S. Departmen
   of Commerce, Washington, D.C. 20234.
5. *The British Computer Society Data Dictionary Systems Working Party Re
   port*, Vol. 9, No. 2 (Fall 1977).

Data Base Design (Conceptual Model and Logical Model)

Data Models

A data base management system (DBMS) uses a data model as its underlying structure. A data model embodies the relationships between the entities. Today most data base implementations use hierarchical and network data models. Another data model that is gaining importance is called a relational data model. A number of experimental relational systems have been developed, and a few commercial packages have emerged.

In addition to these three data models in today's market, there are many data base management systems that use file inversion on multiple keys. These DBMSs can frequently be categorized into hierarchical or network; but in the real world they are used to construct simple files and use multiple key retrieval. File inversion is more a matter of physical implementation. The issue of physical implementation is treated in Part III of this book. (In that part we will discuss data base management systems that use file inversion.)

This chapter discusses the three data models: relational, hierarchical, and network. The data models are presented with help of an example: a "pseudo-hospital" environment.

4.1 WHAT IS A DATA MODEL?

One of the major responsibilities of the data base administration function is to develop a conceptual model, also called an enterprise model, of the organization. The model embodies the entities and their relationships and is the tool used to represent the conceptual organization of data. The conceptual model is a communications tool between the various users of data, and as such is developed without any concern for physical representation. The conceptual model is used to organize, visualize, plan, and communicate ideas. It is (or should be) independent of a data base management system.

The entities of an organization and the relationships between them can be represented by a data model. The commercial data base management systems available today are based either on a hierarchical data model, a network data model, a relational data model, a combination of the three, or some subset of the three.

The conceptual model (also called the "enterprise model") has to be mapped to the logical model used as an underlying structure for a data base management system, and the logical model must be mapped to the physical model (also called the "internal model" or the "physical structure"). The logical model is either a relational, a hierarchical, or a network data model. We use the term "data model" in the generic sense, that is, it may be a conceptual or a logical or an internal (physical) model.

The data base management system is not a factor in designing a conceptual model, but designing a logical model is dependent on the DBMS to be used. In the real world, the DBMS is frequently given, and the data base administrator has no choice. The reason why this occurs is that a particular computer (central processing unit) may support only one or two DBMS. Ideally, the DBMS should be a dominant factor when selecting the computer, but this is seldom the case. Again ideally, the choice of the DBMS should be made after the conceptual model is designed. The process of mapping from the conceptual model to the logical model should be examined while evaluating different DBMS packages.

The main difference among the three types of data models lies in the representation of the relationships between the entities. We would like to distinguish between a relationship among entities, and between a relationship among attributes of the same entity and among attributes of different entities. The next section deals with these relationships.

4.2 RELATIONSHIPS WITHIN A DATA MODEL

A relationship is a mapping or linkage between two sets of data. It can be "one-to-one," "one-to-many," or "many-to-many." The following examples will illustrate these relationships.

In the hospital environment to be considered, a number of patients are admitted to the hospital. If the patient is "new" to the hospital, medical information about his/her history is recorded for the first time. If the patient has been admitted to the hospital previously, existing medical information is updated. The patient keeps the unique identification number regardless of the number of times he/she enters the hospital. The information about the patient will include his/her name, the assigned patient number, and an address. Thus the attributes of the entity PATIENT are patient's number, patient's name, and patient's address.

Another entity we are interested in is SURGEON. The attributes representing the entity SURGEON in the example are surgeon's license number and surgeon's name.

The hospital environment in the example is only a surgical environment, that is, only surgeries are performed in the hospital and the patients receive medical attention by the surgeons after surgery.

The third entity we consider is BED. The hospital room number and the bed number are the attributes of the entity BED.

4.2.1 "One-to-One" Relationship (between Two Entities)

At a given point in time, one patient is assigned to one bed. The relationship between PATIENT and BED is "one-to-one." A "one-to-one" relationship can be denoted by single-headed arrows. (See Figure 4.1.)

4.2.2 "One-to-Many" Relationship (between Two Entities)

At a given point in time, zero, one or many patients are assigned to one hospital room (i.e., a hospital room may have zero, one, or many patients), but a patient is assigned to only one hospital room. A "one-to-many" relationship can be denoted by a single-headed arrow going in the "one" direction and a double-headed arrow going in the "many" direction. (See Figure 4.1.)

4.2.3 "Many-to-Many" Relationship (between Two Entities)

In the example we are using, a surgeon may have operated on several patients. On the other hand, a patient may have been operated on by several surgeons on several visits to the hospital. The relationship

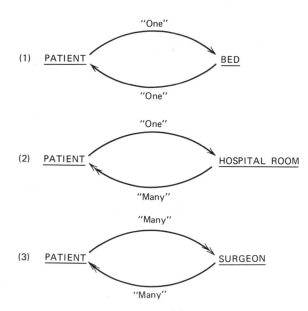

Figure 4.1 Relationships between two entities.

1. *"One-to-one" relationship.* At a given point in time one patient is assigned to one bed.
2. *"One-to-many" relationship.* At a given point in time zero, one, or many patients are assigned to one hospital room, that is, a hospital room may have zero, one, or many patients, but a patient is assigned to only one hospital room.
3. *"Many-to-many" relationship.* A surgeon may have operated on several patients. A patient may have been operated on by several surgeons on several visits to the hospital.

between PATIENT and SURGEON is "many-to-many." We denote
this relationship by double-headed arrows. (See Figure 4.1.)

The relationships between entities are part of the conceptual
model, and they have to be represented in the data base. Any number of entities can participate in a relationship. On the other hand,
the same entities can participate in any number of relationships.

There also exist mappings between the attributes of an entity.
These mappings, too, can be classified as "one-to-one," "one-to-
many," and "many-to-many."

4.2.4 "One-to-One" Relationship (between Two Attributes)

We are assuming that the patient's number is a unique identifier of
a patient, that is, the patient's number is reused at subsequent admit-
tances. If, together with the patient's number, another unique
identifier of the patient is stored in the data base, the relationship between the two unique identifiers is "one-to-one." The "one-
to-one" relationship can be denoted by single-headed arrows. (See
Figure 4.2.)

4.2.5 "One-to-Many" Relationship (between Two Attributes)

The patient's name and number exist together. There can be many
patients with the same name, but their numbers will be different.
Every patient is assigned a unique patient number, that is, to a given
patient number there corresponds only one name. The "one-to-
many" relationship can be denoted by a single-headed arrow in the
"one" direction and a double-headed arrow in the "many" direction.
(See Figure 4.2.)

4.2.6 "Many-to-Many" Relationship (between Two Attributes)

A number of patients with the same name may have been operated
on by many surgeons. A number of surgeons with the same name
may have operated on many patients. The relationship between the
attributes patient's name and surgeons's name is "many-to-many."
We denote this relationship by double-headed arrows. (See Figure
4.2.)

4.2.7 Overview of the Data Models

The hierarchical and the network data models have been in use as
underlying structures for data base management systems since the

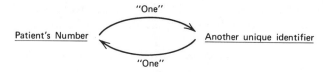

"One—to—one" relationship between two attributes.

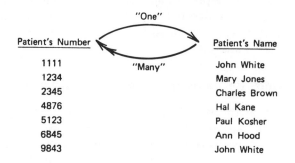

"One—to—many" relationship between two attributes. There can be many patients with the same name, but the patient numbers are unique.

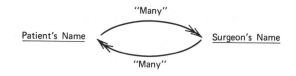

"Many—to—many" relationship between two attributes.

Figure 4.2

early 1960s, whereas the relational data model was proposed as an underlying structure for a data base management system in the early 1970s. The main difference between the three data models is the way they represent the relationships of entities.

In the relational data model, the entities and their relationships are represented with two-dimensional tables, as in Figure 4.3a. The relationships are also considered as entities. Every table represents an entity and is made up of rows and columns. Relational data base management systems have been in use for some time in universities and research laboratories. Some of these prototype packages are System-R (IBM), INGRES (University of California), MACAIMS (R. C. Goldstein and A. L. Strand, "The MacAims Data Management System," *Proceedings of the 1970 ACM—SIGFIDET Workshop on*

PATIENT TABLE		Attribute
Patient's Number	Patient's Name	Patient's Address
1111	John White	15 New Street, New York, N.Y.
1234	Mary Jones	10 Main Street, Rye, N.Y.
2345	Charles Brown	Dogwood Lane, Harrison, N.Y.
4876	Hal Kane	55 Boston Post Road, Chester, Conn.
5123	Paul Kosher	Blind Brook, Mamaroneck, N.Y.
6845	Ann Hood	Hilton Road, Larchmont, N.Y.

Figure 4.3a Representation of data using relational data model. Primary key is patient's number, that is, the patient's number is unique. The PATIENT table has three attributes and at this point in time has six tuples. We do not intend to split the entries in the column headed "Patient's Address" any further into more columns. We are considering the house number, the street, the name of the city, and the name of the state as a single attribute.

Data Description and Access, November 1970, pp. 201–229), and ADMINS (S. McIntosh, and D. Griffel, "Data Management for a Penny a Byte," *Computer Decisions,* May 1973.) Some of the commercial packages available are IBM's Query-By-Example, Tymshare's MAGNUM, Honeywell's MRDM provided with MULTICS, and National CSS's NOMAD. Also, Software AG's ADABAS presents information as if it were a relational system.

The hierarchical data model is made up of a hierarchy of entity types involving a dominant entity type and one or more subordinate entity types at the lower levels, as in Figure 4.5. The relationship established between a dominant and a subordinate entity type is one-to-many, that is, for a given dominant entity there can be many subordinate entity types. At the same time, for a given dominant entity occurrence, there can be many occurrences of a subordinate entity type. Thus the relationships between the entities are like those in a family-tree-like hierarchy, the only difference being that for every child (subordinate entity type) there is only one parent (dominant entity type). Some of the oldest systems are based on the hierarchical data model, some examples are IBM's Information Management System (IMS), Intel's System 2000, and Informatics' Mark IV.

In the network data model, the concept of dominant and subordinate is expanded, any entity can be dominant or subordinate (referred to as owner and member, respectively). In addition, an entity can function as owner (and/or) member simultaneously. This means that any entity can participate in an unlimited number of relationships. There are several commercially available data base management system packages based on the network data model. Some of them are Cullinane's IDMS, Cincom's TOTAL, Honeywell's IDS/II, UNIVAC's DMS 1100, and Digital Equipment Corporation's DBMS-10/20 for its DECSYSTEM-10 and DECSYSTEM-20.

Sections 4.3, 4.4., and 4.5 show in more detail how the three data models represent the relationships between the entities and between the data elements. These three data models are the user's view of data and not necessarily the physical mapping.

4.3 THE RELATIONAL DATA MODEL

We shall use the example of a "pseudo hospital" to discuss the various relationships between the entities of an enterprise. A hospital has data requirements for medical and insurance purposes, peer review, and research study of drug reactions. It has patients, physicians, facilities, drugs, and so on. The "pseudo-hospital" example will serve also to illustrate the various approaches to creating a data model.

Consider the sample data base shown in Figure 4.3a. This data is represented in a two-dimensional table, which is called a relational model of the data. In the relational data model terminology, a table like the one in Figure 4.3a is called a *relation*. But to avoid confusion between a relation and a relationship between the entities, sometimes a relation is called a "table." Every column in a relation is an *attribute*. The values in the column are drawn from a *domain*, that is, a domain is a set of all the values an attribute may have. For example, the domain for patient's number is made up of all the four-digit integers (0000, 0001, 0002, . . . , 9999), but the actual values taken in the PATIENT table at this time are 1111, 1234, 2345, 4876, 5123, and 6845. (See Figure 4.3a.) The rows of the table are called *tuples.*

We could roughly say that the columns of the table represent data elements and the rows of the table represent the data records in conventional terminology.

The SURGEON table in Figure 4.3b represents the entity SURGEON. The PATIENT-AND-SURGEON table in Figure 4.3c

SURGEON TABLE

Surgeon's License Number	Surgeon's Name
145	Beth Little
189	David Rosen
243	Charles Field
311	Michael Diamond
467	Patricia Gold

Figure 4.3b **Representation of data using relational data model. Primary key is surgeon's license number.**

represents the relationship between the patient, the surgeon, and the date of surgery, whereas the table in Figure 4.3*d* represents the entity DRUG with its side effect.

A column or set of columns is called a "candidate key" (often shortened to "key") when its values uniquely identify the rows of the table. (A brief summary of the relational data model terminology is given in Figure 4.3*e*.) It is possible for a relation to have more than one key, in which case it is customary to designate one as the "primary key." In the PATIENT relation, given the patient's number, 1234, which is the value of the key, the patient's name, Mary Jones, and the patient's address, 10 Main Street, Rye, N.Y., are both uniquely determined.

In a table with uniquely assigned names for the columns, the ordering of columns and the ordering of rows are insignificant. No two rows in a table are identical. The ordering of tables is insignificant too. Properties of relations are given in Table 4.1.

The notion of using a relational data model as an underlying structure of a data base management system was introduced by Dr. E. F. Codd in 1970. (See the reference at the end of the chapter.) The process of crystallizing the entities and their relationships in table formats using relational concepts is called the *normalization process*. The normalization theory is based on the observation that a certain set of relations has better properties in an updating environment than do other sets of relations containing the same data. We

PATIENT—AND—SURGEON—TABLE

Patient's Number	Surgeon's License Number	Date of Surgery	Surgery	Postoperative Drug Administered
1111	145	Jan. 1, 1977	Gallstones removal	Penicillin
1111	311	June 12, 1977	Kidney stones removal	— — —
1234	243	April 5, 1976	Eye cataract removal	Tetracycline
1234	467	May 10, 1977	Thrombosis removal	— — —
2345	189	Jan. 8, 1978	Open heart surgery	Cephaldsporin
4876	145	Nov. 5, 1977	Cholecystectomy	Demicillin
5123	145	May 10, 1977	Gallstones removal	— — —
6845	243	April 5, 1976	Eye cornea replacement	Tetracycline

Figure 4.3c **Representation of data using relational data model. Primary key is patient's number + surgeon's license number + date of surgery. One assumption made here is that a patient may receive only one postoperative drug, if any, for a given specific surgery performed.**

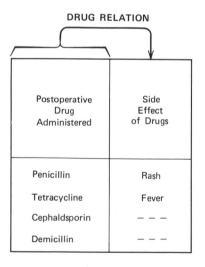

DRUG RELATION

Postoperative Drug Administered	Side Effect of Drugs
Penicillin	Rash
Tetracycline	Fever
Cephaldsporin	— — —
Demicillin	— — —

Figure 4.3d **Representation of data using relational data model. Primary key is postoperative drug administered. One assumption made here is that there can be only one side effect of a drug, if any. Another assumption is that the side effect of a drug depends only on the drug having been administered.**

Terminology: Summary for Relational Data Model

Term	Alternative	Approximate Equivalent
Relation	Table	File (1 record type, fixed number of field types)
Attribute	Column	Field (type, not occurrence)
Tuple	Row	Record (occurrence, not type)
Primary key		Record key, record identifier
Domain		

Figure 4.3e These are only some of the terms used with the relational data model. Anyone interested in other terms used with the relational data model should refer to the bibliography at the end of the chapter.

will use the normalization process in Chapter 5 to build the conceptual model. The conceptual model can be used to develop a logical model, which can then be mapped to a relational, hierarchical, or network model, or to an inverted file with inversion on multiple keys.

One of the major advantages of the relational approach is its simplicity, that is, the ease of understanding for the end user. The end users do not have to be concerned about the physical storage structure; they can be oriented toward the information content of their data and need not worry about the physical representation details. (See Figure 4.3f.) The ability to use the data base without knowing the representation details is called "data independence." We saw the advantages of data independence in Chapter 1.

To establish linkage between tables, some tables must keep some common attributes. For example, the PATIENT table and the PATIENT-AND-SURGEON table have redundancy in the attribute

Table 4.1 Relational Data Model: Properties of Relations

Within any one relation:

1. No duplicate rows.[a]
2. Row order insignificant (a conventional file has some ordering sequence, especially for performance).
3. Column order insignificant (assuming that every column has a unique name).
4. All values atomic, that is, they cannot be split further (without loss of information).

[a]Relation is a set with tuples as elements, and by definition a set is not supposed to have any duplicate elements. In a conventional file there is no reason why two identical records cannot exist.

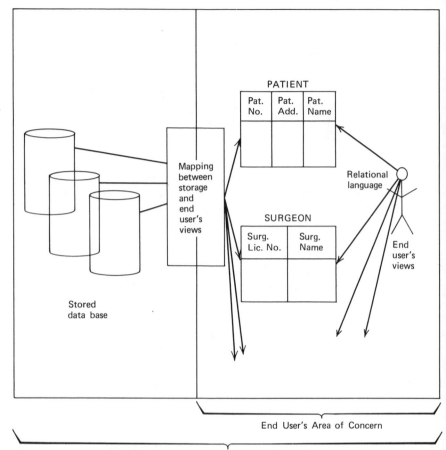

Figure 4.3f A relational data base. The end user is concerned with the "end user's views" supported by the data base management system. The end user is not concerned with how the data is stored, how it is accessed, and in what format it is stored. The data base designer, however, is concerned with the whole spectrum, with the addition of the mapping between the storage and the end user's views.

patient's number. As a result, we have key redundancy between some tables. But the tables are user's view of data and do not necessarily reflect the physical mapping.

4.3.1   Advantages of a Relational Data Model

Simplicity.   The end user is presented with a simple data model. Her/his requests are fomulated in terms of the information content and do not reflect any complexities due to system-oriented aspects. A relational data model is what the user sees, but it is not necessarily what will be implemented physically.

Nonprocedural Requests. Because there is no positional dependency between the relations, requests do not have to reflect any preferred structure and therefore can be nonprocedural.

Data Independence. This should be one of the major objectives of any data base management system. The relational data model removes the details of storage structure and access strategy from the user interface. The model provides a relatively higher degree of data independence than do the other two models to be discussed. To be able to make use of this property of the relational data model, however, the design of the relations must be complete and accurate.

Theoretical Foundation. The relational data model is based on the well-developed mathematical theory of relations. The rigorous method of designing a data base (using normalization, discussed in Chapter 5) gives this model a solid foundation. This kind of foundation does not exist for the other data models.

4.3.2 Disadvantages of a Relational Data Model

Although a few data base management systems based on the relational data model are commercially available today, the performance of a relational DBMS has not been compared with the performance of a DBMS based on a hierarchical data model, network data model, or an inverted file with inversion on multiple keys. As a result, the major question yet to be answered concerns performance. Can a relational data model be used for a DBMS that can provide a complete set of operational capabilities with required efficiency on a large scale? It appears today that technological improvements in providing faster and more reliable hardware may answer the question positively.

4.4 THE HIERARCHICAL DATA MODEL

It is quite easy to understand what a hierarchy is, because we have to deal with a number of hierarchies on a daily basis. Almost every organization has a chief executive officer with a number of executives reporting to him/her. As this hierarchy reaches lower and lower levels, fewer and fewer responsibilities are delegated to the people on these levels.

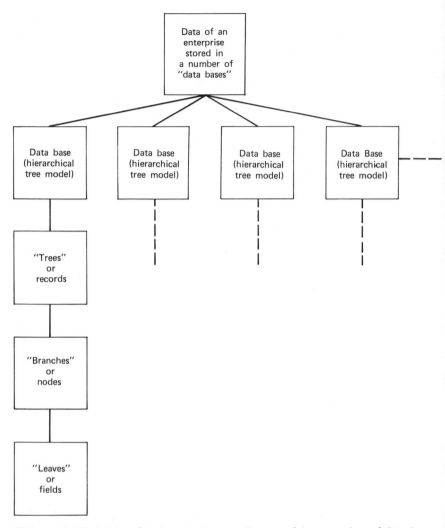

Figure 4.4 The data of an enterprise may be stored in a number of data bases. Every data base has an underlying hierarchical tree model. A number of "trees" or records form a data base. A tree is composed of a number of "branches" or nodes. Every branch has a number of "leaves" or fields.

Consider a family tree, in which the parents can have none, one, or more than one child. If there are children, the children themselves can have their own children. The family tree is a hierarchical tree if we ignore one parent at each node. It is no accident that the hierarchical data model derives much of its terminology from this analogy.

The components of a data base using a hierarchical data model as the underlying structure are shown in Figure 4.4.

4.4.1 A Hierarchical Tree Structure

A hierarchical tree structure is made up of nodes and branches. A node is a collection of data attributes describing the entity at that node. The highest node of a hierarchical tree structure is called a *ROOT* (e.g., the chief executive officer of an organization). The dependent nodes are at lower levels in the tree. The level of these nodes depends on the distance from the root node (See Figure 4.5). (The hierarchical tree is in reverse order as compared to an organic tree, which has its root at the bottom and its branches going up.)

A hierarchical data model is a model that organizes data in a hierarchical tree structure. Every occurrence of the root node begins a logical data base record, that is, a hierarchical data base is made up of a number of trees. In a hierarchical data model the nodes at level 2 are called the children of the node at level 1, and the node at level 1 is called the parent of the nodes at level 2. The nodes at level 3 for a corresponding node at level 2 are called the children of the node at level 2, and the node at level 2 is called the parent, and so on.

A hierarchical tree structure has to satisfy the following conditions:

1. A hierarchical data model always starts with a *root node*.

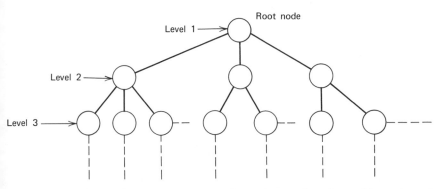

Figure 4.5 A hierarchical tree structure is made up of nodes and branches. A node is a collection of data attributes describing the entity at that node. The highest node of a hierarchical tree structure is called a "root" node (dominant entity type). A root node is at the first level. The dependent nodes (subordinate entity types) are at the second, third, · · · levels.

2. Every node consïsts of one or more attributes describing the entity at that node.

3. Dependent nodes can follow on the succeeding levels. The node on the preceding level becomes the *parent node* of the new *dependent nodes.* The dependent nodes can be added horizontally as well as vertically with no limitation. (See Figure 4.4.) (*Exception:* Level 1 can have only one node, which we called the "root" node.)

4. Every node occurring at level 2 has to be connected with one and only one node occurring at level 1. Every node occurring at level 3 has to be connected with one and only one node occurring at level 2, and so on. Because there can be at most one arc (i.e., connection) between any two nodes, the arcs do not need any labels.

5. A parent node can have one child node as a dependent or many children nodes. If it does not have any node as its dependent, it is not a parent node.

Parent node $\xleftarrow{\text{"one"}}_{\text{"many"}}$ children nodes (one-to-many relationship).

6. Every node except, of course, the root has to be accessed through its parent node. The node represented in a true hierarchy should be retrieved only through its parent, as this is where the true meaning of that data exists. Therefore the access path to every node within a hierarchical data model is unique. (See Figure 4.6.)

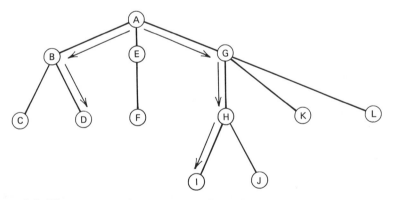

Figure 4.6 The access path to every node within a hierarchical data model is unique. For example, node I can be reached only through the path A to G to H to I. Node D can be accessed only through the path A to B to D. Hence a hierarchical data model consists of linear paths.

(For example, Node I can be reached only through the path A to G to H to I. Node D can be accessed only through the path A to B to D.) Hence a hierarchical data model consists of linear paths.

7. There can be a number of occurrences of each node at each level. Each node occurrence (except the root node occurrence) has to be connected with a parent node occurrence, that is, there can be many occurrences of node A. Every node occurrence of A starts a logical record. There can be zero, one, or many occurrences of node B for every node occurrence of A, and so on.

Consider the example with information from the PATIENT relation, SURGEON relation, PATIENT-AND-SURGEON relation, and DRUG relation as shown in Figures 4.3a, 4.3b, 4.3c, and 4.3d, respectively. A hierarchical data model can represent the information in a number of ways. One possibility is shown in Figure 4.7. The entity PATIENT is the root node, and every patient has a root node occurrence. The data base has, at this time, records for the patients John White (1111), Mary Jones (1234), Charles Brown (2345), Hal Kane (4876), Paul Kosher (5123), and Ann Hood (6845). The data base record for John White (1111) is shown in Figure 4.8. The node at level 2 from Figure 4.7 has two occurrences in Figure 4.8. The hierarchical data model enables us to represent many surgeries and surgeons for a patient.

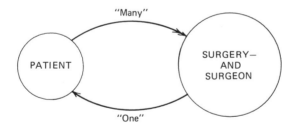

For the hierarchical data model in Figure 4.7, there are five more data base records, for the patients Mary Jones, Charles Brown, Hal Kane, Paul Kosher, and Ann Hood. The data base record for the patient Hal Kane is shown in Figure 4.9.

The information about PATIENT, SURGEON, PATIENT-AND-SURGEON, and DRUG can also be represented with another version of a hierarchical data model, which is shown in Figure 4.10. The entity SURGEON is the root node. Every surgeon has a root node occurrence. The data base has, at this time, records for the surgeons

Level 1
(Root/Parent)

Patient's number	Patient's name	Patient's address

Level 2
(Child to Root)

Surgeon's license number	Surgeon's name	Date of surgery	Surgery	Postoperative drug administered	Side effect of drug

Figure 4.7 **Representation of data using hierarchical data model for PATIENT data base. The entity PATIENT is the root node type. The entities SURGEON, SURGERY, and DRUG are combined into one node type as the dependent of the root.**

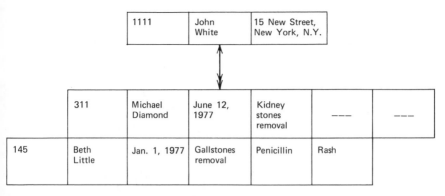

Figure 4.8 A hierarchical data base record occurrence for the hierarchical data model in Figure 4.7. The data base record is for the patient John White. The dependent node type (child to root in this case) has two occurrences for the surgeries gallstones removal and kidney stones removal.

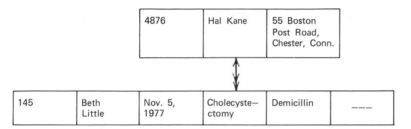

Figure 4.9 A hierarchical data base record occurrence for the hierarchical data model in Figure 4.7. The data base record is for the patient Hal Kane. The dependent node type (child to root in this case) has one occurrence for the surgery cholecystectomy.

Beth Little (145), David Rosen (189), Charles Field (243), Michael Diamond (311), and Patricia Gold (467). The data base record for Beth Little (145) is shown in Figure 4.11. The node at level 2 from Figure 4.10 has three occurrences in Figure 4.11. The hierarchical data model makes possible the representation of many patients for a surgeon.

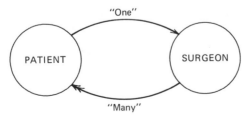

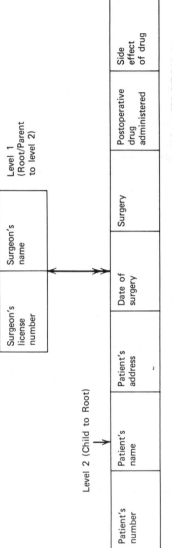

Level 1
(Root/Parent
to level 2)

Surgeon's license number	Surgeon's name

Level 2 (Child to Root)

Patient's number	Patient's name	Patient's address	Date of surgery	Surgery	Postoperative drug administered	Side effect of drug

Figure 4.10 **Representation of data using hierarchical data model for SURGEON data base with all the surgeries performed by the surgeon. Here the SURGEON node type is at a higher level than the PATIENT node type. This structure shows the DBA's intention of implementing the relationship between SURGEON and PATIENT as one-to-many.**

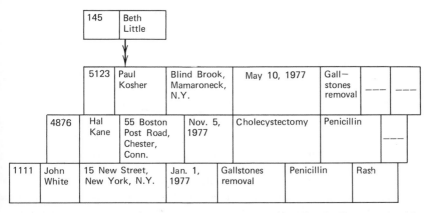

Figure 4.11 A hierarchical data base record occurrence for the hierarchical data model in Figure 4.10. The data base record is for the surgeon Beth Little. The dependent node type (child to root in this case) has three occurrences for the patients John White, Hal Kane, and Paul Kosher.

The hierarchical data models in Figures 4.7 and 4.10 are different, although they are data models of the same hospital environment. The difference is the result of the two ways of looking at the entity relationships. Figure 4.7 has the PATIENT at a higher level than the SURGEON, reflecting the fact that the data base administrator intends to implement the relationship between PATIENT and SURGEON as one-to-many. Figure 4.10 has the SURGEON at a higher level than the PATIENT, showing the data base administrator's intention of implementing the relationship between SURGEON and PATIENT as one-to-many. The choice of the hierarchical data model should be made with performance issues in mind. A detailed discussion of these issues is given in Part III.

The same information can be represented in a different relationship with the help of the data model in Figure 4.12. A data base record occurrence using the data model in Figure 4.12 is shown in Figure 4.13. In this example there is only one occurrence of the node at level 3 for every occurrence of the node at level 2. But there is a possibility that on a specific day a surgeon operated on more than one PATIENT. This hierarchical data model is a simple version with only one node at level 2 and one node at level 3. The hierarchical data model makes possible the representation of many dates of surgery for a surgeon and many patients on whom surgeries were performed on a specific date.

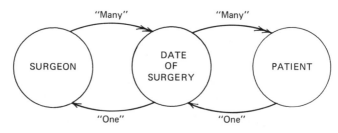

4.4.2   Storage Operations with a Hierarchical Data Model

In the hierarchical data model in Figure 4.7, the PATIENT node is the parent node, and the SURGEON node with the medical information of the patient is the child node. If the same surgeon has operated on more than one patient, the information on the surgeon will be repeated for every patient she/he is treating; for example, in the data base records from Figures 4.8 and 4.9, the information about the surgeon with license number 145 (Beth Little) is redundant.

Insertion.   A child node occurrence cannot exist without a parent node occurrence. If the hierarchical data model is like the one in Figure 4.7, no new surgeon can be added to the data base unless he/she is treating a patient.

Deletion.   When a parent node occurrence is deleted, the child occurrences are deleted too. For example, in the hierarchical data model in Figure 4.10, when a SURGEON node occurrence is deleted, all the node occurrences of the patients operated on by the surgeon

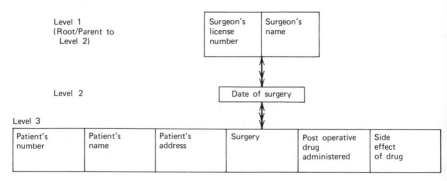

Figure 4.12   Representation of data using hierarchical data model for SURGEON data base with all the days on which the surgeon performed surgeries and all the surgeries performed on the specific day.

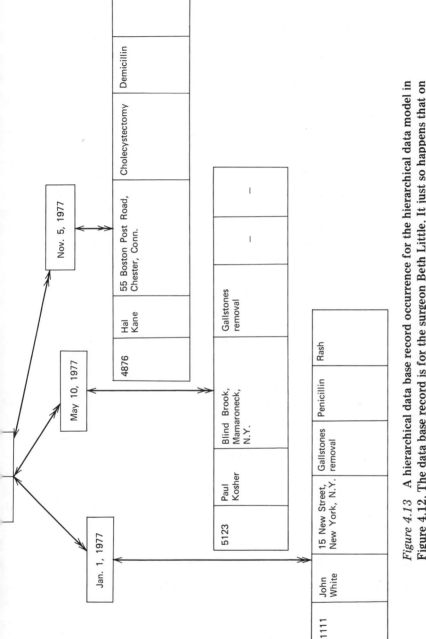

Figure 4.13 A hierarchical data base record occurrence for the hierarchical data model in Figure 4.12. The data base record is for the surgeon Beth Little. It just so happens that on Jan. 1, 1977, on May 10, 1977, and on Nov. 5, 1977, Beth Little performed one surgery each day. On Jan. 1, 1977, the patient was John White; on May 10, 1977, the patient was Paul Kosher; and on Nov. 5, 1977, the patient was Hal Kane.

are also deleted. This results in the loss of information about those patients.

The reason for the storage and update anomalies is that a many-to-many relationship cannot be efficiently represented with one hierarchical data model, which always represents a one-to-many relationship. The anomalies can be partly resolved by introducing two hierarchical data models with a relationship established between the two, as in Figure 4.14. Data model 1 has PATIENT as its root node and SURGERY as the second level node. The second level node is interconnected with the SURGEON node from data model 2. In data model 2, SURGEON is the root node and the SURGERY node is the second level node, which is interconnected with the PATIENT node from data model 1. As a result of these two data models, the information regarding the date of surgery, SURGERY, will still be stored redundantly, but the anomalies of insertion and deletion of PATIENT and SURGEON are removed. The problem of redundancy is solved in data base management systems using a hierarchical data model as the basic data model in different ways.

4.4.3   Advantages of a Hierarchical Data Model

- The major advantage of the hierarchical data model is the existence of proven data base management systems that use the hierarchical data model as the basic structure.
- The relative simplicity and ease of use of the hierarchical data model and the familiarity of data processing users with a hierarchy are major advantages.
- There is a reduction of data dependency. When the two hierarchical data models from Figure 4.14 are used, a number of different views can be provided to the application programmers, as in Figure 4.15.
- Performance prediction is simplified through predefined relationships.

4.4.4   Disadvantages of a Hierarchical Data Model

- The many-to-many relationship can be implemented only in a clumsy way. This may result in redundancy in stored data. We know that redundancy at the logical level is not necessarily bad—on the contrary, it promotes simplicity. Redundancy at the physical level, however, is undesirable.

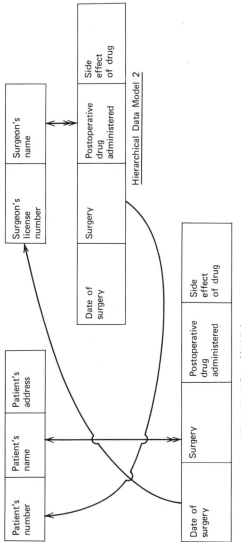

Hierarchical Data Model 1

Hierarchical Data Model 2

Figure 4.14 Representation of data using two hierarchical data models with PATIENT data base and SURGEON data base. Hierarchical data model 1 has PATIENT as its root node and SURGERY as the second level node type. The SURGERY node from hierarchical data model 1 is interconnected with the SURGEON node from hierarchical data model 2. In hierarchical data model 2, SURGEON is the root node and SURGERY is the second level node, which is interconnected with the PATIENT node from hierarchical data model 1.

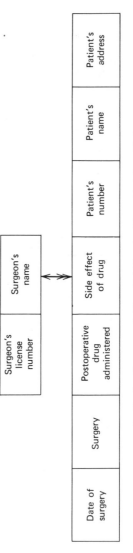

| Date of surgery | Surgery | Patient's number | Patient's name | Patient's address |

| Postoperative drug administered | Side effect of drug | Surgeon's license number | Surgeon's name |

Application Programmer's View 1, Using the Hierarchical Data Models in Figure 4.14

| Surgeon's license number | Surgeon's name |

| Date of surgery | Surgery | Patient's number | Patient's name | Patient's address |

| Postoperative drug administered | Side effect of drug |

Application Programmer's View 2, Using the Hierarchical Data Models in Figure 4.14

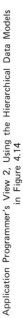

Figure 4.15 **Application programmer's view is called "external model" in ANSI (American National Standards Institute) terminology, as in Figure 1.7.**

- As a result of the strict hierarchical ordering, the operations of insertion and deletion become unduly complex.
- Deletion of parent results in the deletion of children. As a result, users have to be careful in performing a DELETE operation.
- Hierarchical commands tend to be procedural because of the strictness of the structure.
- "Root" is the dominant node type. Any child node is accessible only through its parent node.

4.5 THE NETWORK DATA MODEL

Much of today's awareness of the concepts of the data base can be credited to the work of CODASYL (Conference On Data Systems Languages) and its committees.

CODASYL was established in 1959 in Washington, D.C., at a meeting of the representatives of 40 major computer users, manufacturers, and government departments. It is a voluntary organization and is supported by the enterprises represented. It is not an official government body responsible for standards, nor does it develop standards. The aim of the committee is to develop, design and recommend techniques and languages for data processing systems, analysis, implementation, and operation, and to provide these specifications to the Standards Groups in the form of a *Journal of Development*.

CODASYL's first project was to develop specifications for a Common Business Oriented Language, acronymed as COBOL. In 1966 CODASYL started a new task force, the List Processing Task Force, to extend COBOL for handling data bases. The name of this group was later changed to the Data Base Task Group (DBTG).

The initial specifications of the DBTG were made semipublic in 1969, and were reviewed by a number of interested parties. After their suggestions had been considered, a new report was published in 1971. The DBTG has continued since that date to issue reports. However, because the major implementors of the model are based on the 1971 report, our emphasis will be on it.

After the 1971 report, CODASYL formed a new committee, the Data Description Language Committee (DDLC), to deal with the issues of data description, and replaced the DBTG with the Data Base Language Task Group (DBLTG) for dealing with COBOL extensions to the data base area. These extensions were included in the CODASYL COBOL *Journal of Development.*

The DBLTG's task was to make the DBTG's 1971 report consistent with CODASYL's COBOL specifications. This was accomplished with a report in 1973.

The basic underlying data model in the 1969, 1971, and 1973 reports is a network data model. Implementations conforming to CODASYL are UNIVAC's DMS 1100 for UNIVAC 1108 and 1110 series computers, Cullinane's IDMS for IBM hardware, DEC's DBMS-11 for DEC's PDP11/70, DEC's DBMS-10/20 for its DECSYSTEM-10 and DECSYSTEM-20, and Honeywell's IDS/II, to name just a few.

The components of a data base with a network data model as the underlying structure are shown in Figures 4.16 and 4.17.

Let us study the major components of a network data model, a set, and a record in more detail.

The network data model interconnects the entities of an enterprise into a "network." The graphic notation for this data model

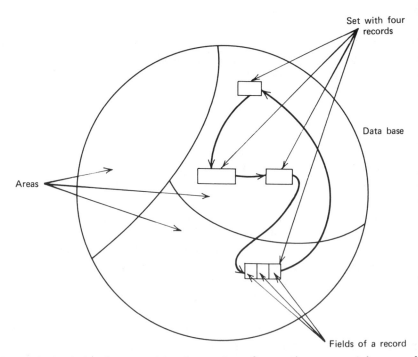

Figure 4.16 A data base consists of a number of areas. An area contains records. In turn, a record may consist of fields. A set, which is a grouping of records, may reside in an area or span a number of areas.

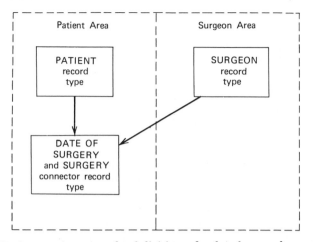

Figure 4.17 An area is a named subdivision of a data base and may contain occurrences of records and sets or parts of sets. Each area can have its own unique physical attributes. Areas can be operated independently of, or in conjunction with, other areas.

uses blocks and arrows. This notation was introduced by C. W. Bachman ["Data Structure Diagrams," *Database*, Vol. 1, p. 2 (Summer, 1969)]. A block represents an entity or record type. Each record type is composed of zero, one, or more attributes (also called 'data elements" or "fields").

Let us distinguish between a record type and a record occurrence. PATIENT is a record type, and "1111 John White 15 New Street, New York, N.Y." is a record occurrence of the record type PATIENT (see Figures 4.18 and 4.19). Thus a record type has one or more "occurrences" in the data base.

A directed arrow connects two or more record types and is used to represent a set type. The record type located at the tail of the arrow functions as the owner record type, and the record type located at the head of the arrow as the member record type. The arrow from owner to member is called a set type. A set type shows a logical one-to-many relationship between an owner and a member (Figure 4.18). Physical storage, that is, closeness between owner and member, is not implied, although, as we shall see in Chapter 8, it can occur.

Every set type is named. The naming of a set type enables the same pair of entities to appear in more than one relationship. (This will be elaborated on as we move along.) The term "set type" has nothing to do with "set theory" in the mathematical sense.

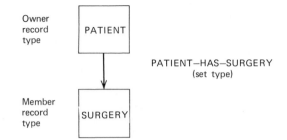

Figure 4.18 A set type PATIENT-HAS-SURGERY based on the owner-record type PATIENT and the member record type SURGERY.

- A set type is a named grouping of related records.
- There is only a single "owner" occurrence in a set occurrence.
- There may be zero, one, or many "member" occurrences in a set occurrence.
- A set type is said to be "empty" when no member record occurrence is associated with the corresponding owner record occurrence.
- A set occurrence exists when an owner record is stored.

Let us distinguish between a set type and a set occurrence. In our example from Figure 4.19, PATIENT-HAS-SURGERY is a set type with an occurrence of the owner record type PATIENT "1111 John White   15 New Street, New York, N.Y." The occurrences of

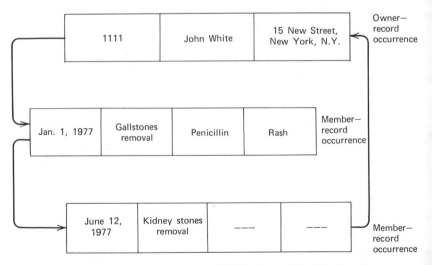

Figure 4.19 A set occurrence of PATIENT-HAS-SURGERY with an owner record occurrence and two member record occurrences implemented as a ring structure. The set occurrence could be implemented in a number of other ways.

he member record type SURGERY are "Jan. 1, 1977 Gallstones emoval Penicillin Rash" and "June 12, 1977 Kidney stones removal - - -." This is a set occurrence. Thus a set occurrence is one occurence of the owner record type, together with zero or more occurrences of the member record type, from a given set type. The elationship between the owner record occurrence and the member ecord occurrence(s) is one-to-many. A given member record occurence cannot simultaneously belong to two or more owner record occurrences of the same set type, that is, a member record occurence cannot violate the rule of unique ownership for a given set ype.

4.5.1 Representation of One-to-Many Relationship

n a data model representing a one-to-many relationship, an owner ecord type owns zero to n occurrences of a member record type. A member record type, in turn, can play the role of an owner record ype with zero to n member record occurrences in a set occurrence. An owner record type can be an owner record type in a number of et types. This type of data model is a hierarchical data model, hat is, a hierarchical data model is a special case of a network data model.

The CODASYL model does not allow direct implementation of a many-to-many relationship. Using the notation developed earlier, we would like to model the structure as shown in Figure 4.20. We would like to represent the information of one patient having undergone many surgeries and a specific kind of surgery performed on many patients. According to the Figure 4.20, a surgery with more han one patient would simultaneously be a member in two or more occurrences of the same set type, violating the rule of unique ownership.

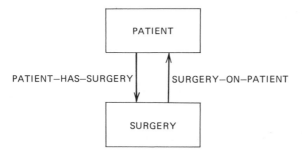

Figure 4.20 A structure of this type would violate the rule of unique ownership because a surgery with more than one patient would simultaneously be a member in two or more occurrences of the same set type.

A many-to-many relationship can be implemented by creating two one-to-many relationships. As we shall see later, this is only one example of the need to alter a conceptual design because of constraints imposed by the DBMS. Let us look at this on the basis of the example.

The entity types here are PATIENT, SURGEON, and SURGERY. A given surgeon may have operated on several patients, and a given patient may have been operated on by several surgeons. PATIENT SURGEON, and SURGERY form a network. The relation between PATIENT and SURGEON is many-to-many. PATIENT can be considered as a record type, and SURGEON as well can be considered as a record type. To transform the many-to-many relationship between PATIENT and SURGEON into two one-to-many relationships, we will use the surgery with date of surgery, surgery, drug, and side effect of drug, which we will call SURGERY, as a "link" or "connector" record type. Note that this is called a connector record type

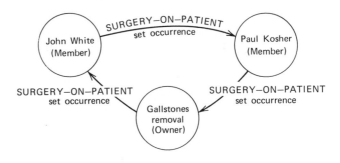

One set occurrence for the owner occurrence of the surgery gallstones removal.

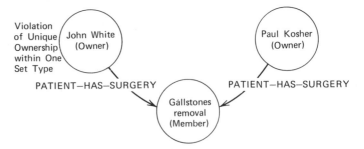

Two set occurrences for the owner occurrence of patient John White and for the owner occurrence of patient Paul Kosher with the same member occurrence, gallstones removal.

Figure 4.21

even if it contains no data itself. In many instances, however, the link record contains information describing the relationship between the other two records.

Figure 4.21 represents two record types, namely, PATIENT record type, and the record type SURGERY.

In the network data model of Figure 4.22, a "set" is constructed with two record types. PATIENT and SURGERY record types create a PATIENT-HAS-SURGERY set. PATIENT record type is called an "owner" record type, and SURGERY record type a "member" record type. SURGEON and SURGERY record types are related by the SURGERY-ON-PATIENT set type. SURGEON record type is called an "owner" record type, and SURGERY a "member" record type.

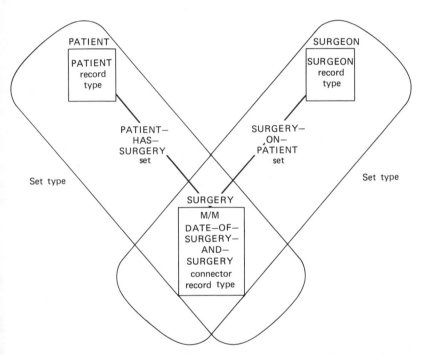

Figure 4.22 Representation of data using network data model. Many-to-many relationship implemented with two set types:

1. PATIENT-HAS-SURGERY with PATIENT as owner record type and SURGERY as member record type.

2. SURGERY-ON-PATIENT with SURGEON as owner record type and SURGERY as member record type.

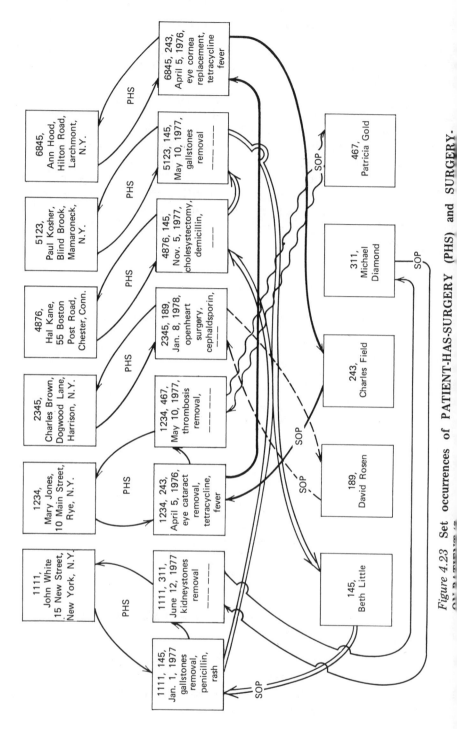

Figure 4.23 Set occurrences of PATIENT-HAS-SURGERY (PHS) and SURGERY-ON-PATIENT (S

116

Each occurrence of the set type PATIENT-HAS-SURGERY represents a hierarchical relationship between the patient and the surgery. The significant difference between the hierarchical data model and the network data model is that in the latter any record type can participate in any number of sets, playing the role of an owner record type or of a member record type.

Figure 4.23 shows the set occurrences of PATIENT-HAS-SURGERY and SURGERY-ON-PATIENT at this time for the hospital environment.

4.5.2 Three More Classes of Set Types

The set types defined in Figure 4.24 are made up of two record types, PATIENT and SURGERY.

A second class of set type is made up of three or more record types, as in Figure 4.25, and is called a "multimember" set type. The owner record type is PATIENT, and the member record types are SURGERY and ILLNESS.

The third class of set type is called a "singular" set type. It is also defined on the basis of an owner record type and a member record type. The difference between this set type and the types previously discussed is that only one occurrence of the set can exist in the data base. This structure is used in two ways:

1. It can join records together into a set where no natural owner record exists.

2. It can hold record occurrences that do not have an owner when they are entered into the data base but will have an owner at some later time. (See Figure 4.26.) When it is time to join the record to its final owner, it is disconnected from the system record and connected into the new owner record's set occurrence.

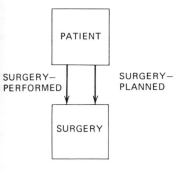

Figure 4.24 Two set types defined on two record types to imply two different contexts. One set type is SURGERY-PLANNED between the two record types PATIENT and SURGERY. Another set type is SURGERY-PERFORMED between the same record types.

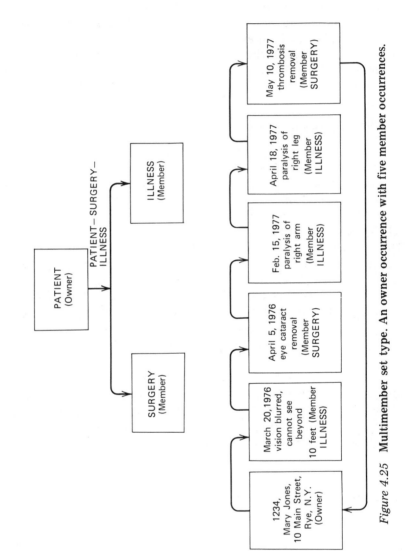

Figure 4.25 Multimember set type. An owner occurrence with five member occurrences.

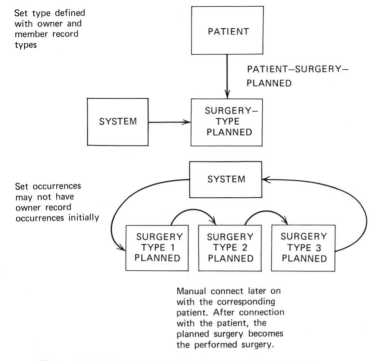

Set type defined with owner and member record types

Set occurrences may not have owner record occurrences initially

Manual connect later on with the corresponding patient. After connection with the patient, the planned surgery becomes the performed surgery.

Figure 4.26   **System-owned set type or singular set type.**

Let us see the various structures that can be built using the set type as a building block.

Case I.   A patient may be admitted to the hospital for observation before surgery is performed (See Figure 4.24). The set type SURGERY-PLANNED between the record types PATIENT and SURGERY is not the same as the set type SURGERY-PERFORMED between the same record types, PATIENT and SURGERY, because of a different perspective.

Case II.   A hierarchical structure can be constructed using a number of set types. (See Figure 4.27.)

Case III.   A Y-structure can be built with the help of a number of set types (See Figure 4.28.)

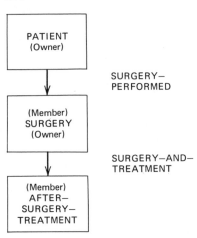

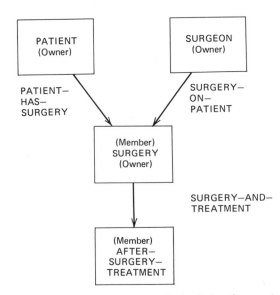

Figure 4.27 Hierarchical structure defined with the help of set types.

4.5.3 Storage Operations with a Network Data Model

Insertion. A new surgeon can be added as an owner occurrence of a SURGERY-ON-PATIENT set occurrence without a member SURGERY occurrence, that is, without having a corresponding patient to operate on. Similarly, the information about a patient can be entered without an assigned surgeon.

Figure 4.28 A Y-structure can be built with the help of a number of set types.

Deletion. If an owner occurrence of a surgeon is deleted, all the pointers connecting the surgeries performed by the surgeon may be deleted for the occurrence of the set type SURGERY-ON-PATIENT. But the information about all the patients operated on by the surgeon remains intact. Only the corresponding surgeon's information is deleted.

Similarly, when an owner occurrence of a patient is deleted, all the pointers connecting the surgeries performed on the patient may be deleted for the occurrence of the set type PATIENT-HAS-SURGERY. But the information about all the surgeons who performed surgeries on the patient remains intact.

4.5.4   Advantages of a Network Data Model

- The major advantage of the network data model is that, as for the hierarchical data model, there are successful data base management systems that use the network data model as the basic structure.

- The many-to-many relationship, which occurs quite frequently in real life, can be implemented easily.

- The network data model is backed by the CODASYL (Conference on Data Systems Languages) Data Base Task Group (DBTG). The reports of DBTG in 1971 and 1978 will certainly influence future national and international standards for data bases.

4.5.5   Disadvantages of a Network Data Model

The main disadvantage of the network model is its complexity. The application programmer must be familiar with the logical structure of the data base, because she/he has to "navigate" through different set occurrences with the help of connector record type occurrences. The connector record types are not invisible to the application programmer. In other words, the programmer has to know her/his position in set occurrences when moving through the data base. Although this can be quite complicated if all operations involve movement through sets, the CODASYL model gives the programmer entry points into occurrences that greatly simplify the programming effort.

An added complication is that, when the data base is reorganized, it is possible, unless great care is taken, to lose data independence. This occurs when sets are removed. Also, because the views supplied to the application programmers are less simple than the views based on the hierarchical data model, the programming may become complex.

Remedy to Gain More Data Independence. The remedy is to have a series of predefined routines that actually navigate the data base. Application programming, then, reduces to calls to these routines.

Having discussed the three popular approaches in the data model area, we would like to concentrate on three of the major responsibilities that the data base administrator has to fulfill. The first responsibility is the designing of a conceptual model of the enterprise's entities and their relationships. The second responsibility is the reduction of that model to a logical model that is compatible with and is managed by the data base management system. The third responsibility is the reduction of the logical model to a physical model (also called an "internal" model) that will satisfy the performance requirements.

The methodology for fulfilling the first and second responsibilities is dealt with in Chapters 5 and 6, and the third responsibility is treated in Part III.

REFERENCES

1. *An Introduction to Database Systems*, 2nd ed., C. J. Date, The Systems Programming Series, Addison-Wesley Publishing Company, 1977.
2. *Data Base Management Systems*, Dioysis C. Tsichritzis and Frederich H Lochovsky, Academic Press—A subsidiary of Harcourt Brace Jovanovich Publishers, 1977.
3. "Principles of Data Base Systems," M. Vetter, paper presented at the International Computing Symposium, Leige, Belgium, April 1977.
4. "A Relational Model of Data for Large Shared Data Banks," E. F. Codd *Communications of the ACM*, Vol. 13, (June 6, 1970).
5. "Further Normalization of the Relational Model," E. F. Codd, *Data Base Systems*, Courant Computer Science Symposia 6, Prentice-Hall, 1972.
6. "The Programmer as Navigator," C. W. Bachman, *Communications of the ACM*, Vol. 16, No. 11 (November 1973).
7. *The Codasyl Approach to Data Base Management*, T. William Olle, A Wiley Interscience Publication, John Wiley & Sons, 1978.
8. *The Art of Computer Programming*, Vol. 3: *Sorting and Searching*, Donald E. Knuth, Addison-Wesley Publishing Company, 1973.
9. *Principles of Data-Base Management*, James Martin, Prentice-Hall, 1976.

10. *Data Base Systems: A Practical Reference*, Ian R. Palmer, Q. E. D. Information Sciences, Inc., Wellesley, Massachusetts, 1978.

11. "Evolution of Data-Base Management Systems," J. P. Fry and E. M. Sibley, *ACM Computing Surveys*, Special Issue: *Data-Base Management Systems*, Vol. 8, No. 1 (March 1976).

12. "COBOL Extensions to Handle Data Bases" (PB 177 682). CODASYL Data Base Task Group, January 1968.

13. Report, CODASYL Data Base Task Group, April 1971 (available from Association for Computing Machinery, 1133 Avenue of the Americas, New York, New York 10036).

14. *The National Symposium on Comparative Data Base Management Systems*, Vol. I, Advanced Management Research International, Inc., June 26-28, 1978.

CHAPTER 5

Data Base Design
(Conceptual Model)

To develop a data base that satisfies today's as well as tomorrow's information needs, a conceptual model must be designed. This conceptual model reflects the entities and their relationships and is based on the data processing needs of the organization. When determining the entities and their relationships, a data analysis is necessary. This analysis can be based on the information about data for existing, as well as future, applications.

For developing the conceptual model, some concepts from the relational approach are used. However, this methodology yields a data base design that is independent of the implementation approach, that is, the conceptual model can be mapped to a relational, hierarchical, or network data model. Unfortunately, it appears that the people implementing hierarchical and CODASYL-DBTG type systems do not necessarily practice the kind of relational normalization process discussed in this chapter. Perhaps data base design would be easier if people did.

DESIGN A CONCEPTUAL MODEL OF A DATA BASE

One major responsibility of a data base administrator is designing a "conceptual model" of the enterprise. This model should represent the entities of the enterprise and the relationships between them.

The conceptual model is not the approach by which an individual application programmer processes the information. Instead, it is a combination of several ways used to process the data for several applications. The view of an individual application programmer is called an "external model." The conceptual model is independent of individual applications, independent of the data base management system, independent of the hardware used for storing the data, and independent of the physical model of the data in the storage media.

When designing the conceptual model, efforts should be concentrated on structuring the data and the relationships between the data elements of the enterprise. At this stage, there should be no concern for the implementation and operation phases of the data base.

The first step in designing a conceptual model is data analysis, which will provide information about the data elements and the relationships between them.

5.1 DATA ANALYSIS

5.1.1 Collecting Information about Data for Existing Applications

Collecting information about data is very time consuming and requires patience on the part of management. The data base administrator should initiate a plan to complete this task. First, the DBA should use a questionnaire or similar vehicle to obtain from each level of management (executive, functional, and operational) a composite list of the data that it needs. The various levels may process the data, or they may store it. Second, the DBA should investigate all the clerical, operational, and data processing uses of the enterprise's data.

One point that should not be overlooked is that forms, bills, reports, existing data files, and old programs are starting points for data collection. The real question, however, is what data is needed in the new data base to support the applications, and the needed data is seldom in a one-to-one correspondence with the data seen on forms and reports.

The questionnaire or data survey form should be addressed to every manager and supervisor within the enterprise who has need of data or supplies data to the repository. It is imperative that the survey be completed by management and not by subordinate personnel. The survey should reflect management's perspective of what it needs. Additional survey forms should be made available to the initial subscribers so that they can add to the survey's breadth if the initial list does not include all data users. A point should be made here: if the initial subscription list to the survey is not complete, the model of the enterprise should be reviewed to determine why omissions occurred in the survey subscription.

The questionnaire should ask for the following information: data entity name, data element name, description, attributes, source and sensitivity (security), value or importance of the data, and relationships of the elements and entities. Every individual supplying information on the questionnaire may not be able to answer all of the entries, but each should provide as much of the information as possible. No one filling out the form should assume that someone else will supply information she/he has omitted. The prime motivational factor which should be emphasized is that an accurate perception of the enterprise's data can be obtained only if everyone answers the questionnaire completely.

A brief description of the entries on the questionnaire follows. There is no best format for the questionnaire, it is important only that the items listed below be included. The format may be dictated by particular data dictionary applications to make the eventual entry to these applications less cumbersome. The enterprise may have data definition standards that it may revise to complete the questionnaire. The specific form the DBA chooses is irrelevant to the actual purpose of the questionnaire.

Questionnaire/Survey Content

1. **Data Entity Name and Description.** List the name and any synonyms by which the data elements (see below) are called. Examples are "orders," "weekly time card," "production log," and "accounts receivable form." Give a description of what the name means even though the name seems to be self-defining or self-explanatory. Describe in general the use or function of the entity, the purpose it serves within the operational or functional unit, and any users outside the unit.

2. **Data Elements.** For each "piece" of information in the entity, provide the following information:

   a. *Element Name and Description.* List the names, acronyms, and mnemonics. Give a full description of the element in prose.

   b. *Element Source.* List the originating source(s) as perceived by the functional or operating unit. Examples include such entries as these: from the customer, from interoffice memos, from the shipping department.

   c. *Element Attributes.* List attributes such as numeric, alphabetic, and textual. Give the unit of measure associated with the data, such as pieces, dollars, and feet. If there are boundaries to the acceptable value ranges for the element, list them, (e.g., the value cannot be less than 100 or greater than 500).

   d. *Element Use.* Describe the use. Examples include the following: to provide addressing information, to determine quantity, to establish the payroll scale rate.

   e. *Element Security/Sensitivity.* List any constraints associated with the element name. These constraints are generally relative to audience restrictions, that is, who may use, access, read, and/or publish the data.

   f. *Importance/Value.* List the importance of the data. Of what value is it in terms of the enterprise's continuing or expanding its functioning? It is no sin to state the value of the data in a negative way (i.e., "We couldn't do business without it!"). Correspondingly, though, the statement relative to the element's use (item d above) should support and elaborate on the value of the element.

   g. *Element Relationship(s).* List the way(s) in which this element is used or paired with other elements. These elements need not be limited to the specific entity being discussed. Such relationships are part number/name, employee number/ name/social security number, production code/job lot, and order number/shipping number.

3. **Retention Criteria and Archiving.** Describe the length of time and the manner in which the data is to be kept. List also, if known, the reason or cause for the retention (e.g., government regulation, company policy).

In conjunction with the completion of the survey, the DBA should investigate the clerical, administrative, and data processing flows of data in the enterprise. The investigation should not be viewed as a "policing" to ensure the correctness of the questionnaire, but rather as an adjunct to the model of the enterprise. The survey should also help the DBA to follow the flow of "paper" through the enterprise, noting the paths and means of data communication, its use, and its purpose.

The next process, and by far the most important, performed by the DBA is analysis of the data repository, which is built from the questionnaire and the data flow investigation. The analysis itself is easily described, but the process of the analysis is not routine or simplistic. The DBA will now create a data map of the entities and elements, showing functional sources and entities and receiving or using functions and their functional entities and elements, as in Figure 5.1.

The diagrams show the flow, although over simplified from any real situation, as it would be initially mapped from the data collection steps, and the ultimate data map structured from the source to

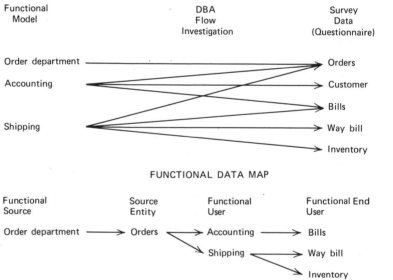

Figure 5.1 The DBA should create a data map of the entities and elements showing:

1. The functional source.
2. The receiving or using functions.

the end user. In the construction of the data map, the DBA will invariably encounter discrepancies, errors, and omissions. He/she must resolve these matters before an accurate picture can be constructed. A handy tool that should be used during the process of data analysis is a data dictionary.

During the reconciliation process, the DBA must determine the value of the data to the end user. The DBA will become aware of the end user's perceived need and the real need for specific entities and elements in the repository. It is important now that the DBA has as much authority and management leverage as possible to implement the elimination, reduction, or redirection of data in the functional units in order to manage the data resource properly.

After the process has been completed, the DBA should review with the functional, operational, and executive levels the data relationships, the functional sources, and the user requirements. Again, it is important that all data users agree with the DBA's perspective of the data.

The DBA may now begin to build a data model or conceptual model of the data base.

5.1.2 Collecting Information about Data for Future Applications

One of the most important and most difficult tasks of the data base administrator is collecting information about the future usage of the data base. Once the data base is put in place, and the users see its value in information processing and decision making, they are going to ask for more in terms of better responsiveness, more functions, more applications, or more cross referencing of the enterprise's data. If the data base was designed based on knowledge of only the current usage of data, it may be difficult to implement new relationships, new entities, and new data elements. To minimize the problems of this nature, the data base administrator must determine other ways in which the information can be used. This is definitely a difficult task to perform, but the DBA has to watch for any overlooked entities, entity relationships, and intrinsic data relationships regardless of functions, and discuss them with the users. Information about the future usage of data not only is necessary for designing the conceptual and logical models but also may have an impact on the physical model. The information about the volume of data anticipated in the future may be an important determinant in the decision regarding the physical model.

5.2 RELATIONAL CONCEPTS FOR THE DESIGN PROCESS

The underlying model of an enterprise representing the entities and the relationships between them is more stable than the different ways in which information stored in a data base is retrieved. An effective way of developing a model, which we would like to call a conceptual model, is by applying the concepts from the relational data model. These concepts are applied to the analysis of the data and relationships information provided by the end users. *The conceptual model need not be implemented with a relational data base management system. Rather, the model can be used as a basis to develop a logical model which can be implemented with a relational, hierarchical, or network data base management system.*

The major concept from the relational data model used in developing the conceptual model is the *normalization process*, that is, the process of grouping the data elements into tables representing entities and their relationships. The normalization theory is based on the observation that a certain set of relations has better properties in an inserting, updating, and deleting environment than do other sets of relations containing the same data.

The reason one would use the normalization procedure is to ensure that the conceptual model of the data base will work. This means, not that an unnormalized structure will not work, but only that it may cause some problems when application programmers attempt to modify the data base. The data base administrator must decide, after locating violations from normalization, whether the modifications will affect how the data base will function.

An unnormalized data model consists of records as they are used by application programs. The first step in normalization consists of transforming the data items into a two-dimensional table. All that is usually required at this step is the removal of repeated occurrences of data items so that a flat file is obtained. For example, if a declaration includes space for an employee name, employee number, spouse, and up to ten children, the result will be a 4 by 10 table, with four columns and ten rows. Every row will have the employee name, employee number, spouse, and the name of one of the ten children. Ten rows will have the names of ten children. This step is just a preliminary one that makes it possible to move to the second normal form.

The second step in normalization is to state what the keys are and to relate the data items to the keys. In the first normal form, the entire row of the table (or tuple) is dependent on all the key items.

In the second normal form, an attempt is made to state what data items are related to parts of the total key. If data items depend only on part of the key, the key and the items connected to the partial key are candidates for removal into separate records. The breaking apart of the first normal table into a series of tables in which each item depends only on the entire key is called the second normal form.

The third step is to separate out data items from the second normal relations that, while dependent only on the key, may have an independent existence in the data base. This is done so that information about these data items can be entered separately from the relationships in which they are involved.

In every data model, one or more data elements are grouped to represent entities and their relations. In the groupings of the data elements, three general types of problems can occur, and the removal of each gives rise to the three normal forms of relations (tables). Thus, the normalization process is a discipline of grouping the data elements into a set of relations (tables). Figure 5.2 shows the three normal forms.

All normalized relations are in the first normal form, some first normal form relations are in the second normal form, and, finally, some second normal form relations are in the third normal form. The normalization process yields the third normal form relations. The third normal form relations represent the entities and the relationships between the entities of an enterprise.

The first, second, and third normal forms provide successive improvements in the insertion, deletion, and update operations against the data base. As we shall see, the normalization process makes the designer understand the semantics of attributes and their relationships and as a result mandates the thought process for data analysis.

The preceding paragraphs have overviewed the steps involved in taking an unnormalized structure and transforming it into the third normal form. The rest of this section shows how to go about doing this.

Consider the example in Figure 5.3. The data elements or attributes are patient's number, patient's name, patient's address, surgeon's license number, surgeon's name, date of surgery, surgery, postoperative drug administered, and side effect of drug. Some restrictive assumptions are made for the "pseudo-hospital" environment. These assumptions, made here for illustration purpose only, are specified as we proceed.

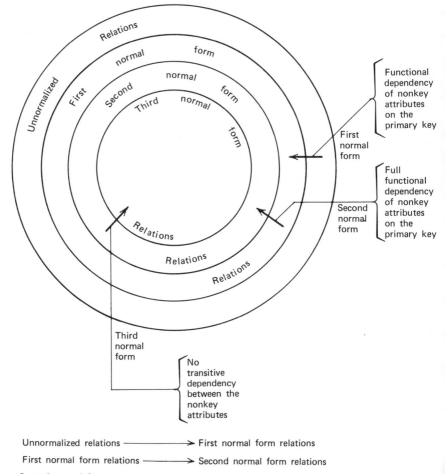

Unnormalized relations ————————→ First normal form relations

First normal form relations ————————→ Second normal form relations

Second normal form relations ————————→ Third normal form relations

Figure 5.2 **Every relation in the first normal form is a special case of an un-normalized relation. But every unnormalized relation is not in the first normal form. Every relation in the second normal form is a special case of the first normal form relation, but not vice versa. Every relation in the third normal form is a special case of a second normal form relation, but every second normal form relation is not necessarily in the third normal form.**

A column or set of columns is called a "candidate key" when its values uniquely identify the row of the relation. Given the patient's number (1234), the surgeon's license number (243), and the date of surgery (Apr. 5, 76), the row (or the tuple) "1234 243 Apr. 5, 1976 Mary Jones 10 Main Street, Rye, N.Y. Charles Field Eye

Patient's Number	Surgeon's License Number	Date of Surgery	Patient's Name	Patient's Address	Surgeon's Name	Surgery	Postoperative Drug Administered	Side Effect of Drug
1111	145	Jan. 1, 1977	John White	15 New Street, New York, N.Y.	Beth Little	Gallstones removal	Penicillin	Rash
1111	311	June 12, 1977	John White	15 New Street, New York, N.Y.	Michael Diamond	Kidney stones removal	---	---
1234	243	Apr. 5, 1976	Mary Jones	10 Main Street, Rye, N.Y.	Charles Field	Eye cataract removal	Tetracycline	Fever
1234	467	May 10, 1977	Mary Jones	10 Main Street, Rye, N.Y.	Patricia Gold	Thrombosis removal	---	---
2345	189	Jan. 8, 1978	Charles Brown	Dogwood Lane, Harrison, N.Y.	David Rosen	Open heart surgery	Cephaldsporin	---
4876	145	Nov. 5, 1977	Hal Kane	55 Boston Post Road, Chester, Conn.	Beth Little	Cholecy— stectomy	Demicillin	---
5123	145	May 10, 1977	Paul Kosher	Blind Brook, Mamaroneck, N.Y.	Beth Little	Gallstones removal	---	---
6845	243	Apr. 5, 1976	Ann Hood	Hilton Road, Larchmont, N.Y.	Charles Field	Eye cornea replacement	Tetracycline	Fever
6845	243	Dec. 15, 1976	Ann Hood	Hilton Road, Larchmond, N.Y.	Charles Field	Eye cataract removal	---	---

Tuple

Attribute

Figure 5.3 Representation of data using a relational data model: "Pseudo-Hospital Environment."

cataract removal Tetracycline Fever" is uniquely determined. Since this is the only candidate key, it becomes the primary key.*

First Normal Form. A relation in the first normal form is a "table." At every intersection of a tuple (row) and a column there can be only one value in the table. No groups of values are permitted at the intersections.

Consider Figure 5.4. This is an "unnormalized" relation. At the crossings of some rows and columns more than one value is present. This implies that in this environment, for a given value of the primary key, the values of the nonkey attributes cannot be determined uniquely.

We transfer the unnormalized relation from Figure 5.4 to a normalized relation in Figure 5.5. In this transformation, we repeated the values taken by patient's number, patient's name, patient's address, and, in one instance, surgeon's license number and surgeon's name. Figure 5.5 represents a relation in the first normal form. At every intersection of a tuple (row) and a column, there is only one value in the table—no groups of values. Figure 5.6 shows the relation in pictorial format.

When the values taken by the patient's number and the surgeon's license number and the date of surgery are known, the values taken by the patient's name, patient's address, surgeon's name, surgery, postoperative drug administered, and side effect of drug are also known. The primary key is thus made up of the patient's number, the surgeon's license number, and the date of surgery. There is no other candidate key for this relation. All the nonkey attributes in the relation are functionally dependent on the primary key, that is, given the value of the primary key, the values taken by the nonkey attributes are uniquely determined.

Storage Anomalies of the First Normal Form. The following anomalies will result if we leave our data in the first normal form. (See Figure 5.5.)

Insertion anomaly. It is possible that a new patient has not undergone any surgery at the hospital and no surgeon has been assigned to the patient. As a result of not assigning a surgeon, the

---

*For simplicity we will assume throughout this section that every relation has only one candidate key. The only candidate key is then the primary key, and every attribute that does not participate in the primary key is a nonkey attribute. In practice, most of the time the primary key identifying an entity is obvious.

Number	License Number	Date of Surgery	Patient's Name	Patient's Address	Surgeon's Name	Surgery	Postoperative Drug Administered	Side Effect of Drug
1111	145	Jan. 1, 1977	John White	15 New Street, New York, N.Y.	Beth Little	Gallstones removal	Penicillin	Rash
	311	June 12, 1977			Michael Diamond	Kidney stones removal	—	—
1234	243	Apr. 5, 1976	Mary Jones	10 Main Street, Rye, N.Y.	Charles Field	Eye cataract removal	Tetracycline	Fever
	467	May 10, 1977			Patricia Gold	Thrombosis removal	—	—
2345	189	Jan. 8, 1978	Charles Brown	Dogwood Lane, Harrison, N.Y.	David Rosen	Open heart surgery	Cephaldsporin	—
4876	145	Nov. 5, 1977	Hal Kane	55 Boston Post Road, Chester, Conn.	Beth Little	Cholecystectomy	Demicillin	—
5123	145	May 10, 1977	Paul Kosher	Blind Brook Mamaroneck, N.Y.	Beth Little	Gallstones removal	—	—
6845	243	Apr. 5, 1976	Ann Hood	Hilton Road Larchmont, N.Y.	Charles Field	Eye cornea replacement	Tetracycline	Fever
		Dec. 15, 1976				Eye cataract removal	—	—

Figure 5.4 This is an "Unnormalized" relation. At the crossings of some rows and columns more than one value is present. It is not easy to identify a primary key. Let us assume that the primary key is patient's number. Given a value of the primary key, there are a number of columns; for example, for "patient's number = 1111," there are a number of values at the crossings with surgeon's license number (145 and 311), date of surgery (Jan. 1, 77 and June 12, 77), and so on. This implies that, in this environment, for a given value of the primary key, the values of the nonkey attributes cannot be determined uniquely. (The reader should try to select a column or a combination of columns as a primary key that will uniquely identify the nonkey attributes.)

Patient's Number	Surgeon's License Number	Date of Surgery	Patient's Name	Patient's Address	Surgeon's Name	Surgery	Postoperative Drug Administered	Side Effect of Drug
1111	145	Jan. 1, 1977	John White	15 New Street, New York, N.Y.	Beth Little	Gallstones removal	Penicillin	Rash
1111	311	June 12, 1977	John White	15 New Street, New York, N.Y.	Michael Diamond	Kidney stones removal	—	—
1234	243	Apr. 5, 1976	Mary Jones	10 Main Street Rye, N.Y.	Charles Field	Eye cataract removal	Tetracycline	Fever
1234	467	May 10, 1977	Mary Jones	10 Main Street Rye, N.Y.	Patricia Gold	Thrombosis removal	—	—
2345	189	Jan. 8, 1978	Charles Brown	Dogwood Lane, Harrison, N.Y.	David Rosen	Open heart surgery	Cepholdsporin	—
4876	145	Nov. 5, 1977	Hal Kane	55 Boston Post Road, Chester, Conn.	Beth Little	Cholecystectomy	Demicillin	—
5123	145	May 10, 1977	Paul Kosher	Blind Brook, Mamaroneck, N.Y.	Beth Little	Gallstones removal	—	—
6845	243	Apr. 5, 1976	Ann Hood	Hilton Road, Larchmont, N.Y.	Charles Field	Eye cornea replacement	Tetracycline	Fever
6845	243	Dec. 15, 1976	Ann Hood	Hilton Road, Larchmont, N.Y.	Charles Field	Eye cataract removal	—	—

Primary Key

patient tuple cannot be entered, that is, no information about the patient can be stored in the first normal form in Figure 5.5.

Suppose that we would like to insert the data about patient's name and patient's address. It should not be necessary to know the surgeon's license number and date of surgery. This means that, to uniquely identify patient's name and patient's address, two components of the primary key, that is, surgeon's licence number and date of surgery, are superfluous. If we separate patient's name and patient's address, together with patient's number, in a different relation, as in Figure 5.7a, this insertion anomaly will be rectified.

Insertion anomaly. It is possible that the hospital has appointed a new surgeon who has not yet operated on any patient at this hospital. As a result, in a tuple for this surgeon, there will not be any value assigned either to the patient's number or to the date of surgery. Only part of the primary key is made up of the surgeon's license number; the rest consists of the patient's number and the date of surgery. As a result, a new tuple for a new surgeon cannot be entered, that is, no information about the surgeon can be stored.* Here the nonkey attribute surgeon's name is uniquely identified by the primary key patient's number + surgeon's license number + date of surgery. But for the unique identification of surgeon's name, the only part of the primary key necessary is surgeon's license number. If

*The reader might suggest the use of null keys or fictitious keys to avoid the problems of insertion. But in relational concepts null or fictitious key values are not permitted, since key values play an important role in searching the data base.

Figure 5.5 Representation of data using a relational data model. First normal form relation. Assumptions made are:

1. A patient receives only one postoperative drug, if any, after surgery, that is, the postoperative drug is uniquely identified by the patient's number, the surgeon's license number, and the date of surgery. Patient's name and patient's address can be uniquely identified by the patient's number only. Patient's number is a part of the whole primary key. Surgeon's name can also be uniquely identified by the surgeon's license number. Surgeon's license number is a part of the whole primary key.
2. Side effect of drug, if any, is dependent only on the drug administered.
3. There can be only one side effect, if any, of the drug administered.

These assumptions are made for the sake of simplicity and for illustration purposes.

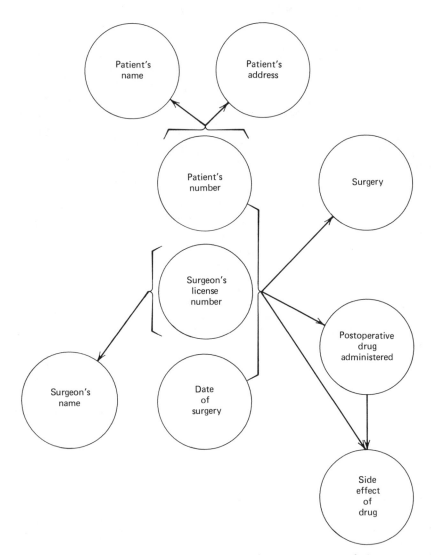

Figure 5.6 **One first normal form relation. Given all three of the values of patient's number and surgeon's license number and date of surgery, one can obtain any of the perimeter values. To find side effect of drug with the given patient's number, surgeon's license number, and date of surgery, one has to find first the postoperative drug administered and then can find the side effect of drug.**

PATIENT Table

Patient's Number	Patient's Name	Patient's Address
1111	John White	15 New Street, New York, N.Y.
1234	Mary Jones	10 Main Street, Rye, N.Y.
2345	Charles Brown	Dogwood Lane, Harrison, N.Y.
4876	Hal Kane	55 Boston Post Road, Chester, Conn.
5123	Paul Kosher	Blind Brook, Mamaroneck, N.Y.
6845	Ann Hood	Hilton Road, Larchmont, N.Y.

Figure 5.7a Second normal form relation. The primary key is patient's number. The nonkey attributes patient's name and patient's address need the full primary key, which is patient's number, for unique identification. Patient's name and patient's address appear only in this relation.

we separate surgeon's name with surgeon's license number, as in Figure 5.7*b*, this insertion anomaly is rectified.

These anomalies occur because some columns depend on only part of the primary key, whereas the entire primary key is necessary to uniquely identify the tuple.

SURGEON Table

Surgeon's License Number	Surgeon's Name
145	Beth Little
189	David Rosen
243	Charles Field
311	Michael Diamond
467	Patricia Gold

Figure 5.7b Second normal form relation. The primary key is surgeon's license number. The nonkey attribute surgeon's name needs the full primary key, which is surgeon's license number, for unique identification. Surgeon's name appears only in this relation.

Update anomaly. If John White enters the hospital for the third time, and if between his second and third visits he has moved, we would like to update his address in all the tuples where he appears. (We want to keep only up-to-date information about the names and addresses for the sake of consistency. We assume that the hospital does not want to keep the old address.) This example shows that it is difficult to update a first normal form relation, because the number of tuples where the change has to be reflected is time-varying. The worst thing could be to have some tuples with the old address and some tuples with the new one.

This update anomaly will be taken care of if patient's address appears only once. If we separate patient's name and patient's address, together with patient's number, as in Figure 5.7a, the anomaly disappears. John White's address will appear only once in the PATIENT table, as in Figure 5.7a.

Deletion anomaly (type 1). Suppose that we wish to delete the information about a patient after she/he is deceased. Let us assume that the patient Charles Brown dies. (See Figure 5.5.) But when we delete the Charles Brown tuple, all facts about the surgeon David Rosen are lost because this was the only surgery that he performed. In some applications, the loss of information of this type could have serious effects. Since the tuple deleted might be the only source of information about David Rosen in our data base, we risk losing all the information about this surgeon. To prevent something like this from happening, we would have to burden the user with the responsibility of checking that the tuple to be deleted is not the only source of information for that "category."

One possibility of resolving a problem of this kind is separating the information about the surgeon that is not dependent on the patient and vice versa. This can be achieved by having two relations, as in Figures 5.7a and 5.7b, for PATIENT and SURGEON, respectively.

Deletion anomaly (type 2). Another type of deletion anomaly is the result of a nonkey attribute from the relation in Figure 5.5 being functionally dependent on another nonkey attribute from the same relation. The side effect of a drug is functionally dependent only on the drug administered. It is possible that the rash resulting from administering penicillin to John White is so severe that this patient receives some other drug. The attribute values for the specific tuple are changed from penicillin to another drug and to some other side effect. As a result of this change, we lose the information that penicillin produced a rash. Since the particular tuple might be the only source of information in the data base for that category, this loss is not desirable.*

To take care of these anomalies, we will separate the patient's information into a PATIENT relation, as in Figure 5.7a, and the surgeon's information into a SURGEON relation, as in Figure 5.7b. The primary key in the PATIENT relation from Figure 5.7a is the patient's number, and the primary key in the SURGEON relation from Figure 5.7b is the surgeon's license number. The remaining attributes comprise the PATIENT-AND-SURGEON relation shown in Figure 5.7c, with the primary key composed of patient's number, surgeon's license number, and date of surgery.

The relations in Figures 5.7a, 5.7b, and 5.7c are said to be in the second normal form. These three second normal form relations for our data are more desirable than the one first normal form relation in Figure 5.5, because a second normal form relation removes some of the storage anomalies encountered with a first normal form relation. Figure 5.8 represents the three second normal form relations in a pictorial format.

Second Normal Form Relation. A relation is said to be in the second normal form when every nonkey attribute is fully functionally dependent on the primary key, that is, every nonkey attribute needs the full primary key for unique identification. Conversely, a relation is not in the second normal form if there is a nonkey attribute that is not fully functionally dependent on the primary key.

Every relation in the second normal form is also in the first normal form.

Storage Anomalies of the Second Normal Form Relation. Figures 5.7a, 5.7b, and 5.7c represent three second normal form relations. Some of the anomalies with the first normal form, as in Figure 5.5, have been removed with the second normal form relations.

*The reader can think of some realistic examples of this type. The restrictive assumptions made here are for illustration purposes only. The reader may change the assumptions about the "pseudo-hospital" environment as follows:
1. A patient may receive more than one postoperative drug.
2. A postoperative drug may have more than one side effect.
3. The side effect depends not only on the drug administered but also on the patient.
With the changed assumptions the reader will develop a different set of third normal form relations.

PATIENT—and—SURGEON Table

Patient's Number	Surgeon's License Number	Date of Surgery	Surgery	Postoperative Drug Administered	Side Effect of Drug
1111	145	Jan. 1, 1977	Gallstones removal	Penicillin	Rash
1111	311	June 12, 1977	Kidney stones removal	———	———
1234	243	Apr. 5, 1976	Eye cataract removal	Tetracycline	Fever
1234	467	May 10, 1977	Thrombosis removal	———	———
2345	189	Jan. 8, 1978	Open heart surgery	Cephaldsporin	———
4876	145	Nov. 5, 1977	Cholecystectomy	Demicillin	———
5123·	145	May 10, 1977	Gallstones removal	———	———
6845	243	Apr. 5, 1976	Eye cornea replacement	Tetracycline	Fever
6845	243	Dec. 15, 1976	Eye cataract removal	———	———

Figure 5.7c Second normal form relation. The primary key is patient's number + surgeon's license number + date of surgery. Every nonkey attribute, (i.e., surgery, postoperative drug administered, and side effect of drug) requires the full primary key patient's number + surgeon's license number + date of surgery for unique identification.

Insertion. We can enter a new patient who has not undergone any surgery at the hospital and to whom no surgeon has been assigned by simply entering the patient's information in the relation in Figure 5.7a.

Insertion. The information regarding a new surgeon who has not yet operated on any patient at the hospital can be entered by simply introducing a new tuple into the relation in Figure 5.7b.

Deletion (type 1). If Charles Brown dies, the corresponding tuple from the relations in Figures 5.7a and 5.7c can be deleted. The information about the surgeon David Rosen will remain in the relation in Figure 5.7b.

Update. If John White enters the hospital for the third time with a new address, the only place where the address change will

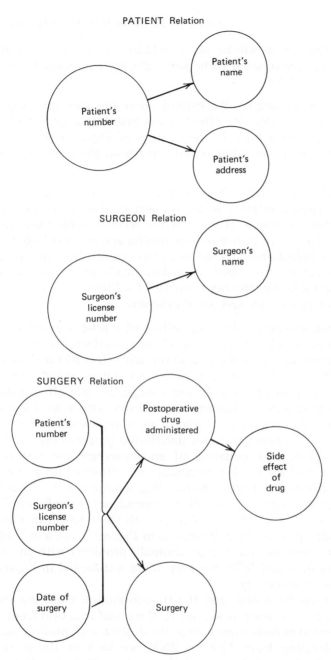

Figure 5.8 Three second normal form relations. The primary key of the PATIENT relation is patient's number. The primary key of the SURGEON relation is surgeon's license number. The primary key of the SURGERY relation is patient's number + surgeon's license number + date of surgery.

have to take place will be in the relation in Figure 5.7a and *not* in Figure 5.7c. There seem to be some storage anomalies with the relation in Figure 5.7c.

Insertion anomaly. We cannot enter the fact that a particular drug has a particular side effect unless that drug is given to a patient. We cannot enter a tuple in the relation of Figure 5.7c until we have a patient who is operated on and to whom the particular drug can be given.

Deletion anomaly. The deletion anomaly where a nonkey attribute from a relation is functionally dependent on another non-key attribute remains. If John White receives some other drug as a result of the severe rash due to penicillin and the attribute values for the drug administered and the side effect of the drug are updated, we lose the information that penicillin produced a rash. Since that particular tuple was the only source of information in the data base for that category, this loss is not desirable.

Update anomaly. The side effect of a drug appears in the relation in Figure 5.7c many times. If the manufacturer of a particular drug changes the formula so that the side effect of the drug changes, we are faced with two approaches: (1) either search through the whole relation in Figure 5.7c and change the side effect value every time the drug was administered, or (2) live with some inconsistency as a result of changing the value in some tuples and not changing it in others. (This example is for illustration purposes only.) The insertion, deletion, and updating of anomalies are the results of the dependency of the nonkey attribute "side effect of drug" on another nonkey attribute, "postoperative drug administered." This type of dependency is called a "transitive" dependency. (See Figure 5.9.)

The solution to these problems with the relation in Figure 5.7c is to replace it with two relations, as in Figures 5.10c and 5.10d.

Since there are no storage anomaly problems with the relations in Figures 5.7a and 5.7b, we keep them untouched in Figures 5.10a and 5.10b, respectively.

It should be noted that the transformation from the second to the third normal form is similar to the transformation from the first to the second normal form except for dealing with nonkey attributes. In transforming from 1NF to 2NF, we look at the relationships between the key attributes and the nonkey attributes. In transforming from 2NF to 3NF, however, we look at the relationships between the nonkey attributes.

Transitive Dependency

Patient's Number	Surgeon's License Number	Date of Surgery	Surgery	Postoperative Drug Administered	Side Effect of Drug
1111	145	Jan. 1, 1977	Gallstones removal	Penicillin	Rash
1111	311	June 12, 1977	Kidney stones removal	— — —	— — —
1234	243	Apr. 5, 1976	Eye cataract removal	Tetracycline	Fever
1234	467	May 10, 1977	Thrombosis removal	— — —	— — —
2345	189	Jan. 8, 1978	Open heart surgery	Cephaldsporin	— — —
4876	145	Nov. 5, 1977	Cholecystectomy	Demicillin	— — —
5123	145	May 10, 1977	Gallstones removal	— — —	— — —
6845	243	Apr. 5, 1976	Eye cornea replacement	Tetracycline	Fever
6845	243	Dec. 16, 1976	Eye cataract removal	— — —	— — —

Figure 5.9 Representation of data using a relational data model:

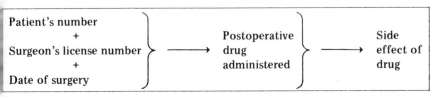

Postoperative drug administered, which is not a part of the primary key, uniquely identifies the nonkey attribute side effect of drug. This type of dependency between the nonkey attributes is called "transitive" dependency.

The relations PATIENT, SURGEON, PATIENT-AND-SURGEON, and DRUG, as in Figures 5.10a, 5.10b, 5.10c and 5.10d, respectively, are in the third normal form. Figure 5.11 shows the four third normal form relations in the pictorial format.

Note, also, that DRUG can be a key to answering questions such as, "Who is taking or took tetracycline?"

Third Normal Form Relation.   A relation is said to be in the third normal form if *there is no transitive functional dependency between the nonkey attributes.* (When one nonkey attribute can be determined with

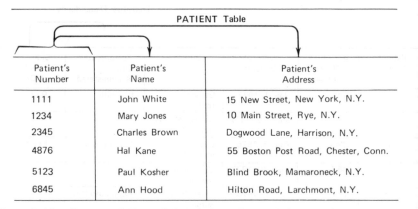

PATIENT Table

Patient's Number	Patient's Name	Patient's Address
1111	John White	15 New Street, New York, N.Y.
1234	Mary Jones	10 Main Street, Rye, N.Y.
2345	Charles Brown	Dogwood Lane, Harrison, N.Y.
4876	Hal Kane	55 Boston Post Road, Chester, Conn.
5123	Paul Kosher	Blind Brook, Mamaroneck, N.Y.
6845	Ann Hood	Hilton Road, Larchmont, N.Y.

Figure 5.10a Representation of data using relational data model. Third normal form relation. The primary key is patient's number.

one or more nonkey attributes, there is said to be transitive functional dependency between the two. The side effect of a drug can be determined from the drug administered. The side effect of a drug is thus transitively functionally dependent on the drug administered.) Alternatively, if there are any nonkey attributes with functional dependency between them, the relation is not in the third normal form.

As a result of creating two relations, as in Figures 5.10c and 5.10d from the relation in Figure 5.7c, the storage anomalies are removed.

SURGEON Table

Surgeon's License Number	Surgeon's Name	
145	Beth Little	
189	David Rosen	
243	Charles Field	
311	Michael Diamond	
467	Patricia Gold	

Figure 5.10b Representation of data using relational data model. Third normal form relation. The primary key.is surgeon's license number.

PATIENT—and—SURGEON Relation

Patient's Number	Surgeon's License Number	Date of Surgery	Surgery	Postoperative Drug Administered
1111	145	Jan. 1, 1977	Gallstones removal	Penicillin
1111	311	June 12, 1977	Kidney stones removal	— — —
1234	243	Apr. 5, 1976	Eye cataract removal	Tetracycline
1234	467	May 10, 1977	Thrombosis removal	— — —
2345	189	Jan. 8, 1978	Open heart surgery	Cephaldsporin
4876	145	Nov. 5, 1977	Cholecystectomy	Demicillin
5123	145	May 10, 1977	Gallstones removal	— — —
6845	243	Apr. 5, 1976	Eye cornea replacement	Tetracycline
6845	243	Dec. 15, 1976	Eye cataract removal	— — —

Figure 5.10c Representation of data using relational data model. Third normal form relation. The primary key is patient's number + surgeon's license number + date of surgery. The nonkey attributes are surgery and postoperative drug administered.

DRUG Relation

Postoperative Drug Administered	Side Effects of Drug
Penicillin	Rash
Tetracycline	Fever
Cephaldsporin	— — —
Demicillin	— — —

Figure 5.10d Representation of data using relational data model. Third normal form relation. The primary key is Postoperative Drug administered.

147

148

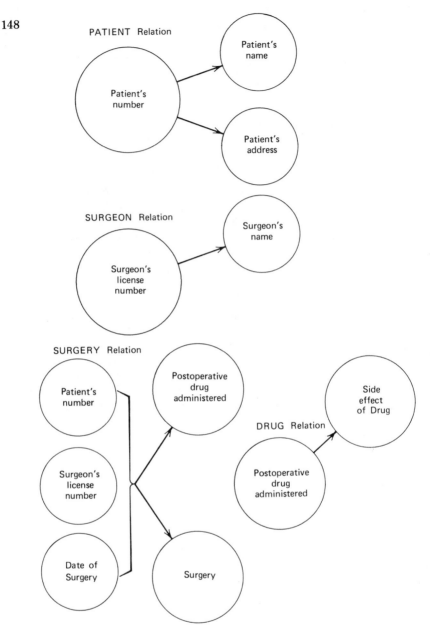

Figure 5.11 **Four third normal form relations.**

1. PATIENT relation. The primary key is patient's number.
2. SURGEON relation. The primary key is surgeon's license number.
3. SURGERY relation. The primary key is patient's number + surgeon's license number + date of surgery.
4. DRUG relation. The primary key is postoperative drug administered.

Insertion. We can enter the fact that a particular drug has a particular side effect in the relation in Figure 5.10*d*, without a patient being administered the drug.

Deletion. If John White receives some other drug as a result of severe rash due to penicillin, he may be administered another drug. The fact that penicillin caused severe rash can be recorded in the relation in Figure 5.10*d*.

Update. The side effect of every drug will appear only once in the relation in Figure 5.10*d*, thus taking care of the update anomaly.

It is important to notice that, in the process of reduction from the first normal form relation to a set of third normal form relations, we did not lose any information. This means any information that can be derived from the relation in Figure 5.5 can also be derived from the relations in Figures 5.10*a*, 5.10*b*, 5.10*c*, and 5.10*d*. The relation in Figure 5.5 can be constructed by combining the relations in Figures 5.10*a* to 5.10*d*. *Another point that needs to be stressed here is that the reduction process is not a function of the data values that happen to be in the relations at some particular point in time, but is a function of the relationships between the attributes.*

To follow the normalization process, it is absolutely necessary that the data base designer understands the semantics of the information. Depending on the assumptions about the functional dependencies between the attributes, the set of third normal form relations for the enterprise will be different.*

As a result of the normalization process, four third normal form relations are derived. They represent the entities and their relationships and correspond well with the intuitive idea of the entities: PATIENT, SURGEON, SURGERY, and DRUG. For the enterprise in our example, four relations represent the conceptual model.

5.3 GRAPHICAL REPRESENTATION

It is well known that a picture can communicate much better than words. For describing our process of developing a conceptual model,

---

*There have been some publications about a fourth normal form, which should eliminate the problem of multivalued dependence. The author considers the normalization process up to the third normal form of sufficient practical value and refers any interested reader to the bibliography for the literature on the fourth normal form.

we will use a notation for the two basic elements of any data base model: the entity and the mapping.

Consider the following example.

In a university environment a student can take many courses, and a course can be taken by many students. For every course taken, a student will receive some grade. The information about only the student and the grade is insufficient because it is not clear in which course the student received the specific grade. On the other hand, the information about only the course and the grade is not sufficient either. We would like to know which student received the specific grade in which course. (See Figure 5.12.)

Figure 5.13 represents the underlying conceptual model of Figure 5.12 and can be interpreted as follows:

- Any STUDENT may take any number of courses.
- Any one COURSE can be taken by any number of students.
- A specific GRADE can, and must, be related to one and only one student *and* to one and only one course.
- The double-headed arrow joining STUDENT and GRADE represents the fact that a student may have none, one, or many

Student \ Course	CS601	MA123	GY456	PH387	CH890
Robert Braun	A	B	A		
Helen Plain		A		A	
Harry Klein		A	B		
Jim White	A				A
John Flunk	C			C	

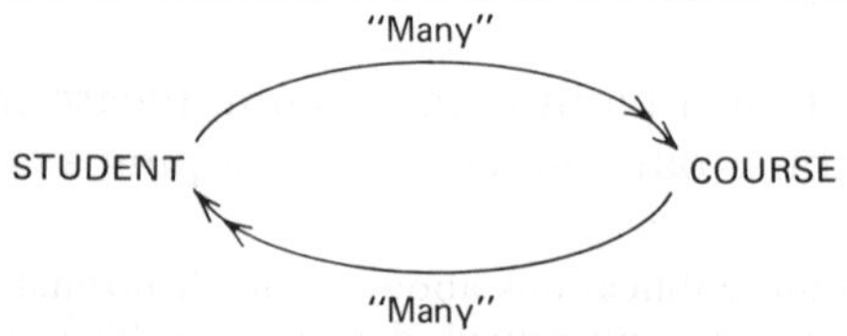

"Many"

STUDENT ⟷ COURSE

"Many"

Figure 5.12 Relationships between STUDENT, COURSE, and GRADE. A given student may take many courses. A given course may be taken by many students. A specific grade tells more about the student and the course.

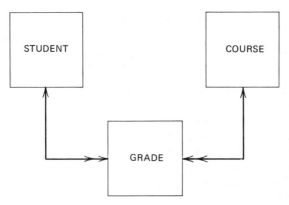

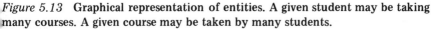

Figure 5.13 **Graphical representation of entities. A given student may be taking many courses. A given course may be taken by many students.**

grades, depending on none, one, or many courses taken by the student.

The double-headed arrow will be used to denote this type of relationship, which is described as "many," throughout the book.

The schematic representation for the conceptual model will be used in this chapter. We must determine how to extract the entities, the relationships between the data elements representing the entities, and the relationships between the entities themselves. The next section will discuss these issues.

5.4 DESIGN PROCESS

It is desirable to examine systematically the purpose, the inputs, and the desired outputs of the application that will use the data base as a repository of information. The approach of the design procedure is outside-in.

Here the application of the normalization process is demonstrated with a subset of a university environment. A complete treatment is given in Appendix B as a case study.

The elements and the relationships between the elements will be extracted from the conceptual requirements, and it will be determined which elements can be considered as key data elements. This determination will help the data base administrator to develop the model of the enterprise.

In this section we will apply the relational concepts to designing

STUDENT SCHEDULE LIST/SEMESTER

DATE: SEPTEMBER 7, 1979

SEMESTER: FALL 1979:   SEPTEMBER 10, 1979
TO DECEMBER 22, 1979

SCHOOL:	STATE UNIVERSITY
STUDENT:	123456789
NAME:	JOHN F. SMITH
STATUS:	UNDERGRADUATE
MAJOR:	COMPUTER SCIENCE
MINOR:	GYMNASTICS
FACULTY—ADVISOR:	JOSEPH A. CORRIGAN

NO—COURSE	COURSE—TITLE	NAME—INSTR	CREDITS	CAMPUS	DAY—TIME	BLDG—NO ROOM
CS601	INTRO TO COMP SCIENCE	A.B. ADAMS	3	WHITE PLAINS	W6—8 P.M.	AL201
CS605	INFO STRUCT ALGORITHMS	J.S. FINK	3	BROOKLYN	TH8—10 A.M.	MAIN 605

Figure 5.14 Every registered student at the school receives the report at the beginning of every semester. It is a confirmation of the courses for which the student has registered. This report is a "conceptual requirement" of an "end user."

a data base with the help of only one end user's view in the university environment of Appendix B. The end user's view is represented in Figure 5.14, Data base design for the university environment is done for all the end users' views in Appendix B.

The data elements referenced in the conceptual requirement of Figure 5.14 are represented in Figure 5.15.

The assumptions about the conceptual requirement in Figure 5.14 are as follows:

1. A student has one student identification number.

2. The student identification number uniquely determines the student's name, the student's status, the major discipline, the minor discipline, and the faculty advisor.

SEMESTER	
DSTRTSEM	Date of start of semester.
DENDSEM	Date of end of semester.
NO-STUDENT	Number of student.
NAME-STUDENT	Name of student.
STATUS	Status of student.
MAJOR	Major discipline.
MINOR	Minor discipline.
FACULTY-ADVISOR	Faculty advisor.
NO-COURSE	Number of course.
COURSE-TITLE	Course title.
NAME-INSTR	Name of instructor.
CREDITS	Credits for which the student has registered.
CAMPUS	Campus where the course will be taught.
DAY-TIME	Which day and what time the course will be taught.
BLDG-NO-ROOM	Building number and room number where the course will be taught.

Figure 5.15 The data elements representing the entities of the conceptual requirement in Figure 5.14.

3. A course with the same number can be offered in different semesters and at different campuses. At the time of an offering the title of the course may be changed. Also, the instructor teaching the course may be changed from one semester to another. The campus, the period, and the room may be changed from one semester to another.

4. In a specific semester a specific course will be taught by a specific instructor, at a specific campus, in a specific period, and in a specific room for a specific number of credits.

5. A student may choose the number of credits to be taken for a specific course in a specific semester. Auditors, that is, the students who will not appear for examinations, will receive fewer credits.

The purpose of stating the assumptions is not to solve the environment's problems regarding these assumptions but to reflect them in our conceptual model.

The relationships between the data elements from Figure 5.15 are as follows:

1. SEMESTER ←——→ DSTRTSEM, DENDSEM. For a given SEMESTER there is only one date of start of semester (DSTRTSEM) and also only one date of end of semester (DENDSEM) and vice versa. This is a one-to-one mapping, represented as ←——→ or as $\overset{one}{\rightleftarrows}$. The primary key picked is SEMESTER from the candidate keys SEMESTER, DSTRTSEM, and DENDSEM.

2. NO-STUDENT ←——→ NAME-STUDENT, STATUS, MAJOR, MINOR, FACULTY-ADVISOR. For a given number of student (NO-STUDENT) there is only one NAME-STUDENT, STATUS (of the student), MAJOR (discipline of the student), MINOR (discipline of the student), and FACULTY-ADVISOR. But for a given status there can be many students. There can be many students with the same major and minor disciplines. And a faculty advisor may be advising more than one student. This is a one-to-many mapping, represented as ←——→ or $\overset{one}{\underset{many}{\rightleftarrows}}$.

3. SEMESTER*NO-COURSE ←——→ COURSE-TITLE, NAME-INSTR, CAMPUS, DAY-TIME, BLDG-NO-ROOM. In a given SEMESTER and for a given number of course (NO-COURSE) there is only one COURSE-TITLE, one instructor teaching the course (NAME-INSTR) (if more than one instructor is teaching the course, we consider it one team of instructors), one CAMPUS, and one DAY-TIME and one BLDG-NO-ROOM where the course will be taught.

   But there may be a number of courses with the same course title (e.g., Introduction to Computer Science, taught in different sections with course numbers CS601.1, CS601.2, etc.). The same instructor may be teaching a number of courses in a semester, and a number of courses may be taught on a specific campus in a specific semester at the same time on the same day and in the same room in the same building.

   This is a one-to-many mapping with SEMESTER and NO-COURSE being the compound key and represented as ←——→ or .

3a. NO-STUDENT*SEMESTER ◄◄——►► NO-COURSE, CREDITS.
A given student (NO-STUDENT) may be taking in a given
SEMESTER many courses (NO-COURSE) and also a set of
CREDITS. A given course may also be taken by many students
in a specific semester, and a given number of credits may be
taken by many students as well. This is a many-to-many map-

ping, represented as ◄◄——►► or $\overset{\text{many}}{\underset{\text{many}}{\rightrightarrows}}$.

Relations 1, 2, and 3 are in the third normal form, because the
nonkey data elements from these relations require the full keys for
their identification. There is no transitive dependency between the
nonkey data elements as well. But relation 3a is not even in the first
normal form, because the mapping is many-to-many. The first normal form requires the mapping between the primary key and the
nonkey data elements to be one-to-many (◄◄——►) or one-to-one
(◄——►). The second normal form requires that the nonkey data
elements have the full primary key for their unique identification.
And the third normal form requires that there be no transitive
dependency between the nonkey data elements.
Relation 3a can be transferred into a third normal form relation
if the primary key is further qualified, that is, if the primary key is
further "compounded" with NO-COURSE.

3b. NO-STUDENT*SEMESTER*NO-COURSE ◄◄——► CREDITS.
Relation 3b is now in the third normal form. A given student
(NO-STUDENT), in a given SEMESTER and for a given course
(NO-COURSE), takes a specific number of CREDITS.

Drawing the Conceptual Model. The relations 1, 2, 3, and 3b are
renumbered as 4, 5, 6, and 7. The relations 4, 5, 6, and 7 (Figure
5.16) can be represented in a pictorial format as follows:

1. Each relation for which the primary key consists of only one
    data element represents an entity. Relations 4 and 5 represent
    the entities SEMESTER and STUDENT, respectively. All entities
    of this type are placed on level 1. In Figure 5.17 the boxes
    SEMESTER and STUDENT on level 1 represent the entities in
    relations 4 and 5. The data elements are written inside the
    boxes. The primary keys of the entities are underlined. If a box
    cannot hold all the data elements representing an entity, the
    omissions are shown by three dashes, ---.

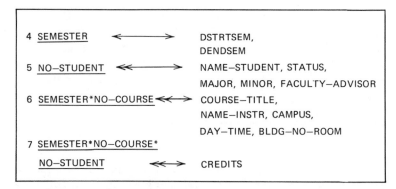

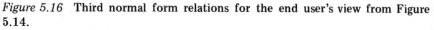

Figure 5.16 **Third normal form relations for the end user's view from Figure 5.14.**

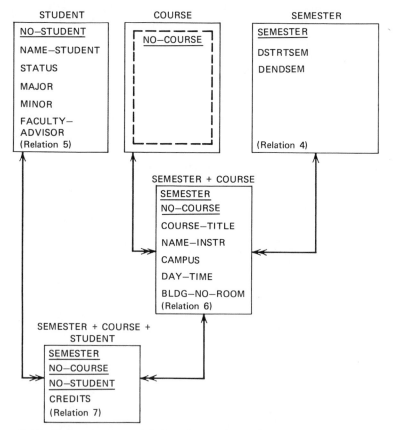

Figure 5.17 **Conceptual model for the end user's view from Figure 5.14. Created relations are shown in dashed boxes.**

2. Relations with a primary key of two data elements represent relationships between two entities. Relations of this type are placed on the second level. If a part of a primary key is not represented as an entity, a new entity relation will be generated; for example, the compound key of relation 6 is SEMESTER*NO-COURSE. This key represents the relationship between the two entities SEMESTER and COURSE. There is a box for the entity SEMESTER on level 1, but no box for the entity COURSE on level 1. To represent the relationship between the entities SEMESTER and COURSE on level 2, a new entity relation for COURSE will be created on level 1, because no relation in Figure 5.16 is defined only with number of course (NO-COURSE) as the primary key. The box with relation 6 on level 2 interconnects the relation SEMESTER and the newly created relation COURSE on level 1. The newly created box is represented with dashed lines.

The single-headed and double-headed arrows between relations 4 and 6 and the dashed box COURSE from Figure 5.17 indicate that in a given semester many courses may be taught, and a given course may be taught in many semesters.

3. The procedure for level 2 will be repeated for level 3 with relations with a primary key of three data elements, and so on.

The resulting diagram for relations 4, 5, 6, and 7 is shown in Figure 5.17.

After the conceptual model is determined, the data base administrator can develop a logical model with the underlying structure of a relational, hierarchical, or network data model. Designing a logical model is presented in the next chapter, and the determination of a physical model on the basis of cost, size, and performance is treated in Part III.

REFERENCES

1. *An Introduction to Data Base Design*, John K. Lyon, The Wiley Communigraph Series in Business Data Processing, John Wiley & Sons, 1971.

2. *An Introduction to Database Systems*, 2nd ed., C. J. Date, Addison-Wesley Publishing Company, 1977.

Data Base Design
(Logical Model)

This chapter demonstrates a procedure for mapping a conceptual model into a logical model. Because today's data base management systems use a relational, a hierarchical, or a network data model, or a combination of these data models, the steps for mapping the conceptual model to each of these data models are given.

DESIGN A LOGICAL MODEL OF A DATA BASE

In developing a logical model of the data base, the first consideration is deciding which data model will be the best one for the particular conceptual model. Commercial data base management systems are based on one data model or on a combination of data models. The three major data models are known as relational, hierarchical, and network, and a detailed discussion of these data models was given in Chapter 4.

The conceptual model of Chapter 5, Figure 5.17, is shown here for convenience as Figure 6.1. The boxes at the first level, STU-DENT, COURSE, and SEMESTER, represent the basic entities. As explained in Chapter 5, the primary key of an entity at the first level consists of only one attribute. For example, the key of the STUDENT entity is NO-STUDENT. The box SEMESTER + COURSE at the second level has a primary key composed of SEMESTER and

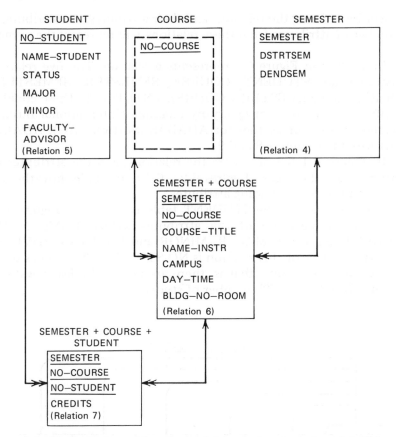

Figure 6.1 Conceptual model to be used to map to a logical model. This conceptual model is taken from Figure 5.17.

NO-COURSE. This box connects the basic entities SEMESTER and COURSE. The primary key of the box at the third level, SEMESTER + COURSE + STUDENT, is made of three attributes: SEMESTER + NO-COURSE + NO-STUDENT.

The following discussion gives versions of the logical model using a relational, a hierarchical, and a network data model.

6.1 MAPPING TO A RELATIONAL DATA MODEL

A relational data model consists of a number of relations (tables). In mapping the conceptual model from Figure 6.1 to a logical model, we will be defining the relations and their attributes. An attribute, or a number of attributes from these relations will represent the primary key.

Every box in Figure 6.1 represents a relation. The five relations illustrated are STUDENT, COURSE, SEMESTER, SEMESTER + COURSE, and SEMESTER + COURSE + STUDENT. These could be specified as relations for Query-By-Example (International Business Machines Corp.) or as files for ADABAS (Software AG). ADABAS is discussed in Chapters 8 and 9.

In Figure 6.1 the boxes are the relations, and the attributes are written inside the boxes. Figures 6.2a, 6.2b, and 6.2c show the relations with the corresponding attributes.

The user view of the STUDENT table is shown in Figure 6.2a. The table is made up of the attributes NO-STUDENT, NAME-STUDENT, STATUS, MAJOR, MINOR and FACULTY-ADVISOR. The primary key of this relation is NO-STUDENT. The values of the primary key are unique, that is, there are no two tuples (rows) with the same NO-STUDENT (number of student).

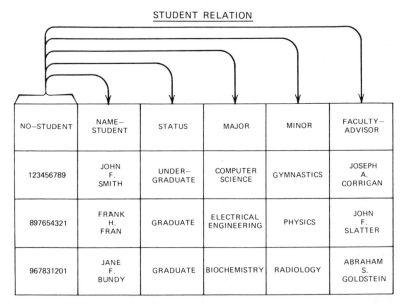

STUDENT RELATION

NO–STUDENT	NAME–STUDENT	STATUS	MAJOR	MINOR	FACULTY–ADVISOR
123456789	JOHN F. SMITH	UNDER–GRADUATE	COMPUTER SCIENCE	GYMNASTICS	JOSEPH A. CORRIGAN
897654321	FRANK H. FRAN	GRADUATE	ELECTRICAL ENGINEERING	PHYSICS	JOHN F. SLATTER
967831201	JANE F. BUNDY	GRADUATE	BIOCHEMISTRY	RADIOLOGY	ABRAHAM S. GOLDSTEIN

Figure 6.2a STUDENT relation (table). The key attribute is NO-STUDENT (number of student). The nonkey attributes are NAME-STUDENT, STATUS, MAJOR, MINOR, and FACULTY-ADVISOR.

The COURSE relation in Figure 6.2b consists only of the attribute NO-COURSE (number of course), which is the key attribute. This table shows the numbers of all the courses taught at the university. Every course number appears only once.

The SEMESTER relation from Figure 6.2b has the attributes SEMESTER (number of semester), DSTRTSEM (date of start of semester), and DENDSEM (date of end of semester), with SEMESTER being the primary key. Given the value of SEMESTER, there is only one tuple with that value, that is, there is only one DSTRTSEM and only one DENDSEM. The semester FALL, 1979 starts on September 10, 1979, and ends on December 22, 1979.

The relation that links the two relations SEMESTER and COURSE is SEMESTER + COURSE. The key attributes of that relation are SEMESTER and NO-COURSE, and the nonkey attributes are COURSE-TITLE, NAME-INSTR, CAMPUS, DAY-TIME, and BLDG-NO-ROOM. The key is called a compound key because it is composed of more than one attribute. For a given SEMESTER and for a given NO-COURSE, there is only one COURSE-TITLE and one NAME-INSTR, CAMPUS, DAY-TIME, and BLDG-NO-ROOM. This table gives a user view of all the courses taught in a given semester and all the semesters where a given course is taught. For example, in FALL, 1979, the courses taught are CS601, CS605, CS623, and PH500, whereas the course CS623 is taught in the semesters SUMMER, 1979 and FALL, 1979. The combination of the values of NO-COURSE and SEMESTER uniquely identifies the values taken by the nonkey attributes.

Finally, the SEMESTER + COURSE + STUDENT relation in Figure 6.2c establishes the linkage at the third level in Figure 6.1 between SEMESTER, COURSE, and STUDENT. The primary key is composed of SEMESTER, NO-COURSE, and NO-STUDENT. The nonkey attribute is CREDITS. In one semester many courses may be taught, and one course may be taken by many students. On the other hand, a student may take many courses in a specific semester. This table reflects the many-to-many relationships between SEMESTER, NO-COURSE, and NO-STUDENT. In a given semester (e.g., FALL, 1979), a given student, 123456789 (JOHN F. SMITH), has elected three credits for a specific course, CS601.

The five relations from Figures 6.2a, 6.2b, and 6.2c are the user views or the logical model of the data base. This logical model is derived from the conceptual model in Figure 6.1. The key attributes are redundant in some of the user views. For example, NO-COURSE appears in three of the five relations. However, the relations in Figures

NO-COURSE Relation

NO-COURSE
CS601
CS603
CS605
CS618
CS623
EE101
PH500
...

COURSE Relation

SEMESTER Relation

SEMESTER	DSTRTSEM	DENDSEM
SPRING, 1978	JANUARY 12, 1978	APRIL 29, 1978
SUMMER, 1978	MAY 11, 1978	AUGUST 16, 1978
FALL, 1978	SEPTEMBER 9, 1978	DECEMBER 21, 1978
SPRING, 1979	JANUARY 10, 1979	APRIL 30, 1979
SUMMER, 1979	MAY 12, 1979	AUGUST 15, 1979
FALL, 1979	SEPTEMBER 10, 1979	DECEMBER 20, 1979
...	...	...

SEMESTER + COURSE Relation

SEMESTER	NO-COURSE	COURSE-TITLE	NAME-INSTR	CAMPUS	DAY-TIME	BLDG-NO-ROOM
SUMMER, 1979	CS608	COMPILER	A.B. ADAMS	BROOKLYN	THU 8-10 pm	MAIN601
SUMMER, 1979	CS623	SWITCHING AND DIGITAL SYSTEMS	J.N. DOLM	WHITE PLAINS	TU 6-8 pm	ACCT389
SUMMER, 1979	PH500	FIELD & WAVES	A.T. FRIEDMAN	BROOKLYN	MO 8-10 pm	AL302
FALL, 1979	CS601	INTRO TO COMP SCIENCE	A.B. ADAMS	WHITE PLAINS	W 6-8 pm	AL201
FALL, 1979	CS605	INFO STRUCT & ALGORITHMS	J.S. FINK	BROOKLYN	THU 8-10 pm	MAIN605
FALL, 1979	CS623	SWITCHING & DIGITAL SYSTEMS	A.M. JONES	LONG ISLAND	TU 6-8 pm	MAIN238
FALL, 1979	PH500	FIELD & WAVES	A.B. ADAMS	BROOKLYN	THU 8-10 am	ACCT389
:	:	:	:	:	:	:

Figure 6.2b

6.2*a*, 6.2*b*, and 6.2*c* are user views, and are not necessarily implemented physically in that way.

The mapping of the conceptual model onto a relational data model is a relatively easy process. Every box from the conceptual model becomes a relation or a table, and the user is supplied with the userview, which is in a table format. This is due to using a relational approach to designing the conceptual model.

6.2 MAPPING TO A HIERARCHICAL DATA MODEL

Deriving a logical hierarchical data model from a conceptual model is not a straightforward process in that many seemingly arbitrary choices can be made, and there is no one "right" result. However, the steps to be followed can be grouped into categories with rules and guidelines for the choices to be made within each category. These categories are as follows:

A. Derive a hierarchical data model without regard for a particular data base management system (DBMS).
B. Modify the data model to eliminate conflicts with the rules of the DBMS to be used.
C. Refine the modified data model according to some "obvious" performance considerations.
D. Simplify key names.
E. Add relationships that exist between data but have not surfaced in the logical model so far.

Figure 6.2b   **Three relations are shown:**

1. COURSE relation. The only attribute, NO-COURSE, is the key attribute.
2. SEMESTER relation. The key attribute is SEMESTER, and the nonkey attributes are DSTRTSEM and DENDSEM.
3. SEMESTER + COURSE relation linking the two relations SEMESTER and COURSE. The key attributes are NO-COURSE and SEMESTER. The nonkey attributes are COURSE-TITLE, NAME-INSTR, CAMPUS, DAY-TIME, and BLDG-NO-ROOM.

SEMESTER	NO–COURSE	NO–STUDENT	CREDITS
SUMMER, 1979	CS608	967831201	4
SUMMER, 1979	CS608	897645123	2
SUMMER, 1979	CS623	967831201	3
SUMMER, 1979	PH500	967831201	4
FALL, 1979	CS601	123456789	3
FALL, 1979	CS601	897645123	2
FALL, 1979	CS605	123456789	2
FALL, 1979	CS623	967831201	3
FALL, 1979	PH500	897645123	3

Figure 6.2c SEMESTER + COURSE + STUDENT relation. SEMESTER, NO-COURSE, and NO-STUDENT comprise the primary key. The nonkey attribute is CREDITS.

A Derive a hierarchical data model without regard for a particular DBMS.

A.1 Eliminate transitivity.

Transitivity exists in the conceptual model if the relationship between A and C (Figure 6.3) can be removed without any loss of essential information. The relationship between

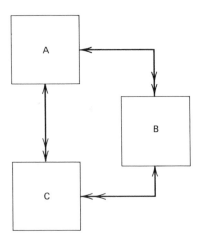

Figure 6.3 The relationship between A and C is superfluous if the same relationship can be derived from the relationships between A, B and B, C.

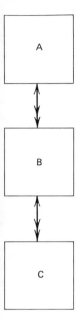

Figure 6.4 Direct relationship between A and C was removed from Figure 6.3. The relationships between A, B and B, C are intact, and the relationship between A and C can be derived through B.

A and C can be derived from the relationships between A, B and B, C.

After removal of the relationship between A and C, Figure 6.3 can be redrawn as Figure 6.4.

Before the removal of any relationship, it should be examined to determine whether any information could be lost. For example, consider Figure 6.5, where relationship ① between FACULTY and STUDENT is that of ACADEMIC ADVISOR and ACADEMIC ADVISEE. Relationship ② between FACULTY and STUDENT is "over" PROJECT. A faculty member may be an academic advisor or counselor for one group of students and also a project advisor for a specific project of another group of students. In this situation relationship ① is not superfluous and cannot be removed.

A.2 Derive parent-child relationships.

In the conceptual model, the boxes represent node types and the arrows represent parent-child relationships between these node types. In Figure 6.1 the root node types are the boxes at the first level, that is, STUDENT, COURSE, and

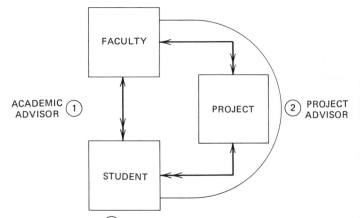

Figure 6.5 Relationship ① between FACULTY and STUDENT is that of ACADEMIC ADVISOR and ACADEMIC ADVISEE. Relationship ② between FACULTY and STUDENT is "over" PROJECT, that is, that of PROJECT AD-VISOR and PROJECT ADVISEE.

SEMESTER. The box at the second level is SEMESTER + COURSE, which can be a child node type of SEMESTER or of COURSE. Here we have two root node types, that is, two hierarchical trees with the interconnecting node type SEMESTER + COURSE, as in Figure 6.6. A decision has to

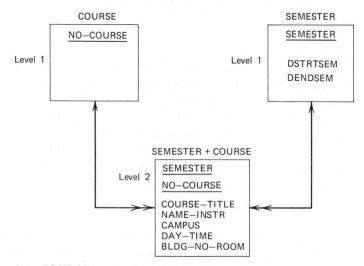

Figure 6.6 COURSE and SEMESTER are the two root node types. SEMES-TER + COURSE is a node type that could be a child of either SEMESTER or COURSE.

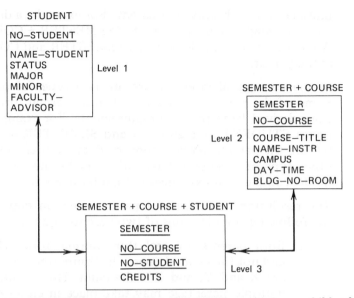

Figure 6.7 SEMESTER + COURSE + STUDENT could be a child of either STUDENT or SEMESTER + COURSE.

be made whether SEMESTER + COURSE should be a child of SEMESTER or of COURSE.

Let us further take a part of Figure 6.1 with the node types STUDENT, SEMESTER + COURSE, and SEMESTER + COURSE + STUDENT, as in Figure 6.7. The node type SEMESTER + COURSE + STUDENT could be a child of SEMESTER + COURSE at the second level or of STUDENT at the first level.

In this stage, the possible parent-child relationships are identified. These relationships are resolved in the next stage.

A.3   Resolve multiple parentage.

In the conceptual model as presented in Figure 6.1 and as seen in its subsets as in Figures 6.6 and 6.7, there may be several nodes with two or more parents. In Figure 6.6, SEMESTER + COURSE has SEMESTER and COURSE as parents. In a hierarchical data model, however, a child can have only one parent (see Chapter 4). To map the conceptual model onto a hierarchical data model, every child node type must be left with only one parent. For example, a decision has to be made about the parent of SEMESTER + COURSE. A choice must be made between SEMESTER and COURSE as the parent.

In the conceptual model, there are two types of parents. Some of the parents represent real third normal form relations derived from the data requirements. For example, the boxes STUDENT in Figure 6.7 and SEMESTER in Figure 6.6 are the parents derived from the data requirements. The other type of parents is "created" to make the conceptual model complete, as explained in Chapter 5, Section 5.4.

The resolution procedure for parent selection depends on the following combinations of two parents at a time.

A.3.1 **Both parents are real third normal form relations and not the created ones.** In Figure 6.8, the parents are X and Y, and Z is the child. The resolution of multiple parentage may take place in either of two ways: X as a parent, Y and Z combined as a child; or Y as a parent, X and Z combined as a child. In both cases, redundancy may be introduced by making Y a part of a child of X, or, in the alternative solution, X a part of a child of Y. Thus, in resolving the multiple parentage of "real" parents, it must be decided whether both parents are necessary or

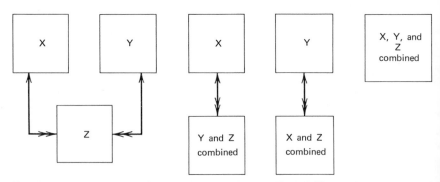

Figure 6.8 Resolution of multiple parenthood. X and Y are the parent node types. Z is the child node type. The resolution of multiple parentage may take place with X as the parent, Y and Z combined as a child. It may take place with Y as the parent, X and Z combined as a child. It may also take place with X, Y, and Z combined into one node.

whether one of them can be integrated into the child node at the cost of some redundancy. The third possibility is to integrate both parents and child in one node type, for example, X, Y, and Z combined as in Figure 6.8.

A.3.2 **One parent is a real third normal form relation, and the other parent is a created one.** The most probable candidate for removal may be the created parent. In Figure 6.9a, the child at the second level, SEMESTER + COURSE, has SEMESTER, which is a result of a real third normal form relation, as one parent, whereas the other parent is COURSE, which is a created one. The box COURSE has only one attribute, NO-COURSE. The same attribute is represented also in SEMESTER + COURSE. There will not be any loss of data or of relationships if we eliminate the box COURSE and make SEMESTER the only parent of SEMESTER + COURSE, as in Figure 6.9b. One precaution to be taken while eliminating the boxes is that no other relationships with the other "boxes" are left unresolved, as in Figure 6.9c.

After making the change indicated in Figure 6.9b to Figure 6.1, the logical model at this stage appears as in Figure 6.10.

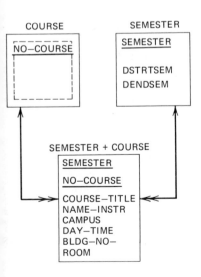

Figure 6.9a SEMESTER is a "real" parent, whereas COURSE is a "created" parent of SEMESTER + COURSE.

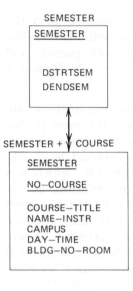

SEMESTER

SEMESTER
DSTRTSEM
DENDSEM

SEMESTER + COURSE

SEMESTER
NO–COURSE
COURSE–TITLE NAME–INSTR CAMPUS DAY–TIME BLDG–NO–ROOM

Figure 6.9b The "created" parent is removed, and the only parent left of SEMESTER + COURSE is SEMESTER.

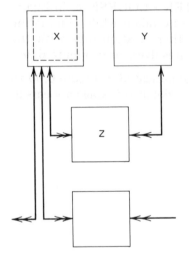

Figure 6.9c X is a "good" candidate for removal, as a parent of Z, because it is a "created" parent. Before removing the parent X, however, the other relationships indicated by the arrows pointing to X must be taken care of.

A.3.3 **Both parents are created ones.** The most probable candidates for removal may be both parents. In Figure 6.10*a*, the "created" parents are X and Y, and the child is Z. X, Y, and Z may be integrated into one node type. Because both X and Y are removed, the combined node X, Y, and Z moves one level higher in the hierarchy, as in Figure 6.10*b*.

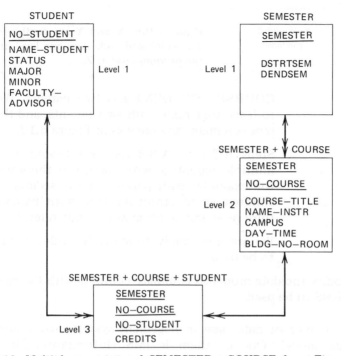

Figure 6.10 **Multiple parentage of SEMESTER + COURSE from Figure 6.1 is resolved. Multiple parentage of SEMESTER + COURSE + STUDENT is not yet resolved.**

A.3.4 If no decision can be reached with A.3.1 to A.3.3, the choice is arbitrary. The remaining parents of the child can be considered in the same way until either only one parent per child node is left, or a decision is made that the multiple parents are necessary. In such a situation, a DBMS has to be chosen that will support multiple parentage. The node SEMESTER +

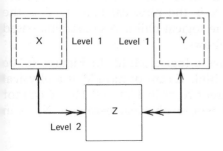

Figure 6.10a **X and Y are the "created" parents. Both are candidates for removal for parent resolution.**

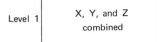

Level 1 | X, Y, and Z combined

Figure 6.10b **X and Y are combined with Z. The combined node goes one level higher than the previous level of Z.**

COURSE + STUDENT has two parents. We decide to leave that node with two parents, and the logical model remains the same as in Figure 6.10.

Steps A.3.1 to A.3.3 can be repeated in resolving multiple parentage with parents at the lower levels, for example, with parents at the second level and children at the third level, or with parents at the third level and children at the fourth level.

We are now ready to apply the rules of the DBMS to be used.

B Modify the data model to eliminate conflicts with the rules of the DBMS to be used.

A number of data base management systems use a hierarchical data model. One of them is IMS (Information Management System), marketed by International Business Machines Corporation. IMS also provides some network capabilities. When IMS is used as the DBMS, some constraints are imposed on the model that may require modifications.

1. There can be no more than 255 node types (called "segment types" in IMS).
2. There can be no more than 15 hierarchical levels.
3. A child segment type can have at the most two parents. (A more detailed discussion of IMS will be given in Chapter 8). One parent, in whose hierarchy the child is placed, is called a "physical" parent, and the other parent is called a "logical" parent. In Figure 6.10c, X is the physical parent, Y is the logical parent, and Z is the logical child. A constraint based on the logical child is as follows.
4. A logical child cannot have a logical child. In Figures 6.10c and 6.10d, Z is a logical child. Z cannot have M as a physical child that has a logical parent N, as in Figure 6.10c. Z cannot have M as a logical child whose physical parent is N, as in Figure 6.10d.

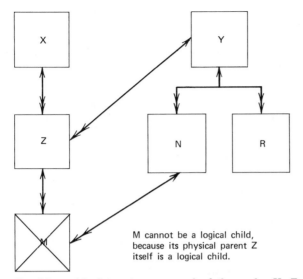

M cannot be a logical child,
because its physical parent Z
itself is a logical child.

Figure 6.10c One hierarchical tree is composed of the nodes X, Z, and M. Another hierarchical tree consists of the nodes Y, N, and R. The node Z has X as its physical parent and Y as its logical parent, that is, Z is a logical child. The node M cannot be a logical child, that is, it cannot have two parents, Z and N. Z, being a logical child, cannot have a physical child M that has another parent, N.

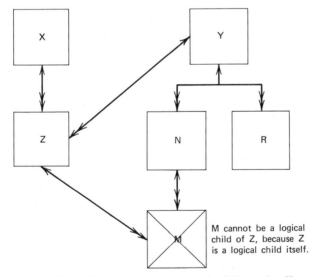

M cannot be a logical
child of Z, because Z
is a logical child itself.

Figure 6.10d One hierarchical tree is composed of the nodes X and Z. Another hierarchical tree consists of the nodes Y, N, R, and M. The node Z has X as its physical parent and Y as its logical parent, that is, Z is a logical child. The node M cannot be a logical child, that is, it cannot have two parents, N and Z. Z, being a logical child, cannot have a logical child M.

173

In Figure 6.10, none of the constraints listed above are violated; hence no modifications are required. The logical model to be used for IMS is thus as shown in Figure 6.10. The only decision yet to be made concerns the placement of the logical child SEMESTER + COURSE + STUDENT. This logical child has to be placed as the physical child of either STUDENT or SEMESTER + COURSE.

C   Refine the modified data model according to some "obvious" performance considerations.

We are still working with the view of Figure 6.11 which is identical to Figure 6.10. This view will provide the functional capabilities required. The question now is, can performance capabilities be enhanced by combining segments to reduce the number of levels, splitting segments to provide more efficient data transfer or more security, combining hierarchies, splitting hierarchies, or making other types of arrangements?

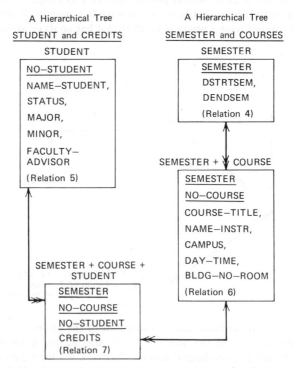

Figure 6.11   **Logical model with two hierarchical trees for the conceptual model** from Figure 6.1.

Considerations of this type cannot be fully resolved without quantitative performance information, such as frequency of use of the various hierarchical paths, average number of occurrences of each segment type, and segment length. Thus a thorough treatment of these considerations belongs to physical design rather than to logical design. However, a few "obvious" choices can be made as part of the logical design process.

C.1   Parents having only one child segment type are potential candidates for combination with their children.

In Figure 6.11, SEMESTER has only one child, SEMESTER + COURSE. The trade-off is between redundancy and performance. Here SEMESTER has only two fields, DSTRTSEM (date of start of semester) and DENDSEM (date of end of semester). If we keep the segment SEMESTER as the parent of SEMESTER + COURSE, there will be only one occurrence of the SEMESTER segment per semester, that is, date of start of semester and date of end of semester will be stored only once each semester. But there will be at least one pointer from the semester occurrence to its first course occurrence. There will also be pointers between the semester occurrences. The time required for updating the pointers and the time required for accessing separate segments, SEMESTER and SEMESTER + COURSE, have to be considered.

The alternative here is to combine the SEMESTER segment with the SEMESTER + COURSE segment, as in Figure 6.12. By combining the two segments, we are introducing redundancy on DSTRTSEM (date of start of semester), and DENDSEM (date of end of semester). If 50 courses are offered in a specific semester, there will be 50 occurrences of the SEMESTER + COURSE segment, and in each occurrence the fields DSTRTSEM (date of start of semester), and DENDSEM (date of end of semester) will appear for every course. This is redundancy of data, that is, more space will be used. The real problem could be maintaining integrity of data if the same data is stored more frequently than necessary. The major issue to be considered when introducing redundancy of data is volatility. If the data is volatile, it should not be stored redundantly. In this case, "date of start of semester" and "date of end of semester" are not volatile data elements for a given semester. Updating of the

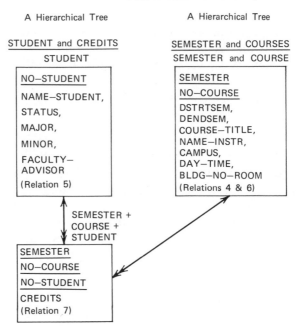

Figure 6.12 Logical model with two hierarchical trees. A modification of Figure 6.11.

two fields will not occur too frequently. Thus combining SEMESTER with its child SEMESTER + COURSE seems intuitively to be a good move.

We have decided to make the segment SEMESTER + COURSE + STUDENT a physical child of the parent STUDENT and a logical child of SEMESTER + COURSE.

C.2 Should there be a logical relationship, or should the logical parent be combined with the logical child in order to eliminate the logical relationship?

In Figure 6.12 SEMESTER + COURSE + STUDENT is the logical child of the logical parent SEMESTER + COURSE. In IMS every root segment type starts a new data base. We have two hierarchical trees and two data bases. Every time an application program needs information about course taken by a student, IMS will have to access two separate data bases, the STUDENT data base and the SEMESTER and COURSE data base. If we combine the logical child SEMESTER + COURSE + STUDENT with the logical par ent SEMESTER + COURSE, the hierarchical tree will appear as in Figure 6.13.

The major consideration here for not having the hierarchical tree as in Figure 6.13 is the redundancy of volatile data about courses. A data base with this hierarchical tree will have redundancy of course occurrences for every student who has taken a particular course. For example, if students FRANK H. FRAN and JANE F. BUNDY have taken the same course, CS608, the course, with all the data about COURSE-TITLE, INSTR-NAME, and so on, will appear twice in the same data base. This type of redundancy may have adverse effects on data integrity. We do not choose to have one hierarchical tree, as in Figure 6.13, but prefer to have two hierarchical trees, as in Figure 6.12.

If we have a choice of having one hierarchical tree, as in Figure 6.13, we will have eliminated one physical data base, SEMESTER and COURSES, as in Figure 6.12. Elimination of a physical data base is a strong consideration from

A Hierarchical Tree
STUDENT, CREDITS, and COURSES
STUDENT

| NO–STUDENT |
| NAME–STUDENT, STATUS, MAJOR, MINOR, FACULTY– ADVISOR (Relation 5) |

SEMESTER + COURSE +
STUDENT combined

| SEMESTER, NO–COURSE, NO–STUDENT |
| CREDITS DSTRTSEM, DENDSEM, COURSE–TITLE, NAME–INSTR, CAMPUS, DAY–TIME, BLDG–NO–ROOM (Relations 4, 6, and 7) |

Figure 6.13 **Logical model with one hierarchical tree. Logical child and logical parent from Figure 6.12 are combined into one segment type.**

the viewpoint of performance. Further performance considerations are discussed in more detail in Chapter 9, with quantitative information such as frequency of use of the various hierarchical paths, average number of occurrences of each segment type, and segment length.

D   Simplify key names.

Segments in a hierarchical path may now have key names as follows:

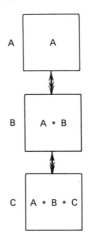

For each child segment, these key names may be simplified by removing the subsets that occur in the parent segment. We get:

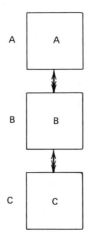

In a hierarchy the key of a child (called a physical child) is implied. But compound keys that represent logical children, which relate parents in different paths, are retained:

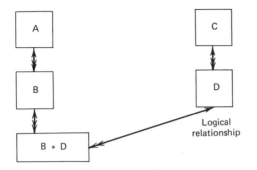

In Figure 6.12 the only segment where the key can be simplified is SEMESTER + COURSE + STUDENT. The segment is a logical child and relates parents in different paths. As a result we would like to keep the compound key SEMESTER, NO-COURSE, and NO-STUDENT.

E   Add relationships that exist between data but have not surfaced in the logical model so far.

The refined logical model in Figure 6.12 satisfies the functional data requirements, and it possesses "intuitively" better performance characteristics than the original conceptual model of Figure 6.1. At this point, the logical design with mapping to a hierarchical data model could be considered complete.

However, the designers may want to strengthen the logical design by adding some inherent (also called intrinsic) data relationships. These are data relationships that exist intrinsically because of the organizational or physical characteristics of the enterprise being modeled or because of the working relationships within the enterprise, but that were not explicitly requested in the data requirements. The reason for adding intrinsic relationships is to obtain a data base that is more likely to support ad hoc queries as well as additional future functions.

It is not necessary to add any relationships to the logical model in Figure 6.12.

The logical model for IMS may look as in Figure 6.12, and an external model that enables an application programmer to gen-

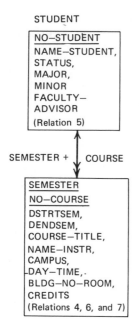

STUDENT

NO–STUDENT
NAME–STUDENT, STATUS, MAJOR, MINOR FACULTY– ADVISOR (Relation 5)

SEMESTER + COURSE

SEMESTER
NO–COURSE
DSTRTSEM, DENDSEM, COURSE–TITLE, NAME–INSTR, CAMPUS, DAY–TIME, BLDG–NO–ROOM, CREDITS (Relations 4, 6, and 7)

Figure 6.14 **An external model that enables an application programmer to generate the report Student Schedule List/Semester is based on the logical model from Figure 6.12 for IMS.**

erate the report in Student Schedule List/Semester may look like the one in Figure 6.14.

6.3 MAPPING TO A NETWORK DATA MODEL

Mapping the conceptual model to a network data model is also not a straightforward process. Many arbitrary choices have to be made, and there is no one "right" result. The following major steps, similar to those used in mapping to a hierarchical data model, may be taken:

A. Derive a network data model without regard for a particular data base management system (DBMS).

B. Modify the data model to eliminate conflicts with the rules of the DBMS to be used.

C. Refine the modified data model according to some "obvious" performance considerations.

D. Simplify key names.

E. Add relationships that exist between data but have not surfaced in the logical model so far.

A Derive a network data model without regard for a particular DBMS.

A.1 Derive owner-member relationships.

In the conceptual model, the boxes represent record types and the arrows ◀──▶ represent mappings between the record types. We would like to use the "Bachman arrow" while discussing the network data model. If we redraw the conceptual model from Figure 6.1 with Bachman arrows, it will look like Figure 6.15. We also have named the set types as follows:

Set Type I STUDENT-HAS-CREDITS with owner STUDENT and member SEMESTER + COURSE + STUDENT.

Set Type II STUDENT-COURSE-CREDITS with owner SEMESTER + COURSE and member SEMESTER + COURSE + STUDENT.

Between set types I and II, the member record type SEMESTER + COURSE + STUDENT is the link.

Set Type III SEMESTER-WITH-COURSES with owner SEMESTER and member SEMESTER + COURSE.

Set Type IV COURSE-TAUGHT-IN-SEMESTER with owner COURSE and member SEMESTER + COURSE.

Between set types III and IV, the member record type SEMESTER + COURSE is the link.

The record type SEMESTER + COURSE is the member record type in set types III and IV and is simultaneously the owner record type in set type II.

Translating the conceptual model from Figure 6.1 into a logical model that is based on a network data model seems to be a relatively easy step so far. The network data model from Figure 6.15 is not based on any DBMS.

A.2 Resolve any violations of unique ownership.

From Chapter 4, Section 4.5, we know that a member cannot have more than one owner in the same set. This is a unique ownership criterion. Figure 6.15 does not have to be modified because unique ownership will not be violated.

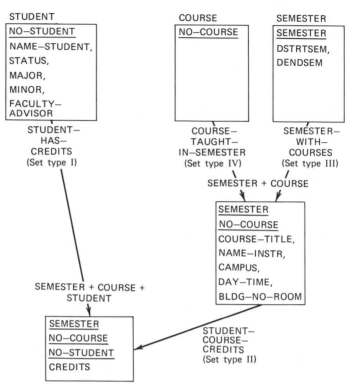

Figure 6.15 Conceptual model from Figure 6.1, redrawn using Bachman arrows. This figure could be used as a starting point for drawing a logical model. The following assumptions are made:

1. COURSE-TITLE is accompanied by SEMESTER and NO-COURSE. It is possible that for the same NO-COURSE the COURSE-TITLE may vary from one semester to another.
2. CREDITS is accompanied by SEMESTER, NO-COURSE, and NO-STUDENT. A student has a choice of selecting the number of credits in a semester and for a course.

B   Modify the data model to eliminate conflicts with the rules of the DBMS to be used.

A number of data base management systems are based on the CODASYL–Data Base Task Group specifications. Some examples are Honeywell's IDS/II, Cullinane's IDMS, DEC's DBMS-10 and DBMS-20 for its DECSYSTEM-10 and DECSYSTEM-20, and Univac's DMS 1100, to name a few. All four set constructs from

Figure 6.15 follow the CODASYL-DBTG specifications. Some modifications to the network data model from Figure 6.15 may be necessary if the DMBS selected does not support all the CODASYL-DBTG specifications for a data model.

C Refine the modified model according to some "obvious" performance considerations.

The logical model of Figure 6.15 will provide the functional capabilities required. Now we would like to consider whether the performance capabilities are enhanced by combining record types to reduce the number of set types, whether more security can be provided by splitting the record types and increasing the number of set types, or whether some other type of arrangement will be more beneficial for the data base to be implemented.

With the network data model, unlike the other data models, the DBA should be aware of how record occurrences will be stored, because the record definition must say how this is done. Choices made at this time can have a profound impact on the data base performance. For example, we could specify that the CREDITS record will be stored via the STUDENT-HAS-CREDITS set or the STUDENT-COURSE-CREDITS set. The choice is determined by which way access will be fastest. (No matter which one is chosen, occurrences still can be accessed through either set.) See Chapter 8 for more information.

Considerations of this type can be more effectively resolved with the help of quantitative performance information, such as frequency of use of the various sets, average number of occurrences of each record type, and record length. Thus a thorough treatment of these considerations belongs to physical design rather than logical design. There are, however, some "obvious" performance considerations, as follows.

C.1 Don't overstructure.

STEP 1 Owners or members that are not providing any data in their own right may be removed. The best candidates for this consideration are the "created" record types. In Figure 6.15, the owner record type from set type IV is not providing any data in its own right. The data provided by the COURSE record type is NO-COURSE. The same data can be found in the member SEMESTER + COURSE. The resulting diagram after removal of the owner course from set type IV is shown in Figure 6.16. The three set types left are:

Set Type I STUDENT-HAS-CREDITS with owner STUDENT and member SEMESTER + COURSE + STUDENT.

Set Type II STUDENT-COURSE-CREDITS with owner SEMESTER + COURSE and member SEMESTER + COURSE + STUDENT.

Between set types I and II, the member record type SEMESTER + COURSE + STUDENT is the link.

Set Type III SEMESTER-WITH-COURSES with owner SEMESTER and member SEMESTER + COURSE.

STEP 2 Owners providing only trivial data and participating in only a "small" number of set types as owners are candidates for combination with their members if their contents are not volatile, that is, are not subject to much

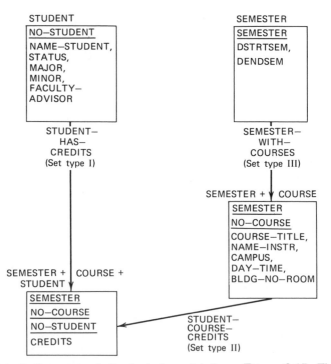

Figure 6.16 Refinement of the logical model from Figure 6.15. The owner COURSE from Figure 6.15 is removed. Only three set types are left.

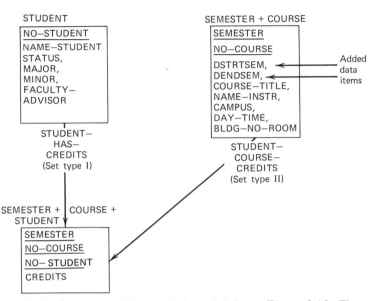

Figure 6.17 Refinement of the logical model from Figure 6.16. The record types SEMESTER and SEMESTER + COURSE are combined into one record type, SEMESTER + COURSE.

The reader should notice one fact. The relationship between SEMESTER and COURSE is many-to-many. We combined the two record types SEMESTER and COURSE into one record type. If the question "Which courses are taught in a given semester?" is asked quite frequently, the designer must give thought to combining the two record types into one record type.

change. The owner record type SEMESTER from set type III in Figure 6.16 provides only DSTRTSEM (date of start of semester) and DENDSEM (date of end of semester) and participates in only one set type, III. SEMESTER from Figure 6.16 seems to be a good candidate for combination with the member record type SEMESTER + COURSE. The resulting diagram is shown in Figure 6.17. (In reality, semester dates would not be part of a data base because they are not used very frequently. The dates may be stored in a separate table.) The owner record type STUDENT does not seem to be a good candidate for combination with the member SEMESTER + COURSE + STUDENT in set type I. The STUDENT record type provides data in its own right about STUDENT.

The combined record type SEMESTER and SEMESTER + COURSE from Figure 6.17 is also not a good candidate for combination with the member SEMESTER + COURSE + STUDENT in set type II.

Figure 6.17 has two set types.

Set Type I STUDENT-HAS-CREDITS with owner STUDENT and member SEMESTER + COURSE + STUDENT.

Set Type II STUDENT-COURSE-CREDITS with owner SEMESTER + COURSE   and   member   SEMESTER + COURSE + STUDENT.

Between set types I and II the member record type SEMESTER + COURSE + STUDENT is the link.

D   Simplify key names.

Record types in a set construct may have key names as follows:

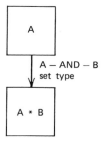

For each member, these names may be simplified by removing the subsets that occur in the owner record. We get:

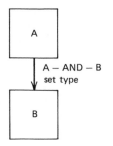

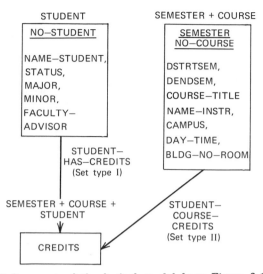

Figure 6.18 Refinement of the logical model from Figure 6.17. The elements SEMESTER, NO-COURSE, and NO-STUDENT have been removed from the record type SEMESTER + COURSE + STUDENT.

After simplifying the key names from Figure 6.17, the logical model is reflected in Figure 6.18.

The resulting logical model has two set types:

Set Type I STUDENT-HAS-CREDITS with owner STUDENT and member SEMESTER + COURSE + STUDENT.

Set Type II STUDENT-COURSE-CREDITS with owner SeMESTER + COURSE and member SEMESTER + COURSE + STUDENT.

Between set types I and II the member record type SEMESTER + COURSE + STUDENT is the link with the data item CREDITS.

E   Add relationships that exist between data but have not surfaced in the logical model so far.

It is not necessary to add any relationships to the logical model in Figure 6.17.

An external model that enables an application programmer to generate the report in Student Schedule List/Semester is identical to the logical model in Figure 6.17.

DATA BASE DESIGN (LOGICAL MODEL)

REFERENCES

1. *An Introduction to Data Base Design*, John K. Lyon, The Wiley Communi-graph Series in Business Data Processing, John Wiley & Sons, 1971.
2. "Data Structure Diagrams," C. W. Bachman, *Data Base*, Journal of ACM Special Interest Group British Data Processing, Vol. 1, No. 2 (Summer 1969).
3. *IMS/VS System/Application Design Guide*, IBM Corporation, 1133 West-chester Avenue, White Plains, New York.
4. *The Codasyl Approach to Data Base Management*, T. William Olle, A Wiley-Interscience Publication, John Wiley & Sons, 1978.

Data Base Performance

CHAPTER 7

Data Storage
and Access Methods

One of the major factors affecting the performance of programs interacting with the data base is the manner in which data is stored and accessed. A generalized data base management system uses some internal model access methods, in addition to the specialized access methods made available through the external model. The internal model is the physical model, and the external model is a userview. Some internal model access methods are identical to the access methods provided by the operating system. In most DBMS packages, the data base designer has the flexibility of choosing one or a combination of several access methods provided. To design a data base for efficient storage and access performance, the designer should be familiar with the internal model (physical model), as well as the external model (userview), access methods.

7.1 INTERFACES BETWEEN USER AND DATA BASE(S)

One can almost say that, as the number of physical inputs/outputs necessary for retrieving data to satisfy a user request increases, performance decreases.

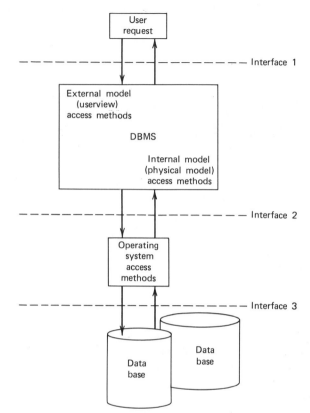

Figure 7.1 Fulfillment of a user request through the data base management system, external model access methods, internal model access methods, and operating system access methods.

To complete the loop beginning with the user request and ending with the satisfaction of that request, the system has to pass through a number of interfaces. (See Figure 7.1.)

Interface 1. After a user request is passed on to the data base management system, the DBMS "knows" the description of the userview, of the application program, and of the security and privacy conditions. On the basis of the userview, it knows which physical data base(s) may be accessed. From the description of the physical data base(s), it also knows which internal model access method(s) may be used. This may differ from implementation to implementation, but most implementations support more than one userview of the data base.

Interface 2. The data base management system in turn uses an internal model access method. This method (or methods) differs from one implementation to another. Some of these internal model access methods are specialized methods provided by the DBMS, and some are composed of the generalized access methods provided by the operating system. Two examples are ISAM (indexed sequential access method) and BDAM (basic direct access method).

Interface 3. The internal model access methods, together with the operating system access methods, access the physical data base record(s). Once access to the physical data base record(s) is gained, the requested data base record(s) may be found by using the access method(s) that describe the logical relationship between different parts of the data base record.

By using the operating system access methods and the internal and external model access methods, data from the physical data base(s) may be retrieved and presented to the DBMS. Then it is up to the DBMS to decide which part of the data may be presented to the user, in which format it will be presented, and so on. Descriptions of all these features must be provided to the DBMS by the data base administrator prior to data base implementation.

Since the performance of a data base depends to a large extent on the internal as well as the external model access methods, we discuss them in this chapter. This discussion is intended to provide the reader with a conceptual knowledge of these access methods. The designer will need to study the implementation details of the different access methods of the specific data base management system purchased or leased.

7.2 INTERNAL MODEL (PHYSICAL MODEL) ACCESS METHODS

The internal model access methods discussed here are: physical sequential, indexed sequential, indexed random, inverted, direct, and hashing. (See Figures 7.2, 7.3, and 7.4.) For every internal model access method, we will consider two measures:

1. *Access Efficiency.* This measure is the inverse of the average number of physical accesses required per logical access. A logical access is a request for a specific data base record. Physical accesses take place to satisfy the request. For example, if the

Physical Sequential	Indexed Sequential·
• Key values of the physical records are in logical sequence.	• Key values of the physical records are in logical sequence.
• Main use is for "dump" and "restore."	• Access method may be used for storage as well as retrieval.
• Access method may be used for storage as well as retrieval.	• Index of key values is maintained with entries for the highest key values per block(s).
• Storage efficiency is near 100%.	• No duplicate key values are permitted.
	• Access efficiency depends on levels of index, storage allocated for index, number of data base records, and amount of overflow.
	• Storage efficiency depends on size of index and volatility of data base.

Figure 7.2 Two of the internal model access methods: Physical Sequential and Indexed Sequential

- The access efficiency of the physical sequential leaves much to be desired. Every data base record has to be verified until the desired one can be retrieved.
- The access method in which only the key values are verified before the data base records are accessed is called the "indexed sequential access method."

system needs to access two records to find the one desired, the access efficiency is 0.5.

2. *Storage Efficiency.* This measure is the inverse of the average number of bytes of secondary storage space required to store each byte of raw data. Space is required for the raw data, as well as for tables, control information, free space left for expansion, and space that is unusable because of fragmentation. A data base designer usually finds a trade-off between the access and storage efficiencies. As we move into the on-line environment, access efficiency becomes the primary issue. Some data base management systems are optimized for on-line updating. As we will see in Chapter 9, access efficiency is indirectly dependent also on storage efficiency.

Figures 7.2, 7.3, and 7.4 provide an overview of the internal model access methods.

Indexed Random	Inverted
• Key values of the physical records are not necessarily in logical sequence.	• Key values of the physical records are not necessarily in logical sequence.
• Index may be stored and accessed with indexed sequential access method.	• Access method may be used for retrieval only.
• Index has an entry for every data base record. These entries are in ascending order. The index keys are usually in logical sequence. If they are not in logical sequence, the index is accessed via a hashing algorithm. Data base records are not necessarily in ascending sequence.	• An index for every field to be inverted may be built.
• Access efficiency depends on number of data base records, levels of index, and storage allocated for any index.
• Access method may be used for storage as well as retrieval.	

Figure 7.3 Two of the internal model access methods: Indexed Random and Inverted.

- With the indexed random access method the records are stored at random. A separate file is created with entries of the actual key values, together with the physical addresses of the records stored.
- The inverted access method is used, in general, for retrieval only. Some other access method is used for storage.

7.2.1 Physical Sequential

With the physical sequential access method, the physical records are stored in logical sequence. If the storage medium to be used is a tape, the programmer has to present the physical records in logical sequence. If the storage medium is a direct access one, the system will interconnect the physical records so that they are in logical sequence, even if they were not presented in logical sequence.

Access Efficiency   Let us assume that one physical record has been retrieved and another physical record with a higher key value is to be retrieved. In the worst case, the whole data base has to be accessed to retrieve the desired data base record, whereas in the best case only the next physical data base record must be retrieved to satisfy the requirement. On average, the number of data base records to be accessed for retrieval of the desired record is half the size of the data base.

Direct	Hashing
• Key values of the physical records are not necessarily in logical sequence.	• Key values of the physical records are not necessarily in logical sequence.
• There is one-to-one correspondence between a record key and the physical address of a record.	• Many key values may share the same physical address (block).
• Access method may be used for storage as well as retrieval.	• Access method may be used for storage as well as retrieval.
• Access efficiency is always 1.	• Access efficiency depends on distribution of keys, algorithm used for key transformation, and space allocated.
• Storage efficiency depends on density of keys.	
• No duplicate keys are permitted.	• Storage efficiency depends on distribution of keys and algorithm used for key transformation.

Figure 7.4 Two of the internal model access methods: Direct and Hashing.

- With the direct access method the storage and retrieval of the physical record can be done at a unique storage location. For one record key there is a unique storage location.
- There is a similarity between the direct access method and the hashing access method. With the hashing access method the address of the physical record is derived from the record key with the help of an algorithm.

Storage Efficiency If a tape is used as a storage medium, the programmer has to present the data base records in logical sequence. As a result there is no waste of storage on a tape. On the other hand, if a direct access device is to be used, the system assigns the next available physical storage to the next physical record presented. The data base records are then interconnected so that they can be retrieved in logical sequence.

The access efficiency of the physical sequential method leaves much to be desired. Every data base record has to be verified until the desired one can be retrieved. The fact that the physical records are stored in logical sequence can be used for faster access. It would be beneficial if only the key values could be verified before the data base records were accessed. The access method based on this concept is called "indexed sequential," and the repository of the key values is called an "index".

7.2.2 Indexed Sequential

There are a variety of indexed access methods. The basic principle for any such method is that a separate file or structure is created with entries of the actual key values. The entry of the actual key is called an "index entry," and the entire actual key file, as mentioned above, is termed an "index." The index file is much smaller than the data base itself and therefore can be searched much more rapidly because a number of entries may fit in memory.

In the indexed sequential access method, the index file is always sequential based on a key called the "primary key." The primary key is the major attribute of the physical record. On the basis of the value of the primary key, the physical records can be identified. As far as possible, records are stored in the same logical sequence as the index (hence the name "indexed sequential" access method). The index therefore needs a reference, not for every record in the data base, but only for the range of the records stored in one physical block. For example, if ten records are stored in a block, only one entry in the index file is necessary, not ten entries. In this case, the size of the index file will be reduced by a factor of 10.

Because the index file is sequentially ordered, it is possible to build an index on top of the index files. The index records can be grouped into blocks. In turn, these blocks can be indexed. For large files, this arrangement can be used effectively for better access performance.

Since the actual keys do not necessarily behave uniformly, it is not advisable to preassign the key values to the blocks in the data file. Instead, the data file is created by initially loading it with the physical records in the order of the primary key. The key value of the last record in the block, which is either the highest or the lowest (most vendor-supplied indexed sequential access methods load the data file in ascending sequence of the primary key value) is entered in the index file. (See Figure 7.5).

In practice, how does the access method cope with the insertions of new records? Depending on the values of the added records, the index entries may have to be changed. What happens when a block does not have any more room for a new record?

There are two ways of handling this problem:

1. The record is stored in a separate area called an "overflow area," and the block is chained in the overflow area with the initial block where the record logically belongs. The access of the

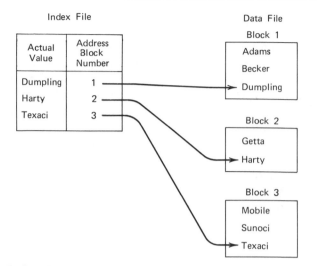

Figure 7.5 Indexed sequential access method. Index file and data file are in sequential order. Index file has only the highest value of the primary key in each block.

records in the overflow area may reduce the access efficiency considerably.

2. When a block cannot accommodate any insertion, the block is divided in half. One new block contains half of the records of the initial block, and the other block contains the remaining half. (Sometimes the block is divided into two blocks such that one block contains two thirds, and the other block the remaining one third, of the records of the initial block.) A new entry is then made in the index file. In most cases, the access efficiency is better with this method as compared to chaining the records in the overflow area. But if the same blocks have to be split repeatedly, the file should be unloaded and reorganized and a new index file created. An example of this approach is IBM's VSAM (virtual storage access method).

In the case of a very large file, it may be advisable to build a number of index files. Another level of index file can be built pointing to these index files. The building of this type of indexing may be done so that the final index file is of reasonable size and can be kept in processor storage. Figure 7.6 shows the building of higher level index files.

The following major points must be considered in trying to achieve the best performance with ISAM files.

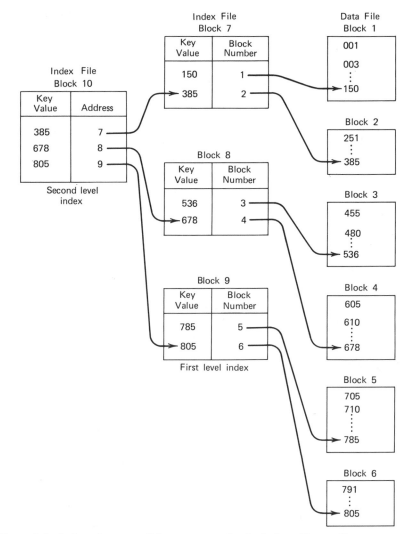

Figure 7.6 Indexed sequential access method. Index files with two levels. Because the index file is sequentially ordered, it is possible to build an index on top of the index files. The index records can be grouped into blocks. In turn these blocks can be indexed. This arrangement can be used effectively for large files for better access performance.

Access Efficiency

1. **Size of the Data Base.** As the size of the data base increases, more entries are made in the index. This probably results in a higher level of indexing. However, a large index file or a higher

level of indexing decreases access efficiency. In a large data base, the selection of primary and secondary keys is crucial.

2. **Record Size.** There is a trade-off between the size of the average record and the number of records in a data base. The bigger the size of the record, the smaller is the number of records in the data base, resulting in a smaller number of entries in the index. But the time required for transferring the big data base records across the channels must be considered too. Determination of the optimum data base record size should be considered.

3. **Activity in the Data Base.** A higher level of insertion and deletion activity on the data base degrades access efficiency, that is, reorganization of the data base, together with the index files, should be planned from time to time. In some systems, this kind of activity does not significantly degrade access efficiency. However, the methods that make it possible to maintain access efficiency increase the size of the data base, that is, they decrease storage efficiency.

4. **Highest Level Index in the Processor Storage.** The allocation of enough processor storage for the highest level index increases access efficiency.

Storage Efficiency

1. **Size of the Data Base.** As new records are added to the data base subsequent to the initial loading, the free space provided at the time of initial loading will be used. Storage efficiency depends on the percentage of free space provided. Since the records must preserve logical sequence, storage efficiency also depends on which part of the data base has the highest activity of addition and deletion of data base records. An analysis providing the value of free physical blocks and parts of blocks has to be carried out.

2. **Record Size.** The two factors affecting storage efficiency are record size and number of records. Larger records use less space for index entries. The number of records decreases as the size of the records increases. More levels of indexes are required as the number of records increases.

A final point that should be mentioned about the indexed sequential access method is that most vendors commonly restrict index keys to unique values.

For some applications, it is not necessary to process the data base records in logical sequence. In fact, it may be necessary to process the records in a random way. Nevertheless, the access method, called "indexed random," still relies on an index.

7.2.3 Indexed Random

For this access method, the records are stored at random, and a separate file is created with entries of the actual key values, together with the physical addresses of the records stored. The entry of the actual key, together with the address, is called an "index entry" and the entire file is termed an "index." In this access method there is an entry in the index for every data base record.

There are two major ways in which the index of the indexed random access method is created and accessed. In one way, the index is kept in collating sequence [e.g., IBM's Information Management System provides this facility, and it is called "secondary indexing" (see Figure 7.7)]. Access to the index is sequential. The sequential index makes it possible to process the records sequentially.

In the other way, the index itself is not kept in sequential order

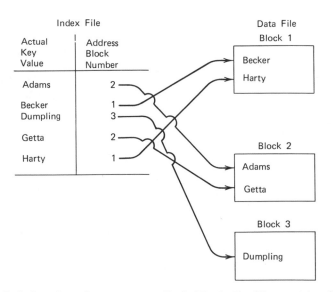

Figure 7.7 Indexed random access method. The index file consists of an entry for every record, and the index entries are in ascending sequence. The target file is not necessarily in ascending sequence. Access to the index is sequential.

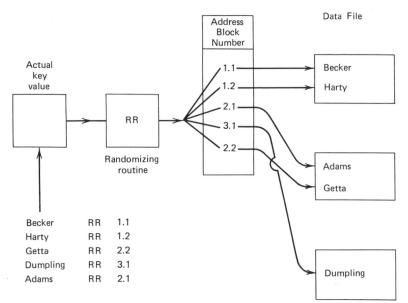

Figure 7.8 Indexed random access method. The actual key values go through the randomizing routine (RR), and the addresses for the records in the data file are calculated. There is a one-to-one correspondence between the address created and the physical record. Access to the index is through a randomizer.

but a random access to the index is provided [e.g., Burrough's DMS-II provides random access to the index entries (see Figure 7.8)].

One aspect common to both ways of creating and accessing the index is that the records are not stored sequentially by the index key. That is the reason for calling this the "indexed random" access method.

The indexed random access method enables one to keep an index file on any field of the record, not necessarily on the primary key field. If duplicate key values exist, maintenance of the index file can be cumbersome.

Two major drawbacks of the indexed random access method are:

1. If the index is not kept in a sequential order, it is not possible to process the records sequentially with the help of the index only.

2. Because one entry exists for every record in the index file, the index file may become quite large.

To overcome these two major problems of the indexed random access method, the indexed sequential access method (ISAM) is widely used.

Access Efficiency.

1. **Random Processing.** Because the index contains one entry for each record, the access efficiency is 1. This is true for only the primary key.
2. **Sequential Processing.** Because data base records are stored at random, and not necessarily in the logical sequence, the efficiency of sequential processing cannot be predicted. To mitigate the problem, the index may be kept in logical sequence.

Storage Efficiency.

Size of the data base. The index will be quite large as a result of having one entry for every data base record. This may result in high levels of indexing.

If more than one attribute or a field of a record should be considered for retrieval by different applications, it may be necessary to build indices for the various attributes. The method based on this concept is called an "inverted" access method.

7.2.4 Inverted

The inverted access method is used, in general, for retrieval only, although some implementations do provide inverted updating capability too. In general, some other access method is used for storage. For example, a data base is loaded using any of the external model access methods discussed in this chapter. For each "inverted" field an entry is made in a table. The entry consists of the field name, the field value, and the record address. After the initial loading of the data base, sorting is performed on the field name and within the field name on the field value. For every field name, a separate index can be built. All the records with the same value for a field are grouped together, with the common value pointing to all the records with that value. As new records are added, entries are made to the appropriate index and to the appropriate value. And as records are deleted, the index entries from the appropriate index and for the appropriate values are removed. Figure 7.9 shows an example of the use of the inverted access method for the retrieval of records.

Access Efficiency. Before accessing the records from the data base, the index file(s) has to be accessed. As a result, the access efficiency of the inverted access method depends on the access method used for

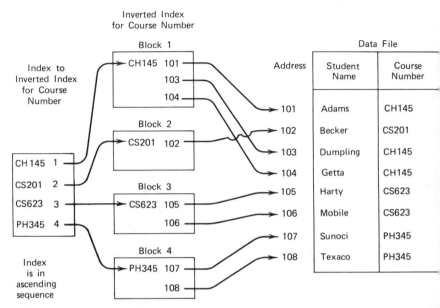

Figure 7.9 **Inverted** access method. Data file is inverted on the field "course number." **For each** "inverted" field an entry is made in a table, also called an "index." **The entry** consists of the field name, the field value, and the record address. **For every** field a separate index can be built. This means that the data file is **inverted on that field.**

the index. In any event, at least one access is required to the index and at least one access to the data base record itself. The access efficiency is thus less than 0.5, at least two physical accesses being required for accessing one record. An analysis should be carried out to determine the access method for the index file(s). The access efficiency improves tremendously if the inverted index is kept in the storage during the data base processing.

Storage Efficiency. The storage efficiency depends on the access method used for storing the data. If the only retrieval method to be used is the inverted one, the direct method, discussed in Section 7.2.5, using system-assigned keys can result in very efficient storage. The storage required for the index file will depend on the storage method used and the number of fields to be inverted.

7.2.5 Direct

The main characteristic of the direct access method is direct correspondence between the record key and the physical address of the record. The storage and retrieval of the physical record can be done at a unique storage location. The physical location of the record is derived from the key itself.

Access Efficiency. The access efficiency is always 1 if the method is used in a direct way because of the one-to-one correspondence between the key value and the physical address of the record. If the physical records are not retrieved using this correspondence, the retrieval access efficiency will depend on the method of retrieval.

Storage Efficiency. The storage efficiency depends on the density of the keys. If the keys are not dense, storage is wasted, because storage locations will be reserved for the missing keys. (See Figure 7.10.)

In the example of Figure 7.10, the algorithm used is: Strip off the "X1" of all the source keys beginning with "X1," and take the last two digits of the source key as the target key and the storage location. For the source keys that start with "Y," strip off the "Y" and use the last three digits as in the target key and the storage location. Note that the physical record with the key "Y102" is

Student Numbers (source keys)	Keys Transformed (target keys)	Storage Locations (relative block numbers)	
X101	01	01	X101
X102	02	02	X102
X103	03	03	X103
•	•	•	•
•	•	•	•
•	•	•	•
X199	99	99	X199
Y100	100	100	Y100
Y101	101	101	Y101
(Missing)	(Missing)	Empty	
Y103	103	103	Y103

Figure 7.10 Direct access method. Keys transformed (target keys) are based on the student numbers (source keys) giving the unique storage locations. The main characteristic of the direct access method is direct correspondence between the record key and the physical address of the record.

missing and that a storage location for that record will be reserved. Another drawback of this access method is that the keys have to be unique.

It is conceivable that, for some data bases, a one-to-one correspondence between the record key and the physical address of the record is not necessary. It may suffice to have a group of records point to the same physical address. This type of access method called "hashing," is described in Section 7.2.6.

7.2.6 Hashing

There is a similarity between the direct access method and the hashing access method in that the address of the physical record is derived from the record key with the help of an algorithm. The main difference between the two is the one-to-one mapping between the key and the address in the direct access method, and the potential many-to-one mapping between the keys and the address in the hashing access method (i.e., more than one key value may share the same address or the block.)

The algorithm performing the key-to-address transformation is often called a "randomizing" or "hashing" routine. With this routine, the same key will always be transformed to the same address. The randomizing routine attempts to map a larger set of source key values to a smaller set of address places (usually relative block numbers). The keys mapped to the same physical address are called "synonyms." Since only one record can be stored in the randomized address, the synonyms have to be stored elsewhere. At the same time, some mechanism has to be provided to retrieve these synonyms. In most cases, the records with the synonym keys randomizing to the same physical address are chained, and the chain is called a "synonym chain." (See Figure 7.11.)

In Figure 7.11, the source key is Getta. The transformed key is 415, which is the address of the first record in the synonym chain. The Getta record points to the Mobile record at the address 423. The Mobile record points, in turn, to the Sunoci record with the address 852. And the Sunoci record points to the Texaci record at 900. This is the last record in the chain pointing to 0.

One major consideration when using a randomizing routine is the order of the transformed keys, that is, the order of the physically stored records does not match the order of the original keys. This may result in major difficulty in processing the physically stored records in sequential order by the original keys.

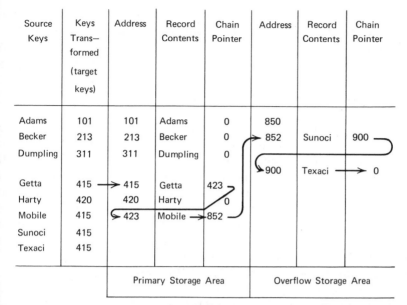

Source Keys	Keys Trans— formed (target keys)	Address	Record Contents	Chain Pointer	Address	Record Contents	Chain Pointer
Adams	101	101	Adams	0	850		
Becker	213	213	Becker	0	852	Sunoci	900
Dumpling	311	311	Dumpling	0	900	Texaci	0
Getta	415	415	Getta	423			
Harty	420	420	Harty	0			
Mobile	415	423	Mobile	852			
Sunoci	415						
Texaci	415						

Primary Storage Area	Overflow Storage Area

Figure 7.11 Hashing access method. The algorithm performing the key-to-address transformation is often called a "randomizing" routine. It is also called a "hashing" routine. Note the synonym chain for the records with the keys Getta, Mobile, Sunoci, and Texaci.

Access Efficiency. The access efficiency of the random access method depends on three factors:

1. **Original Key Distribution.** In many environments, the original key distribution is not totally random. The more the designer knows about the distribution, the better position he/she is in to select the number of blocks and the number of home addresses per block. The optimum selection of these factors will enable the designer to reduce the average length of the synonym chain. The access efficiency of the hashing access method depends greatly on the length of the synonym chain. In most data base management systems, the vendor-supplied hashing routines seem to do an excellent job and there is very little need for user-written routines.

2. **Space Allocated.** The key issue for access efficiency is even distribution of the actual keys over the number of blocks (i.e., the space allocated). If the output of the randomizing routine assigns many keys in one area, the result is a larger number of

synonyms. Increasing the allocated space increases the numbe of addresses to which the randomizing routine can randomize.

3. **Randomizing or Hashing Routine** (also called "algorithm" o "module"). A good randomizing routine should distribute th actual keys evenly over the space allocated, thus reducing th average length of the synonym chain.

Storage Efficiency. The storage efficiency depends on the spac allocated and the randomizing routine. When using the hashing ac cess method, it is advisable not to specify any free space within th blocks, as well as any free blocks. The reason is that the randomizin routine may randomize to the free blocks and to the free spac within a block; this will result in putting the corresponding record into the overflow area. Determination of the page size also seems t be a major performance issue. Once the desired page is in the storage searching the synonym chain is trivial compared to the physica input/outputs necessary if that is not the case.

Other, more complex access methods may be built with the hel of the six internal model access methods described in Section 7.2.

7.3 EXTERNAL MODEL (USERVIEWS) ACCESS METHODS

Access methods that describe the logical relationship may be calle "external model access methods." Based on the data model used b the DBMS (e.g., relational, hierarchical, network, or some combina tion), different userviews may be provided for describing the logica relationship(s) between different parts of a physical record.

After gaining entry to the data base with the internal mode access methods, the external model access methods are used fo further retrieval of the data base records or of the parts of them The external model access methods store or retrieve records on th basis of the relationships between the records. The relationship between the records depend on the data model used as an underlyin data structure by the particular data base management system. It i possible that there are a number of external model access method by which a record may be retrieved. But there is only one externa model access method by which the record is stored.

7.3.1 Relationships between Two Records

To discuss the relationships between two records, let us examine th following case.

Consider two records, X and Y. Record X is stored, and record
´ is to be stored. Or record X is retrieved, and record Y is to be
etrieved. If there is any relationship between the two records, X
nd Y, the possibilities are as follows for hierarchical and network
lata models:

. **Sequence Field Relationship.** Two records are related based on
the key sequence field, that is, Y's key sequence field is next in
sequence to X's key sequence field.

!. **Dependency Relationship.** There is a dependency relationship
between X and Y, that is, Y is a dependent of X.

Hierarchical Data Model. Y may be a child, and X may be a
parent.

Network Data Model. Y may be a member record, and X may
be an owner record.

!. **Parent Relationship.** This is a dependency relationship with
reversed roles of X and Y.

Hierarchical Data Model. The retrieved record X may be a child,
and the record Y to be retrieved may be a parent.

Network Data Model. The retrieved record X may be a member,
and the record Y to be retrieved may be the owner.

!. **"Near" Relationship.** This relationship simply specifies that
record Y should be stored near record X.

Hierarchical Data Model. There may or may not exist any specific relationship based on sequence field, dependency, or parentage between X and Y.

Network Data Model. There may or may not exist any specific
relationship based on sequence field, dependency, or ownership
between X and Y.

⌐.3.2 External Model Access Methods

3ased on the four types of relationships between two records, there
ɹre four types of external model access methods. Two subcategories
•f these access methods are storage and retrieval. We will discuss the
·xternal model access methods for hierarchical and network data
nodels.

.. **Sequence Field Access Method.** Record Y to be stored is the
one whose sequence field is next in sequence to record X.

Hierarchical Data Model. X and Y are of the same node type.

If there is no node occurrence to establish the relationship, sequential next has no meaning.

Network Data Model. X and Y are of the same record type. If there is no record occurrence to establish the relationship, sequential next has no meaning.

The access methods for establishing the relationship based on the sequence field are as follows:

- *Prior*

  Hierarchical Data Model. Either insert (store) or retrieve a node occurrence Y PRIOR to the node occurrence X.

  Network Data Model. Either insert (store) or retrieve a record occurrence Y PRIOR to the record occurrence X.
- *Next*

  Hierarchical Data Model. Either insert (store) or retrieve a node occurrence Y NEXT to the node occurrence X.

  Network Data Model. Either insert (store) or retrieve a record occurrence Y NEXT to the record occurrence X.
2. **Dependency Access Method.** Dependency access methods may be used for storage as well as retrieval of dependent nodes for hierarchical data model and of records for the network data model.

The following options may be specified (see Figure 7.12):

- *First*

  Hierarchical Data Model. Insert the most recent child as the first child Y of the parent X.

  Network Data Model. Insert the most recent member as the first member Y of the owner X.
- *Last*

  Hierarchical Data Model. Insert the most recent child as the last child Y of the parent X.

  Network Data Model. Insert the most recent member as the last member Y of the owner X.
- *Sorted*

  Hierarchical Data Model. The dependent child should be inserted in the sorted sequence of the key. The child with the lowest sequence field is, therefore, logically the first one.

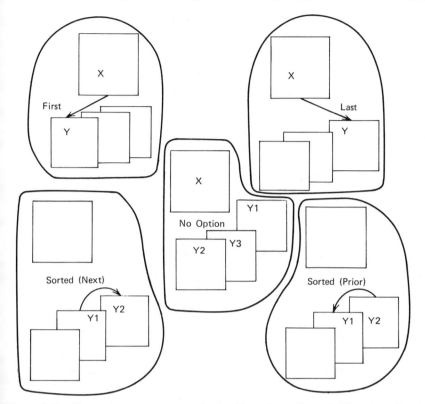

Figure 7.12 Dependency access methods: First, Last, Sorted (Next and Prior), and No Option. Dependency access methods may be used for storage as well as retrieval of dependent nodes for the hierarchical data model and of records for the network data model.

Network Data Model. The dependent member should be inserted in the sorted sequence of the key. The member with the lowest sequence field is, therefore, logically the first one.

- *No Option*

   The data base management system will not maintain any dependency order.

The options for retrieval using the dependency access methods are as follows:

- *First*

   Hierarchical Data Model. Retrieve the first child. See Figure 7.12.

Network Data Model. Retrieve the first member. See Figure 7.13.

- *Last*

Hierarchical Data Model. Retrieve the last child.

Network Data Model. Retrieve the last member.

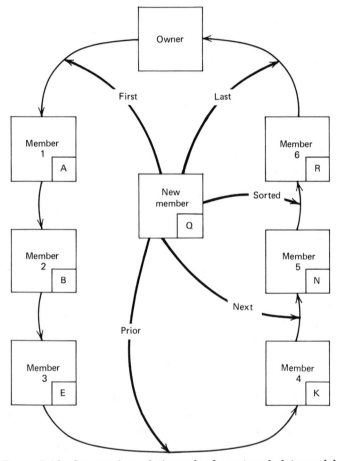

Figure 7.13 Set member relation rules for network data model.

- First.
- Last.
- Prior.
- Next.
- Sorted (for insertion only).

- *Prior*

   Hierarchical Data Model. Retrieve the prior child, with respect to the most recent retrieved.

   Network Data Model. Retrieve the prior member, with respect to the most recent retrieved. (The most recent member retrieved was Member 4 in Figure 7.13.)

- *Next*

   Hierarchical Data Model. Retrieve the next child with respect to the most recent one retrieved.

   Network Data Model. Retrieve the next member with respect to the most recent one retrieved. (The most recent member retrieved was Member 4 in Figure 7.13.)

- *Qualified:*

   Hierarchical Data Model. Retrieve the child based on the qualification specified.

   Network Data Model. Retrieve the member based on the qualification specified.

When the dependency access method is used, the way in which node (or record) Y is inserted or retrieved depends on how the dependents are ordered, how the access is qualified, and which reference node (or record) was inserted or retrieved previously.

3. **Parent or Owner Access Method.** The parent or owner access method is the reverse of the dependency access method.

   Hierarchical Data Model. A child cannot exist without its parent. This implies that the child cannot be stored before the parent. The parent access method thus cannot be used for the storage of the child and of the parent. This access method can be used, however, for retrieval of the parent from the child. (See Figure 7.14.)

   Network Data Model. In some implementations of the network data model, a member may exist without its owner. In such implementations the owner access method may be used for storage as well as for retrieval of the owner from the member. (See Figure 7.14.)

4. **"Near" Access Method.** The "near" access method is a storage-only data model access method.

   Hierarchical Data Model: A child is to be stored physically near its parent in a given hierarchical relationship.

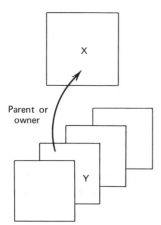

Figure 7.14 **Parent or owner access methods. Retrieval of the parent or owner X from the child or member Y (hierarchical data model).**

Network Data Model. A member is to be stored physically near its owner in a given network relationship.

The external model access methods are often implemented with pointers. There are three types of pointers:

1. **Direct Pointer** (see Figure 7.15). The direct pointer is the actual disk relative block address of record Y "pointed to" and is stored in record X "pointing to" record Y.
2. **Relative Pointer** (see Figure 7.16). The logical pointer is an identifier that can be mapped to an actual disk relative to the block address. For this type of pointer, the first part is the data base page, which can be transformed into a page offset from the

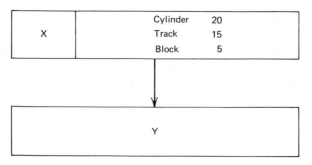

Figure 7.15 **Direct pointer: the actual disk relative to the block address of record Y. For advantages and disadvantages, See Table 7.1.**

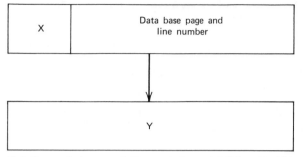

Figure 7.16 Relative pointer: a relative pointer establishes itself in the context of something else. For advantages and disadvantages, see Table 7.2.

beginning of an area. The second part of the pointer gives an offset from the bottom of this page that contains the real position on the page.
3. **Symbolic Pointer** (see Figure 7.17). The key of record Y "pointed to" is stored in record X "pointing to" it. The internal model access method has the responsibility of finding record Y.

The direct, relative, and symbolic pointers each have advantages and disadvantages, as listed in Tables 7.1, 7.2, and 7.3.

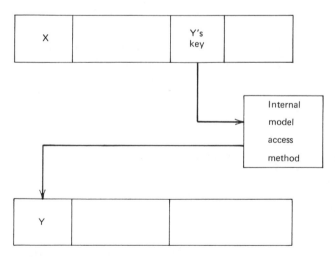

Figure 7.17 Symbolic pointer: The key of record Y. The key makes possible access through one of the internal model access methods. For advantages and disadvantages; see Table 7.3.

Table 7.1   Advantages and Disadvantages of the Direct Pointer

Advantages
Access efficiency is the best. Once the direct address of a record is known, only one access is necessary for its retrieval. In most cases, a direct pointer is shorter than the corresponding symbolic address.

Disadvantages
A direct pointer is device dependent. If a record moves, all the direct pointers pointing to it must be updated.

Table 7.2   Advantages and Disadvantages of the Relative Pointer

Advantages
The advantage that the relative pointer has over the direct pointer is that, when files are moved to different devices (or just copied, for that matter), the only thing that the DBMS has to know is the location of the starting address. No other information has to be changed.
The advantage that the relative pointer has over the symbolic pointer is two-fold: very little processing cost or time is involved in converting the key to a pointer, and the pointer is usually much smaller. The relative key is the concatenation of a data base page and a line number. The DBMS and the monitor then compute which page this is relative to the beginning of the file. After the page is accessed, the DBMS uses the line number as a negative offset on the bottom of the page. This offset contains a second offset, which is the exact location on the page.

Disadvantages
Although a relative pointer is not as device dependent as a direct pointer, it still relies on a preknowledge of the position. With a symbolic key, on the other hand, the records can be moved into a different arrangement, and all that needs to be changed is the algorithm that creates the address. Thus, in a system using symbolic pointers, no updating is necessary.

Table 7.3   Advantages and Disadvantages of the Symbolic Pointer

Advantages
A symbolic pointer is device independent. If a record moves, the symbolic pointers pointing to it do not have to updated.

Disadvantages
Access efficiency may not be the best. The address of the record searched has to be resolved based on the symbolic pointer. A symbolic pointer is usually longer than a direct pointer.

216

REFERENCES

1. *Data Base Management—Access Mechanisms and Data Structure Support in Data Base Management Systems*, Monograph Series, Robert M. Curtice (Staff Member, Arthur D. Little, Inc.), Q.E.D. Information Sciences, Inc., Wellesley, Massachusetts 02181.

Implementations of the Access Methods

A data base management system uses a combination of internal model access methods and external model access methods for storage and retrieval of the records in the data base. A data base designer is faced with a wide variety of options, and the selection of the appropriate ones is crucial because these options affect the performance of the operations on the data base. To be able to appreciate the process of option selection, let us look at some of the implementations of the access methods available for some of today's data base management systems.

8.1 HIERARCHICAL DATA BASE MANAGEMENT SYSTEMS

Some of the oldest data base management systems are based on a hierarchical data model. One of them is IBM's Information Management System, IMS/VS. We shall see how the access methods are implemented in this system.

8.1.1   IMS (Information Management System)

The main component of IMS is Data Language/1 (DL/1). The data model and the access methods are contained in DL/1, which distinguishes between the physical data base(s) (called the "internal model" in Chapter 1), and the logical data bases (called the "external model(s)" in Chapter 1). The logical data bases are the views supplied to the application programmers. These views are always hierarchical. This is the main reason for putting IMS in the category of hierarchical data base management systems, although the logical relationships provide some network data model capabilities to IMS users.

The physical data base consists of a treelike structure. The node types referred to in Chapter 4, Section 4.4 on the hierarchical data model, are called "segment types." The root node type is called the "root segment type." The hierarchy of the segment types is defined as top to bottom and left to right. (See Figure 8.1.) The segment code assigned to the segment types is also in the same order. Every root occurrence starts a new physical record. (See Figures 8.2 and

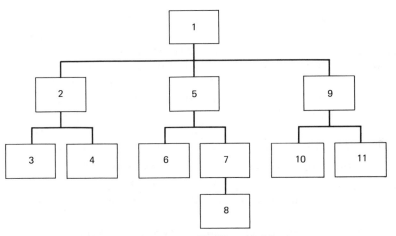

Segment Types Numbered in Hierarchical Sequence

Figure 8.1 **Physical data base structure for IMS. The hierarchy of a physical record starts with the first occurrence of segment type 1. Depending on that occurrence, there is the first occurrence of segment type 2 and all the dependents of types 3 and 4. The hierarchy continues with the next occurrence of segment type 2 and all the dependents of types 3 and 4. When all the occurrences of type 2 are exhausted, the hierarchy continues to the right with segment type 5, and so on.**

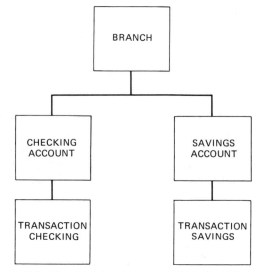

Figure 8.2 **Physical data base record starts with a root.**

8.3.) The child occurrences of the child segment type are called "twin occurrences." The segments in a physical data base are connected with physical relationships; the relationships in a physical hierarchy are physical parent, physical child, and physical twins.

Physical data bases may be split into several files, but a file may not contain segments from different physical data bases. In a physical data base with IMS:

1. The data base contains a single type of root segment.
2. The root may have dependent child segment types.
3. Each child of the root may also have any number of child segment types, up to a maximum of 15 segment types in any one path.
4. There can be up to 255 segment types in one physical data base.
5. For any occurrence of any given segment type, there may be any number of occurrences (possibly zero) of each of its children.
6. No child segment can exist without its parent.

Logical data bases are the views of the application programmers. These views are strictly hierarchical, but they can be constructed with the help of one or a number of physical data bases with the provision of logical relationships. Thus the capability of logical

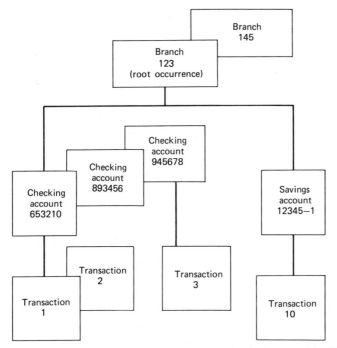

Figure 8.3 Every root occurrence starts a new physical record in IMS. One physical record starts with the occurrence of the root (Branch 123) and further consists of all its dependents (such as checking accounts, transactions on the checking accounts, savings accounts, and the dependent transactions).

relationships in IMS provides some of the network data model properties. The logical relationships are explained later in this section.

Internal Model Access Methods for IMS. For a physical data base, there are four basic access methods, which use two methods for relating the segments:

- *Hierarchical Sequential (HS).* The relationships among the segments of a hierarchy reflect the physical sequence in top-to-bottom, left-to-right order, that is, the segments of a data base record are related by physical adjacency. (See Figure 8.4.)
- *Hierarchical Direct (HD).* The hierarchical relationships among the segments are represented by pointers, called "physical pointers." The pointers are physically stored in the prefixes of the segments. The dependency relationships are parent,

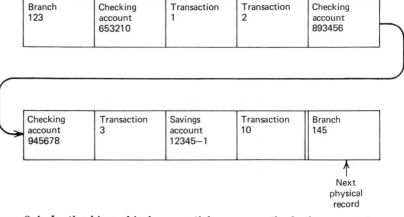

Figure 8.4 In the hierarchical sequential access method, the segments are re-lated by physical adjacency in the top-to-bottom, left-to-right, and front-to-back manners.

child, and twins, and the relationships between parent and child are shown by first child, last child, and physical parent. In IMS terminology, these pointers are physical child first (PCF), physical child last (PCL), and physical parent (PP). The dependency relationship "next" among twins is repre-sented by physical twin forwards (PTF), and the relationship "prior" by physical twin backwards (PTB). (See Figure 8.5.) For a direct organization in IMS, the mandatory physical pointers are PCF and PTF, and the optional direct pointers are PCL, PTB, and PP.

Four internal model access methods which use the two methods, hierarchical sequential and hierarchical direct, for relating the seg-ments, are:

HSAM: Hierarchical sequential access method.
HISAM: Hierarchical indexed sequential access method.
HIDAM: Hierarchical indexed direct access method.
HDAM: Hierarchical direct access method.

HSAM and HISAM use the hierarchical sequential method, and HIDAM and HDAM the hierarchical direct method, for relating the segments.

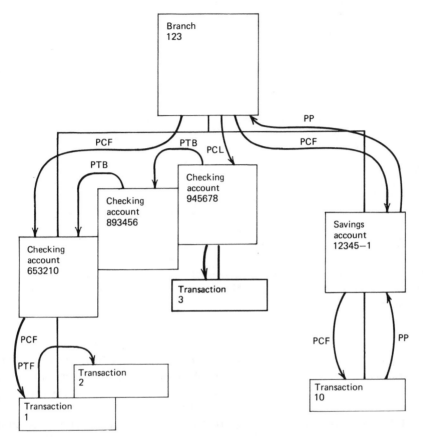

Figure 8.5 Direct pointers are used for relating the segments from the hierarchy in the hierarchical direct access method in IMS.

HSAM can be best described by saying that it is tapelike. The only basic access method used here is physical sequential.

HISAM uses a combination of the basic access methods "indexed sequential" and "physical sequential." There is indexed access to the root and sequential access to the dependents. The index data set is stored and accessed by the indexed sequential access method (ISAM) or the virtual storage access method (VSAM). The index data set consists of root occurrences and as many dependent segments as will fit in a fixed length space in the primary data set (see Figure 8.6), that is, the index is nondense. Other segments are stored in the secondary data set. The segments do not get split, and there are no pointers between them. As a result, when new segments are to be

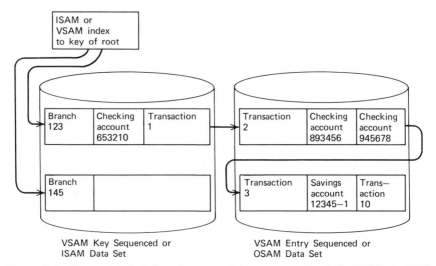

VSAM Key Sequenced or   VSAM Entry Sequenced or
ISAM Data Set   OSAM Data Set

Figure 8.6 Hierarchical indexed sequential access method (HISAM) in IMS. HISAM provides indexed access to the root and sequential access to the dependents.

inserted, the existing stored segments may have to move. At the time of loading, all the root occurrences are inserted in the primary data set. Subsequent additions of new root occurrences are inserted in the secondary data set, which is stored and accessed by the overflow sequential access method (OSAM) or by VSAM.

HIDAM uses indexed access to the root and direct access to the dependents, that is, once the basic access method "indexed" is used to gain access to the root, the data model access methods "first," "last," "next," and "prior" are used for accessing the dependents. The index data set consists of only the root occurrences, that is, the index is dense. The storage and access to the roots are provided by ISAM or VSAM. The dependents of the root are stored in a secondary data set and accessed by OSAM or VSAM. (See Figure 8.7.) Among the root and the dependents, the pointers used are PCF and PTF, these two pointers being mandatory, and PCL, PTB, and PP, these three pointers being optional.

HDAM also uses the hierarchical direct access method for relating the segments of the hierarchy. The major difference between HDAM and HIDAM is that in the former the address where a root is stored is calculated using an algorithm called a "hashing algorithm" or a randomizing routine. The root and a specified number of bytes of the dependents are stored in the "root addressable area (RAA),"

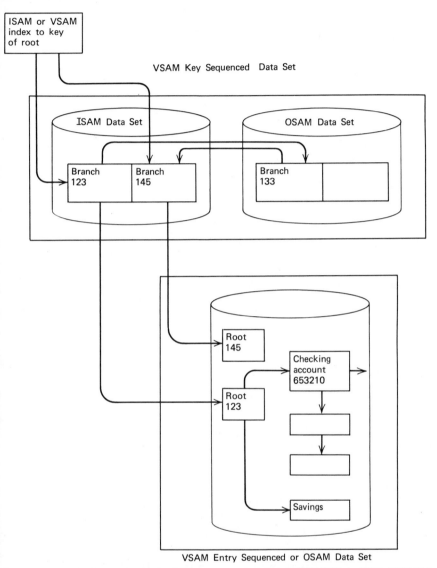

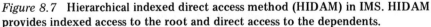

Figure 8.7 Hierarchical indexed direct access method (HIDAM) in IMS. HIDAM provides indexed access to the root and direct access to the dependents.

and the remaining bytes of the dependent segments are stored in the "non-root-addressable area," which is an overflow area. (See Figure 8.8.) The basic access method used for storing and accessing the roots is "random."

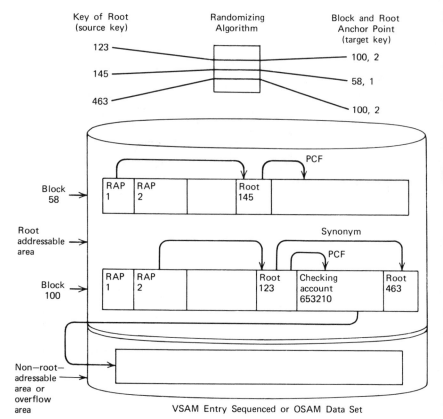

Figure 8.8 Hierarchical direct access method (HDAM) in IMS. HDAM provides random access to the root and direct access to the dependents.

Every block in the RAA has a specified number of root anchor points. The HDAM randomizing algorithm takes the source key and produces the block number and the root anchor point from the block as the target key. If two roots "hash" to the same address, a synonym chain is built.

In HISAM the segments move, but in HIDAM and HDAM they do not. In HISAM, the space used by the deleted segments is not freed until the next reorganization, whereas the deletion of segments in HIDAM and HDAM frees the space. The HDAM organization also provides faster access to the dependent segments in the hierarchy. One drawback of HDAM is that the sequential processing of the root segments is awkward, as compared to HISAM and HIDAM.

HSAM, HISAM, HIDAM, and HDAM use a combination of the

basic access methods and the data model access methods for storing and accessing the data base records using the hierarchical data model. The accessing of a data base record using HSAM, HISAM, HIDAM, or HDAM starts at the root level. To provide an entry at a lower level than the root, or to provide access on a secondary key to the root, IMS provides a capability called "secondary indexing." Secondary indexing is IMS's version of the inverted file structure.

In Figure 8.9, the root is CUSTOMER and the dependent seg-

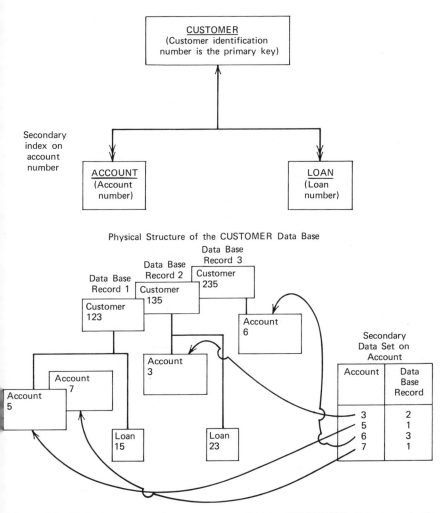

Figure 8.9 **Data base record occurrences of the CUSTOMER data base with inversion on account number.**

Figure 8.10 Logical view based on inversion of account number as provided to application programmer.

ments are ACCOUNT and LOAN. If the data base is "inverted" on account number, a secondary indexing capability can be provided on account number. A secondary data set is maintained by IMS. The logical view provided to the application programmer is shown in Figure 8.10.

IMS also provides some network capability using its "logical relationships."

Logical Relationships with IMS. The external models as explained in Chapter 1 are called "logical views" in IMS. The logical views are provided to application programmers for the coding of programs. In "plain" physical data bases, the segments are related to one another within a hierarchy. A facility provided by IMS called "logical relationships" enables one to span the relationships between segments across two or more physical data bases or between segments in different branches of the physical hierarchy. (See Figures 8.11, 8.12, and 8.13.) A logical view may be a subset of a physical data base or a view from a number of possible views provided by a physical data base(s) using logical relationships. A logical view may provide the user with an alternative view of data.

Two segments involved are said to have a logical relationship. The subordinate segment is called logical child; the other segment, logical parent. There are three possible ways of implementing logical relationships.

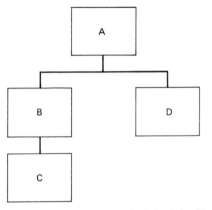

A physical data base without logical relationship

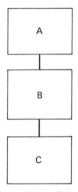

A logical view as a subset of the hierarchy above.

Figure 8.11

Unidirectional logical relationship. A logical parent pointer is used to point from logical child to logical parent. In Figure 8.14 (which is identical to Figure 4.14 in Chapter 4), there are two hierarchical structures with segment B a logical child of segment C, and D a logical child of segment A. Two logical relationships are involved. Pointers used are Physical Child First (PCF), Physical Twin Forwards (PTF), Physical Parent (PP), and Logical Parent (LP). Two of the possible logical views are shown in Figure 8.15. A logical view is the application programmer's view of the data base. There is total redundancy of data in segments B and D in the data bases of Figure 8.14. To have data integrity, the application programmer is respon-

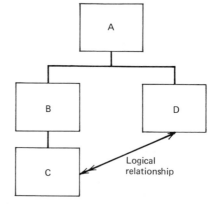

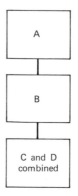

A physical data base with logical relationship between
segments in different branches of the physical hierarchy.

A logical view using the physical data base above with
the logical relationship.

Figure 8.12

sible for updating any part of D if the identical part of B is to be updated and vice versa. IMS can remove this responsibility from the
application programmer by providing a second type of logical
relationship, called the "physically paired bidirectional logical
relationship."

Physically paired bidirectional logical relationship. Segments B
and D in Figure 8.16 are interconnected or "physically paired."
Redundancy of data in B and D is still there. The main difference
between two unidirectional logical relationships, as in Figure 8.14,

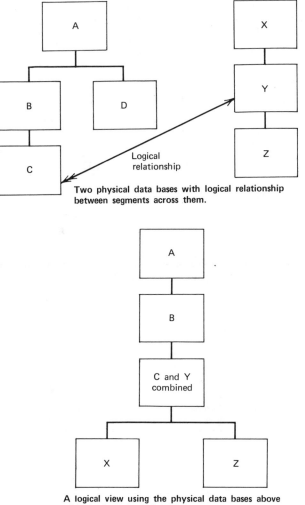

Two physical data bases with logical relationship between segments across them.

A logical view using the physical data bases above with the logical relationship.

Figure 8.13

and a physically paired bidirectional logical relationship, as in Figure 8.16, is that IMS automatically updates D if B is updated and vice versa. The pointers used are physical child first (PCF), physical twin forwards (PTF), physical parent (PP), logical parent (LP), and pair (for pairing B and D). Two of the possible logical views provided to the application programmer are the same as in Figure 8.15. To avoid redundancy between B and D and to avoid the overhead of updating

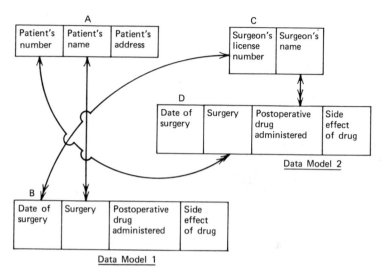

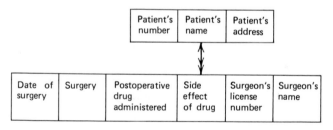

Figure 8.14 Two physical data bases with two unidirectional logical relationships. B is a logical child of C, and D is a logical child of A.

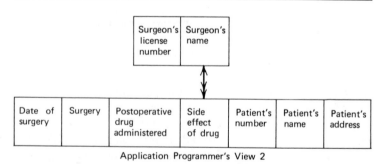

Figure 8.15 Two of the possible logical views based on the physical data bases from Figure 8.14. The logical views are supplied to application programmers.

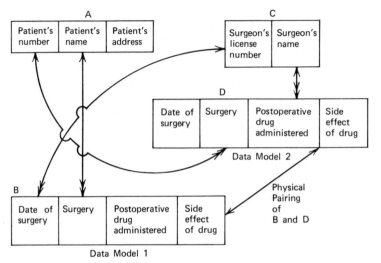

Figure 8.16 Two physical data bases with physically paired bidirectional logical relationship. B and D are physically paired. If B is updated, IMS automatically updates D and vice versa.

D when B is updated and vice versa, there is another way of providing the same logical views, called the virtually paired bidirectional logical relationship.

Virtually paired bidirectional logical relationship. To eliminate redundancy between B and D, one of the two may appear as a physical segment. In Figure 8.17, B is physically present. The pointers used are physical child first (PCF), physical twin forwards (PTF),

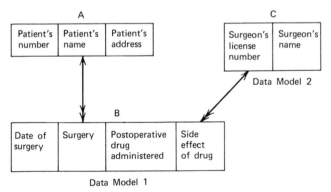

Figure 8.17 Two physical data bases with virtually paired bidirectional logical relationship. B is physically present, and D is virtual.

physical parent (PP), logical parent (LP), logical child first (LCF), and logical twin forwards (LTF). The pair pointer has disappeared because D is not physically present, that is, D is "virtually" paired with B. Two of the possible logical views provided to the application programmer are the same as in Figure 8.15.

A logical data base (LDB) is composed of logical records based on a logical view. A logical record may be identical to a physical record or may be a combination of parts of different physical records from a single physical data base or from a number of them. There are some rules for supporting logical relationships.

Rules for Logical Relationships

1. Every logical view is a hierarchical view. But this hierarchical view may be different from the hierarchical structure represented by the underlying physical data bases.

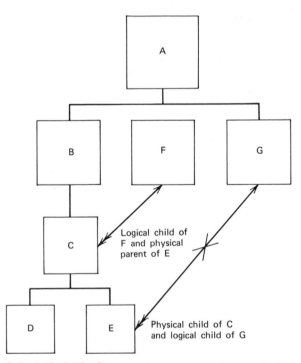

Figure 8.18 A logical child (C) cannot be a physical parent of a segment (E) that is a logical child of G (Rule 6). A logical child (C) can have a physical child (D) (Rule 7).

2. The root of a logical data base must also be the root of a physical data base (except secondary indexing).
3. A logical child can have only one logical parent.
4. The root of a physical data base may be a logical parent, but it cannot be a logical child.
5. A logical child cannot be a logical parent.
6. A logical child cannot be a physical parent of a segment that is a logical child. (See Figure 8.18.)
7. A logical child can have a physical child. (See Figure 8.18.)
8. Physical hierarchy may be traversed while providing a logical view using a logical relationship, that is, a physical parent of a logical parent may appear as a dependent of the concatenated (logical child and logical parent) segment in logical view. (See Figures 8.18a and 8.19.)
9. A physical child of a logical parent may appear as a dependent of the concatenated (logical child and logical parent) segment in logical view. (See Figure 8.19.)
10. Logical relationships may be crossed while constructing logical views.

Figure 8.20 shows a summary of logical views.

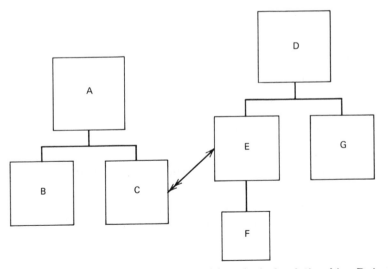

Figure 8.18a Two physical data bases with a logical relationship. D is the physical parent of the logical parent E. F is a physical child of the logical parent E.

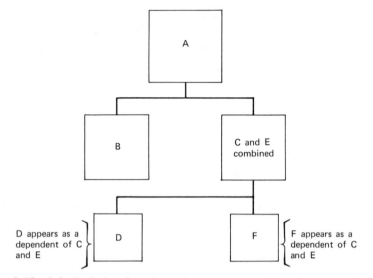

Figure 8.19 A logical view based on the two physical data bases with a logical relationship from Figure 8.18a.

Summary of Internal and External Model Access Methods in IMS/VS

Internal Model Access Methods

- Physical sequential (HSAM).
- Indexed sequential (HISAM, HIDAM).
- Random (HDAM).
- Inverted (secondary index).

External Model Access Methods

- Logical sequential (HSAM, HISAM, HIDAM).
- Physical hierarchy and modified hierarchy with logical relationships:
  Physical child (first, last).
  Physical twin (forwards, backwards).
  Physical parent.
  Logical child (first, last).
  Logical twin (forwards, backwards).
  Logical parent.
  Pair (physically paired bidirectional).

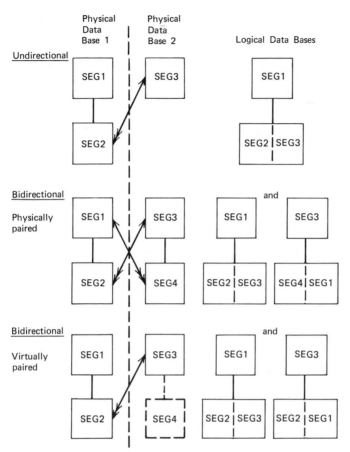

Figure 8.20 **Summary of logical views.**

8.2 NETWORK DATA BASE MANAGEMENT SYSTEMS

As stated in Chapter 4 (Section 4.5), much of today's awareness of the concepts of a data base can be credited to the work of CODASYL (Conference On Data Systems Languages) and its committees (DBTG being a major one). The underlying concepts of CODASYL specifications may be regarded as typical of a network-based system. There are a large number of data base management systems based on network data models, for example, Honeywell's IDS/II, Cullinane's IDMS, DEC's DBMS-10/20 for DECSYSTEM-10 and DECSYSTEM-20, DEC's DBMS-11 for PDP 11/70, and Univac's DMS 1100. Most of these conform to the CODASYL specifications. In this section we shall discuss some implementation details of the CODASYL-DBTG data model.

8.2.1 CODASYL-Data Base Task Group

As discussed in Chapter 4, the basic building block of the network data model is the set type. A set type is made up of an owner record type and one or many member record types. The rules for forming a set type are as follows:

1. A set type has only one owner record type.
2. A set type may have one or more member record types.
3. A record type cannot be an owner and a member of the same set type.
4. A record type can be an owner or a member in any number of different set types.

Internal Model Access Methods

Mapping record types to storage. The term used for placing a record and, in some instances, also finding it is "location mode." There are basically five choices of location mode. Every record type is assigned one of the five location modes.

1. CALC (calculation).
2. DIRECT.
3. VIA SET.
4. SYSTEM (default).
5. INDEX

The relevant DBTG syntax for the assignment of a location mode to a record type is as follows:

1. CALC
   RECORD NAME IS record-name
   LOCATION MODE IS CALC procedure USING data-item, data-item, . . .

The "record-name," "procedure," and "data-item"'s have to be filled in. The term "CALC" is an abbreviation of "CALCULATION." When a record is to be stored in the data base, its data base key is calculated after concatenating the values in the data items specified after "USING" in the LOCATION MODE clause.

In the DBTG's report, CALC implicitly means "hashing." The hashing algorithm may be specified with "procedure" or, if omitted, may be supplied by the data base management system as a default.

To explain how the CALC procedure "determines" where the record should be placed in the data base, we must refer back to the definition of "area" in Chapter 4. An area is a named subdivision of storage space for a data base and may contain occurrences of records and sets or parts of sets. Each record type is assigned to one or more of these areas. Furthermore, each area is divided into a number of equal-sized pages. The CALC algorithm takes the concatenated value of the data items and transforms it into a target key, which is a relative location within an area. The record is then stored somewhere in a page associated with the relative location if there is a space for it. Records with the same target key value are linked into a chain with each record pointing to the next. If there is no room on the page, the last record points to the off-page location where the next record is stored. If the last item on the page already points off-page, that page is accessed.

If the location mode CALC is chosen, it is also necessary to decide how to handle duplicate values of the key. The data base administrator has to decide whether to allow or prohibit duplicate values of the prime key. For "storing" the records, we may want to allow duplicate occurrences of the same key value, for example, if LAST-NAME is chosen as the primary key. If SOCIAL-SECURITY-NUMBER is chosen as the primary key, we may not want to allow duplicate occurrences of the same key value. The duplicate key values are a concern of the programmer as well as of the data base administrator, but the DBMS can edit for duplicates, relieving the programmer and the DBA of this concern. The syntax for the duplicates clause is as follows:

LOCATION MODE IS CALC procedure
      USING data-item, data-item, $\cdots$

$$\text{DUPLICATES are} \begin{bmatrix} \text{NOT} \\ \text{FIRST} \\ \text{LAST} \end{bmatrix} \text{ALLOWED}$$

The problem of "collision" should not be confused with "duplicates." Collision is an aspect of the randomizing module. A collision occurs when two different source key values randomize to the identical target key value. Some people call these records "synonyms." The collision problem concerns only the data base implementor, not the programmer.

2. DIRECT

RECORD NAME IS record-name

LOCATION MODE IS DIRECT $\left\{\begin{array}{l}\text{dbd-name 1}\\ \text{data-item 1}\end{array}\right\}$

The location mode DIRECT means that the application programmer becomes involved in how records of a given type are stored. The application programmer becomes involved by requesting the assignment of a specific data base key to the record when it is stored. Data base keys are unique identifiers that map to relative locations. Thus the location mode DIRECT can be more "direct" than the CALC mode.

In the syntax, two alternatives for the key data items are "dbd-name 1" and "data-item 1." If "data-item 1" is specified, it has to be defined as a "DATA-BASE-KEY," for example, data-item 1 TYPE IS DATA-BASE-KEY.

The key data items must be initialized before the programmer tries to store the records. There are three possibilities as far as the values of the key data items are concerned:

1. Key values are valid because they are not already in use.
2. Key values are invalid, possibly already in use.
3. Key values are null.

In the first two situations, the programmer is trying to be directly involved in the placement of the record. In the third situation, the programmer may not care about the physical storage of the record. The third situation is equivalent to SYSTEM (default), discussed later.

Thus the DIRECT mode is one where application programs rather than the data base management system, control the data base keys. A number of implementors of the DBMS that provide DIRECT mode strongly encourage users to avoid DIRECT because they believe that the function of a DBMS is to automatically maintain the structure of the data base, and that it should always do so in a manner transparent to application programs. Consequently, any programming that requires set or pointer maintenance to be performed by the application program should be discouraged, because any such programming increases the probability of loss of integrity. With any DBMS, such problems exist. However, by relying on the DBMS, one minimizes the incidence of loss of integrity.

It is tempting to use the DIRECT mode because it is the mode that allows quickest access to a record and requires the least amount of space for data base keys. It should be considered, however, that the benefits of leaving the data management functions with the

DBMS may be worth the possible extra time or extra space involved in using the DBMS. For example, consider DEC's DBMS-10/-20. The space argument with DIRECT mode turns out to be so insignificant that it is not worth mentioning. If there is a one-to-two (i.e., one owner and two members) relationship, DIRECT mode would use two words for keys. Declaring the relationship as a set (VIA SET, explained below) would take four words. If a relationship were one-to-fifteen, then DIRECT mode would take 15 words. A set would take 17, and so on. Therefore space constraints are negligible.

In DIRECT mode, one I/O is often considered for each record. With a one-to-two structure, a sample procedure might be to access the owner, the member, and then the second member. Thus there would be three I/O operations. If proper VIA SET clustering occurs, it would be necessary only to access the owner, then the members. The total here might be one I/O operation. Consequently, unless VIA SET clustering is simulated using the DIRECT mode, the performance will be slow.

It appears as if the DIRECT mode is implemented in some data base management systems because the CODASYL-DBTG specifications of 1971 contain the DIRECT mode. The latest report (1978) from CODASYL, however, does not have the DIRECT location mode. (See the reference at the end of the chapter.) The location mode is called the "placement" mode. "Placement" has three options:

- CALC.
- VIA SET.
- SEQUENTIAL . . . (this mode clusters records in a sequential order in a defined page range).

3. VIA SET
    RECORD NAME IS record-name
    LOCATION MODE IS VIA set-name SET

The "record-name" has to be a member in the set type identified by "set-name." The set type "set-name" may have other members, and the "record-name" may be a member or owner in other set types. The choice of the location mode "VIA SET" causes the records to be stored physically close to the other members of the set.

In the example from Chapter 4 and Figure 4.22 (repeated here for convenience as Figure 8.21), let us specify that

    RECORD NAME IS DATE-OF-SURGERY-AND-SURGERY
    LOCATION MODE IS VIA SURGERY-ON-PATIENT SET

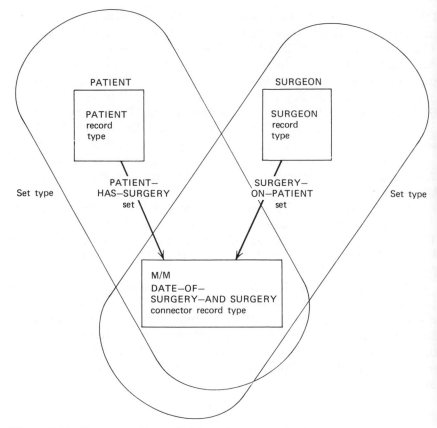

Figure 8.21 Representation of data using network data model (as in Figure 4.22). Many-to-many relationship implemented with two set types:

1. PATIENT-HAS-SURGERY.
2. SURGERY-ON-PATIENT.

Figure 8.21 shows the set types. Set occurrences are given in Figure 8.21a (Figure 4.23 in Chapter 4).

Then the membership of DATE-OF-SURGERY-AND-SURGERY in the set SURGERY-ON-PATIENT must mean something more than its membership in the set PATIENT-HAS-SURGERY. When the connector record of the type DATE-OF-SURGERY-AND-SURGERY is stored, it will be connected into a set of SURGERY-ON-PATIENT as well as into a set of PATIENT-HAS-SURGERY. But an attempt will be made to achieve physical contiguity of the owner and members in the occurrence of the set SURGERY-ON-PATIENT. This is

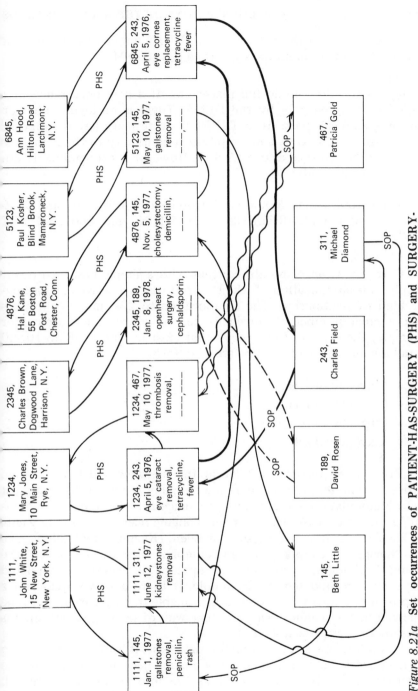

Figure 8.21a Set occurrences of PATIENT-HAS-SURGERY (PHS) and SURGERY-ON-PATIENT (SOP) network data model as in Figure 4.23.

243

the meaning of VIA SET in most DBTG implementations. The default if no location mode is specified is SYSTEM.

4. SYSTEM

With this location mode the placement of a new occurrence of a record is done entirely by the DBMS. There is no involvement on the programmer's part, as in DIRECT, no primary key is supposed to be used as in CALC, and no physical contiguity of the records in a set is to be achieved as in VIA SET. However, most vendors do not implement this mode.

Three topics that should be introduced at this stage are CUR-RENCY, SET OCCURRENCE SELECTION, and SORTED SET FIND.

CURRENCY

Currency is an elaborate concept with a simple basis. To put it simply, it is an indication of which record was just active in a particular kind of relationship. The complication to this simple concept is that a great number of currencies can be active at one time. For example, the classes of currencies that exist in DEC's DBMS-10/-20 data base management systems are as follows:

• Currency of area.
• Currency of record.
• Currency of run-unit.
• Currency of set.

Every area, record, and set in the userview will have its own currency. The reason that there are so many currencies is that most Data Manipulation Language verbs change the placement of a "cursor" in the data base. However, in changing place, one usually wants to keep track of where he/she has been. (Keeping track allows one to "navigate" simply through complex structures.) When the "cursor" changes, currencies are updated; however, only related currencies are updated. For example, if there are two areas and a record in one area is accessed, it is probable that no currency will be changed in the second area. (Another way of looking at currency is to think of it as place holders.)

In finding one's way through a data base, it is often necessary to go from set to set to set, repeatedly moving back and forth from one record which acts as an anchor as the information is processed.

Currencies serve as these anchors. For example, one might have the following structure:

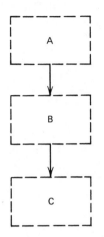

In processing such a tree structure, it is necessary to hang on to where one has been at all times. For example, a typical retrieval procedure might be:

1. Find an occurrence of A.
2. Find all B occurrences related to A.
3. Find all C occurrences related to B.

In doing this kind of processing, one wants to retain all owner record occurrences when member record occurrences are found. A pseudo code for this kind of operation might be (with PL/1):

```
FIND FIRST A RECORD OF SYS_A SET,
            /* This establishes initial currency */
DO WHILE (NOT END_OF_SET SYS_A);
    Process;
    FIND FIRST B RECORD OF A_B SET;
            /* This is the first occurrence of the B record that
               is attached to the current A record */
    DO WHILE (NOT END_OF_SET A_B);
        Process;
        FIND FIRST C RECORD OF B_C SET;
            /* This is the first occurrence of the C record that is
               attached to the current B record */
```

```
    DO WHILE (NOT END_OF_SET B_C);
       Process;
       FIND NEXT C RECORD OF B_C SET,
           /* Now that the currencies are established, process the
           C records */
    END;
    FIND NEXT B RECORD OF A_B SET;
           /* After all the C records are processed, leave the loop
           and process another B record */
    END;
    FIND NEXT A RECORD OF SYS_A SET;
           /* After all the B records of the set occurrence are
           processed, establish a new currency and repeat
           process */
END;
```

This algorithm shows how to work with currency. Its advantage as a concept is that it is relatively transparent. However, by its nature, it allows structures to be processed in a very natural way.

For a more involved data structure, currency is even more important.

Let us discuss now the next topic—SET OCCURRENCE SELECTION.

SET OCCURRENCE SELECTION

The preceding discussion introduced the concept of currency and explained how a program selects set occurrences. Implicit in this discussion is that a program establishes the correct currency. This is forced "navigation" through the data base. In this kind of programming, the program must know the data structure. This is called:

SET OCCURRENCE SELECTION IS THRU
CURRENT OF SET

Another mode of set occurrence selection is less dependent on knowledge of the underlying data structure. However, the user still must know what is linked to what. This mode is called

SET OCCURRENCE SELECTION IS THRU LOCATION
MODE OF OWNER

In this method, the DBMS must establish a currency for the owner record. Based on this currency, it can then establish a currency for the member record. Because the owner can have one of three location modes, there are three cases:

1. If the owner is a CALC record, the programmer must supply the CALC key. The program does not have to locate the record first.

2. If the owner is a DIRECT record, the programmer must supply the DIRECT key. Likewise, the program does not have to locate the owner record first.

3. If the owner is a VIA SET record, the programmer must provide information that tells the DBMS which occurrence of the owner record it should use. In this circumstance, the owner record *must* be part of a sorted set. Thus it is necessary to supply only the sort key. As the DBMS goes on attempting to find occurrences, it checks the owner's owner to see what its location mode is. The only restriction is that the chain of SET OCCURRENCE SELECTION IS THRU LOCATION MODE OF OWNER must terminate in a CALC, DIRECT, or SYSTEM record.

The advantage to application programming of this method is twofold. The programming need not be concerned with navigating through the data base when it attempts to find a record. All that need be supplied are the appropriate sort, DIRECT, and CALC keys. Also, if there are multiple linkages between record types, the programmer need only supply the keys and let the DBMS do the work. The effect is that application program logic is shorter.

The disadvantage of this form is that the owner record or records must be accessed whenever the member is being located. This usually guarantees additional input/output.

SORTED SET FIND

In the majority of data bases using the CODASYL model, there are certain record types that the programmer wants to access directly. For example, if there are employee records, she/he ordinarily wants to access them directly. However, there are also times when the programmer wants to process these records in sequential order. The normal solution to this problem is to CALC the records and have the records also participate in a sorted set. This solution has one disadvantage: in sequentially processing the records, approximately one I/O for every record has to be considered as an average.

5. INDEX

CODASYL has provided one way around this situation. If the record is made a sorted set, a form of the FIND command, called "rse 6" (for record selection expression 6), can be used that is designed exclusively for sorted records. With rse 6, DBMS uses the sorted set index structure to locate the record. The result is that the record can be located fairly quickly, although not as quickly as in CALC. However, there is much better sequential processing.

DEC's DBMS-10/20 allows further sophistication. The index structure can be placed in different buffers than are the records. This means that the DBMS can have the index structure in one set of buffers and the records in other buffers. The result of the separation is very quick access to the index structure (possibly retaining the buffers with index in memory for very long times). This will result in very good sequential processing. Because the records could be VIA records, it is probable that records with similar sort keys are located on the same data base page. Thus, although access to the first record is slower (but not unacceptably so), access to other records is very fast.

Thus the **internal model access methods** used by a DBTG data base management system are:

- Random (CALC).
- DIRECT.
- VIA SET.
- SYSTEM (default).
- Index

Before any operations can be performed on a stored data base record, the record has to be found. The statement "FIND" is a basic building block of any manipulation of data. By the same token FIND as used in the DBTG model can be quite involved. The reader, if interested, is advised to read reference 3 at the end of the chapter for a detailed discussion of FIND.

This has been an overview of the internal model access methods for the DBTG model. Let us now examine the external model access methods for the same model.

External Model Access Methods.   There are many ways in which sets can be implemented. A record type can have only one location mode, but the same record type may participate in a number of set types. Each participation of a record type in a set adds one more access path to the record. In the extreme case, we may say that there is no need to define any set types; only record types must be defined.

In that case, we cannot define the location mode of VIA SET for any record type.

The DBTG has identified two ways to interrelate record types. They are called "chain" and "pointer array."

Chain for a set type. The simplest chain implementation is a chain linked to NEXT. (See Figure 8.22.) The set type in Figure 8.22 is PATIENT-HAS-SURGERY. There are two member record occurrences. The implication is that the owner "John White" record contains a pointer to the "first" member in the set. In practice, the implementation stores the data base key of the "first" member, that is, "Gallstones removal," in the owner record. The last member will contain a pointer to the owner, closing the chain. The closed-ended chain is sometimes called a "ring." Some implementations leave the chain open-ended.

If the PATIENT record was assigned the location mode CALC, it is possible to access the "John White" record independently of the set, and then access the members consecutively with NEXT pointers.

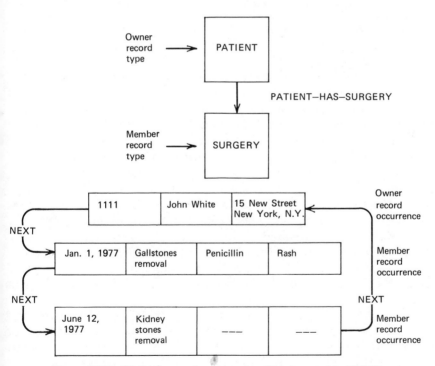

Figure 8.22 Chain for a set occurrence. Pointer used is NEXT.

But if the SURGERY record was stored with the location mode CALC, each member record can also be accessed independently of the set and then processed with the other members of the set.

For a chain structure, the NEXT pointer must be used. It is often advisable to keep chains with NEXT pointers limited in size. If a set has many members, the deletion activity of a member can be time consuming. After a member has been deleted, the preceding member must be accessed to update the NEXT pointer. And the only way to get to the record is by going all the way around the chain, although some data base management systems maintain the address of the preceding record if it was used to process through.

Another consideration for the chain linked to NEXT is whether the location mode VIA SET is used for the member record type. If so, there is a reasonable chance of being on the same page of the area. The data base administrator has to do calculations in terms of page size, set size, and delete frequency.

In most implementations, one must have NEXT pointers whenever there is a set.

NEXT and PRIOR

A PRIOR pointer is used effectively when a member is deleted. There are now two pointers, NEXT and PRIOR, that is two key values, in every record. If a record from a large set is to be deleted, the records on both sides are easily accessible. (See Figure 8.23.)

The PRIOR pointer, in addition to the NEXT pointer, easily takes care of the pointer updating after deletion of a member. But one more problem remains. It arises when the owner is to be accessed from a member. Suppose that the member record SURGERY has the location mode CALC. If one wants to find all the patients who had "Gallstones removal" surgery performed on them, the only way of retrieving the owner records is going all the way around with NEXT or PRIOR pointers. If the data base administrator predicts that the owner will be frequently accessed from the members, an OWNER pointer should be provided, as in Figure 8.24. This is also advisable if the member is not declared "LOCATION MODE VIA THE SET NAME," with which the owner is associated. In some implementations, the index records for sorted sets contain OWNER pointers as well.

An OWNER pointer increases access efficiency of the owner of a set if the member is accessed through other set occurrences or via one of the basic access methods. The owner can also be retrieved via the NEXT or PRIOR pointer, but this may involve retrieval of many undesired records in the set path.

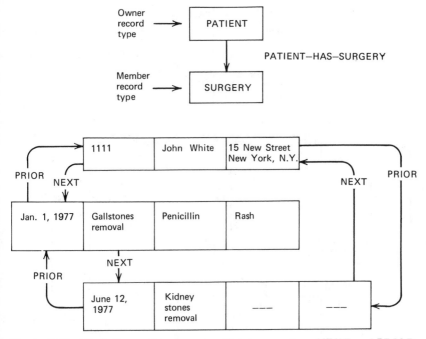

Figure 8.23 Chain for a set occurrence. Pointers used are NEXT and PRIOR.

In addition to the chaining technique, another way of implementing relationships in storage is the pointer array.

Pointer Arrays. The owner contains pointers to all the members and every member points back to the owner. There is no link between the members (See Figure 8.25.) The members may not be physically contiguous to the owner. Where the pointer array is stored and how it is stored are left to the DBMS implementor. Few implementations contain pointer arrays.

Insertion and Retention. There are four combinations for insertion and retention of member record occurrences in a set:

Set Insertion or (Storage Class)	Set Retention or (Removal Class)
1. Automatic	Mandatory
2. Automatic	Optional
3. Manual	Mandatory
4. Manual	Optional

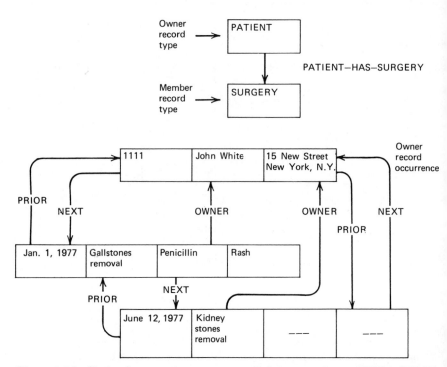

Figure 8.24 Chain for a set occurrence. Pointers used are NEXT, PRIOR, and OWNER.

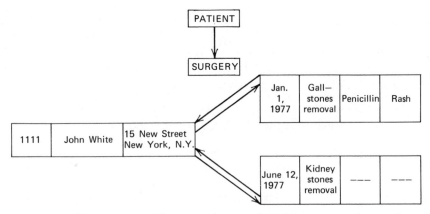

Figure 8.25 Pointer array. The owner has a pointer to every member, and every member is pointing to the owner.

1. **Set Insertion: Automatic; Set Retention: Mandatory.** The member record is linked into a set automatically when it is stored, and the record is retained in that set until it or the owner is deleted. (*Note:* This combination of the options is used quite frequently.)

2. **Set Insertion: Automatic; Set Retention: Optional.** Insertion is the same as above. As far as retention is concerned, however, a member may be disconnected from the set without necessarily deleting it from the data base or other sets. (*Note:* This combination of the options is not used quite so frequently.)

3. **Set Insertion: Manual; Set Retention: Mandatory.** The member record is not linked into the set automatically and must be connected by program logic. Once inserted, however, the member will be retained in the set until it or the owner is deleted. (*Note:* This combination of the options is used very seldom.)

4. **Set Insertion: Manual; Set Retention: Optional.** The member record is not linked into the set automatically and must be connected by program logic. As far as retention is concerned, however, a member may be disconnected from the set without necessarily deleting it from the data base or data sets. (*Note:* This combination of the options is used quite frequently.)

The symbology to illustrate these combinations can be represented as follows:

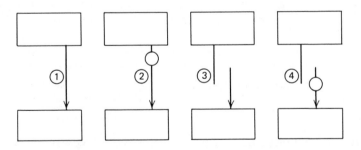

As mentioned in Chapter 4, the graphic notation was introduced by C. W. Bachman. A block represents an entity or a record type. The directed arrow, called the "Bachman arrow," connects two or more record types. The record type at the tail of the arrow is functioning as the owner record type, and the record type at the head of the arrow as the member record type.

INSERT and REMOVE

Along with manual insertion and optional retention come two powerful functions, INSERT and REMOVE. INSERT establishes a set relationship of a member with other members and the owner of the set, whereas REMOVE breaks the chain of a member with other members and the owner of the set. COBOL has implemented these functions through CONNECT and DISCONNECT commands.

STORE and DELETE

STORE. The STORE verb adds a new record to the data base. The DBMS uses whatever is in the key at the time of STORE as the basis for finding a location in the data base for the new CALC record.

For each set type for which the new record occurrence is an automatic member, the DBMS locates a set occurrence according to the SET OCCURRENCE SELECTION clause.

VIA records are stored as near as possible to their logical predecessors. Their location depends on the set ordering of the set of which they are VIA.

DELETE. This verb deletes the current-of-run-unit record from the data base. Other records in the data base may possibly also be deleted or removed from sets by the action of this verb.

When a member of a set is deleted, the pointer(s) of the prior (and the next) record must be changed. If the set has only NEXT pointers, the prior record is not easily determined. In such situations, PRIOR pointers expedite the deletion. DELETE is a deceptively powerful verb and can cause program errors that are difficult to trace.

A number of possible set types, besides the ones specified in Chapter 4, that can be represented in the DBTG network data model are shown in Figures 8.26, 8.27, and 8.28. A data base based on the DBTG model may be a combination of the set types from these figures.

Insertion of Member Records. After a record is stored in a data base, it may also be a member in a number of sets. For each set, a choice must be made regarding how it is to be ordered. Member records of a set can be inserted in the set in the following logical sequences:

- *Logical sequential* within a set (i.e., the members are sorted on a sequence field).

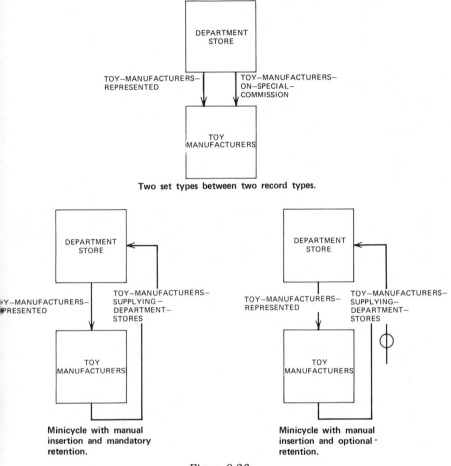

Figure 8.26

- *First:* The record to be added should become the first member of the chain, resulting in the LIFO (last in/first out) method.
- *Last:* The record to be added should become the last member of the chain, resulting in the FIFO (first in/first out) method.
- *Next:* The record to be added should go next to the currently referenced member or owner (same as "First").
- *Prior:* The record to be added should be prior to the currently referenced member or owner (same as "Last").

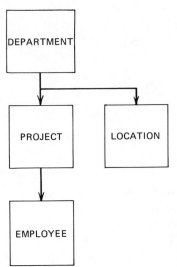

Figure 8.27 A hierarchical structure with three set types, **(DEPARTMENT, PROJECT)**, **(PROJECT, EMPLOYEE)**, and **(DEPART-MENT, LOCATION)**.

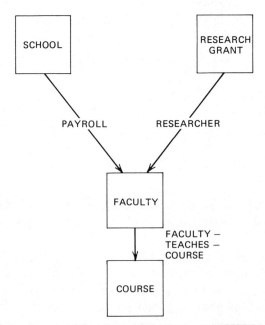

Figure 8.28 Y-structure with three set types, **(SCHOOL, FACULTY)**, **(RESEARCH GRANT, FACULTY)**, and **(FACULTY, COURSE)**.

256

Summary of Internal and External Model Access Methods in DBTG Data Base Management Systems

Internal Model Access Methods

- Random (CALC).
- DIRECT.
- Physical sequential within a set by VIA SET or between any records.
- SYSTEM.
- Index.

External model Access Methods

- NEXT.
- PRIOR.
- OWNER.

Generic functions for modifying the set relationships are as follows:

- REMOVE.
- INSERT.
- STORE.
- DELETE.

8.3 INVERTED FILE DATA BASE MANAGEMENT SYSTEMS

Some data base management systems available today need not impose any specific formal structure on the records. The records do not have to be related by a hierarchy or by a network. There need be no parents, no owners, no children, no members, no twins. In short, the records can be just records. And the records can be inverted on a number of data fields, that is, the data base using such a data base management system is composed of a number of files. The files are inverted on some or all of the data fields and may also be interconnected using the inversion method. The interrelationship may be stored or may be established "on the fly" as a query is being executed. One of the major data base management systems using inversion of files is ADABAS (Adaptable Data Base System), marketed (in the U.S.A. and Canada) by Software AG of North America, Inc.

8.3.1   ADABAS (Adaptable Data Base System)

ADABAS is basically an inverted file data base management system. A data base is composed of a number of files. The files are defined independently. Logical interconnection between files or structured arrangement of files may or may not be imposed.

All records within an ADABAS file have a common definition. In a file any field, subfield, or combination of fields may be defined as a descriptor (key). Descriptors may be defined at the time a file is created or at any later time with the help of a utility.

A unique reference number is assigned to every physical record. The number is called an "internal sequence number" (ISN). At the time of load, the records of a file are loaded in physical sequential manner and an ISN is assigned to every physical record. The ISN is not the physical address but rather a logical record identifier.

Figure 8.29 shows two files. One file describes the Policy, and the other the Policy-Holder. Both files have internal sequence numbers (ISNs). The descriptors in the Policy file are Policy-No and Policy-Type. The descriptor in the Policy-Holder file is Last-Name.

If the Policy-Holder file is expanded with one more field, Policy-No, which is also defined as a descriptor in Figure 8.30, the Policy file can then be related to the Policy-Holder file. The field Policy-No in the Policy file and the field Policy-No in the Policy-Holder file are used as interconnecting descriptors between the two files.

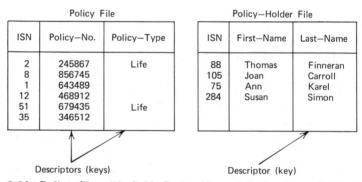

Policy File

ISN	Policy—No.	Policy—Type
2	245867	Life
8	856745	
1	643489	
12	468912	
51	679435	Life
35	346512	

Descriptors (keys)

Policy—Holder File

ISN	First—Name	Last—Name
88	Thomas	Finneran
105	Joan	Carroll
75	Ann	Karel
284	Susan	Simon

Descriptor (key)

Figure 8.29 Policy file with fields Policy-No and Policy-Type. Policy-No and Policy-Type are descriptors (keys).

Policy-Holder file with fields First-Name and Last-Name. Last-Name is a descriptor (key).

For unique identification of the policy holder, we may append the date of birth or address as fields to the Policy-Holder file.

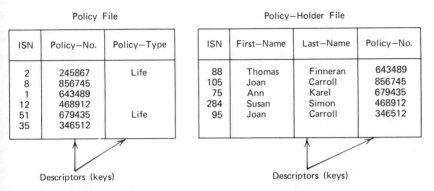

Figure 8.30 Policy-Holder file is expanded with Policy-No as compared to Figure 8.29. Policy-No interconnects the two files, the Policy file and the Policy-Holder file.

A policy holder may hold more than one policy; for example, Joan Carroll holds two policies.

Another way to express this one-to-many relationship is to make Policy-No a multiple valued field, as described later, in the Policy-Holder file. This might be preferable to reduce or eliminate data redundancy.

In Figure 8.30, the field Policy-No interconnects the Policy file and the Policy-Holder file. A Policy-Holder may hold more than one policy, and a policy may be held by more than one person. Such relationships may be many-to-many. Bidirectional access using these relationships is possible. The same person, Joan Carroll, holds two policies with policy numbers 856745 and 346512, as in Figure 8.31.

With this basic capability, ADABAS supports a network data model of multiple files with bidirectional many-to-many relationships between records. Relationships are based on fields that exist in the various files, as in Figure 8.31.

ADABAS also supports hierarchical views based on the common descriptors between the files. The "userviews" ("external models" from Chapter 1) are defined as hierarchical files containing data fields from related data base records. Figures 8.32a and 8.32b show some hierarchical views, based on Figure 8.31.

ADABAS stores data records in compressed form as variable-length byte strings. The data compression is transparent to the user because the system returns field values in userviews. Compression is implemented at the field level and is the default on a field by field basis when a file is loaded. If desired, this default compression may

Policy File

ISN	Policy—No.	Policy—Type	Policy—Holder Last—Name
2	245867	Life	Smith
8	856745		Carroll
1	643489	Life	Finneran
12	468912		Simon
51	679435		Karel
35	346512	...	Carroll
...			...

Policy—Holder File

ISN	First—Name	Last—Name	Policy—No	Rep—No.
88	Thomas	Finneran	643489	2345
105	Joan	Carroll	856745	6748
75	Ann	Karel	679435	1367
284	Susan	Simon	468912	4589
95	Joan	Carroll	346512	6748
...	...	...	...	...

Claims File

ISN	Policy—No.	Claim—Date
855	643489	January 15, 1980
931	346512	March 30, 1980
863	856745	February 18, 1981
845	468912	April 11, 1982
698	643489	March 5, 1980
567	245867	February 8, 1980
...		...

Representative File

ISN	Rep—No.	Policy—No.
581	6748	856745
530	1367	679435
356	4589	468912
289	2345	643489
685	6748	346512
...	...	...

Figure 8.31 **Policy, Policy-Holder, Claims, and Representative files are interrelated on certain descriptors (keys).**

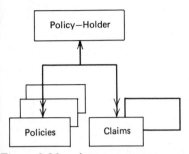

Figure 8.32a **A person may own many policies and may have put in many claims.**

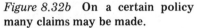

Figure 8.32b **On a certain policy many claims may be made.**

be overridden at file load time. The compression algorithm works as follows:

- Trailing spaces on alphanumeric fields are removed.
- Leading zeros on numeric data are removed.
- Unpacked decimal numeric data is packed.
- A series of consecutive null-valued fields may be represented by a single one-byte "empty field count."

Figure 8.33 shows the result of data compression.

Two basic field types are supported: elementary and multiple-valued fields. An elementary field is limited to one value per record.

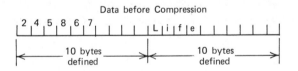

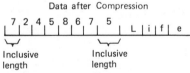

Figure 8.33 **Data compression:**

- **Removes trailing spaces on alphanumeric fields.**
- **Packs unpacked numeric data and removes leading zeros on all.**
- **Reduces one or many null-valued field(s) to a single character.**

A multiple-valued field may have multiple values per record. A series of consecutive fields may be combined into a group. A group that may repeat within a record is called a "periodic" group. Multiple-valued fields may be defined within periodic groups.

Storage of Records.   Each record in an ADABAS file is stored as a compressed variable-length string of field values and is assigned a logical identifier, called the internal sequence number (ISN). The ISN is usually assigned by the data base management system, but it may also be assigned by the user.

The variable-length data records are stored in fixed-length basic direct access method (BDAM) physical data blocks. A certain percentage of free space per block is assigned for growth of the records in blocks. The size of this "padding" area is determined on a file-by-file basis, according to the dynamics of record expansion through update.

Randomized storage mode.   ADABAS provides a direct access method called ADAM (ADABAS direct access method). ADAM uses the field value for computation of the physical block address for record storage, thus bypassing the standard index look-up when this field is used for record selection.

Linear storage mode.   Records may also be stored by linear use of blocks when a file is initially loaded, and in any memory resident block with adequate space when the file is in dynamic use.

Physical ordering of records.   Records may be stored in a physical order in sequence by the value of any descriptor field, thereby optimizing the efficiency of logical sequential access by that descriptor.

Access to Records.   Records are read from ADABAS using either physical sequential access or the inverted list. The ISNs are not the physical addresses. To insulate changes to the inverted list as a result of movement of the physical records (e.g., as a result of increase in size), an *Address Converter* is utilized. This is a way of indirect addressing to the ISNs. (See Figure 8.34.) The address of a record is the relative block number, and the access method used to retrieve a record is basic direct. If the ISN of the record to be retrieved is known, it may be used directly to access the record.

An Address Converter exists for each file in the data base and maps each ISN to its physical record address. The Address Converter is a list containing one entry per record in a file. The logical address

Associator

Inverted List					Address Converter Block Number	Policy File		
Value	Count	ISN	ISN	---	1	ISN	Policy—No.	Policy—Type
					1			
Life	8010	2	51	---		2	245867	Life
						8	856745	
						1	643489	
						12	468912	
					1	51	679435	Life
						35	346512	
					2	:	:	:
					:			

Figure 8.34

- Inverted list for the descriptor Policy-Type in the Policy file. The value Life occurs 8010 times in this file, in records with ISN = 2 and 51, as shown, and some others.

   Address Converter shows that the records with ISN = 1, 2, and 8 are in block 1. The record with ISN = 12 is in block 2.

- Associator consists of the inverted list and the address converter. It contains the general description of the entire data base. It also contains the specific file directory for each file with the file description and field description table. The Associator also consists of the space management tables.

for a record (its ISN) is used as an index to the Address Converter entry for the record, and this entry gives the physical block in which the record is stored.

The records of a file may be read by using the ISNs in sorted order for a specific descriptor value. This results basically in the logical sequential access method. The records with the ISNs 2, 35, 12, 1, 51, and 8 read in results in logical sequential processing of the Policy file from Figure 8.34, based on the descriptor Policy-No.

Inverted List. ADABAS maintains an inverted list for each field in a file that is designated as a descriptor. Descriptors may be defined at the time the file is created or subsequently by use of a utility. A descriptor may be defined as unique, in which case the DBMS ensures that duplicate values do not exist in the file.

The inverted list for each descriptor is in sequence by value. Each entry contains the number of records in which the value occurs and the ISNs of those records. Figure 8.34 shows the inverted list for the descriptor Policy-Type. The value "Life" occurs 8010 times in this file, in records with ISN = 2 and ISN = 51, which are shown in Figure 8.34, and others.

The inverted list is used primarily for record selection. The simplest case is selection by use of a single value of a single descriptor. In the case of Policy-Type=Life, 8010 records will be selected, and they will be retrieved by repeated use of the Address Converter. The record with ISN = 2 is in block 1, whereas the record with ISN = 51 is in block 2. It becomes evident that the selection of fields to be descriptors is a major performance factor in data base design.

Multiple criteria may be specified for selection, for example, Policy-Type=Life and Policy-No=200,000 through 400,000. The DBMS combines the inverted lists for the relevant values, in this case Policy-Type=Life and Policy-No=245867, to form a list of ISNs of those records that meet all criteria. The record with ISN = 2 will be the only one selected. The search criteria are completely resolved using only the inverted lists, without access to data records. The index structure that supports the searching consists of three to six levels of indices, depending on the number of descriptors, lengths of descriptor values, and total number of records in the file. Some of these indices are the hyper-index, the super-index, the main-index, and the normal-index. The index structure is transparent to the user and is the function of the DBMS.

Accessing Interrelated Records from Different Files. If there is a common descriptor between two files, the physical records from these files may be interrelated, based on the value of the common descriptor. This facility, which is called "coupling," is maintained automatically by the DBMS. There is no physical representation of coupling within the data records, but ADABAS supports the bidirectional relationships between records by two additional inverted lists in the Associator. Coupling is bidirectional, that is, it enables one to implement many-to-many relationships. If the Policy file and the Claims file from Figure 8.31 are coupled, the following selection may be resolved:

- Find all policies with Policy-Type=Life and coupled to Claims with Claim-Date=January 1, 1980 thru March 31, 1980.

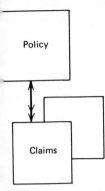

Figure 8.35 Userview: a hierarchical view about possible many claims for a given policy.

The records selected for this inquiry are:

> Policy-No=245867
> > Policy-Type=Life
> > Claim-Date=February 8, 1980
>
> Policy-No=643489
> > Policy-Type=Life
> > Claim-Date=January 15, 1980

There is no limit to the number of records in one file that may be coupled to a single record in another file.

Userviews. The user refers to files and fields. The arrangement of data for a particular user is called a "userview." In the preceding example about coupling for the Policy file and the Claims file from Figure 8.31, the userview supported is as shown in Figure 8.35.

Another data base management system using inverted file structure is System 2000 (INTEL Corporation, marketed by MRI Corporation).

Summary of Internal and External Model Access Methods in ADABAS

Internal Model Access Methods

- Physical sequential.
- Inverted.

- Logical sequential and internal sequence number as a result of inversion.
- Direct with internal sequence number.

External Model Access Methods

- Single-file accessing.
- Multiple files unrelated.
- Many-to-many as a result of coupling.

REFERENCES

1. *Data Base Management*—Access Mechanisms and Data *Structure Support in Data Base Management Systems*, Monograph Series, Robert M. Curtice (Staff Member, Arthur D. Little, Inc.), Q. E. D. Information Sciences, Inc., Wellesley, Massachusetts 02181.
2. *Data Base Management Systems*, Leo J. Cohen, Q. E. D. Information Sciences, Inc., Wellesley, Massachusetts 02181.
3. *The Codasyl Approach to Data Base Management*, T. William Olle, A Wiley-Interscience Publication, John Wiley and Sons, 1978.
4. *IMS/VS System/Application Design Guide*, IBM Corporation, 1133 Westchester Avenue, White Plains, New York.
5. *ADABAS Introduction Manual*, Manual/Order Number: ADA-410-000, Software AG of North America, Inc., Reston International Center, 11800 Sunrise Valley Drive, Reston, Virginia 22091.
6. "Data Structure Diagrams," C. W. Bachman, *Data Base*, Journal of ACM Special Interest Group British Data Processing, Vol. 1, No. 2 (Summer 1969).
7. "Implementation Techniques for Data Structure Sets," C. W. Bachman, from *Data Base Management Systems: Proceedings of the SHARE Working Conference on Data Base Management Systems, Montreal, Canada, July 23-27, 1973*, edited by D. A. Jardine, North-Holland, 1974.
8. *Data Base Management System, Administrator's Procedures Manual*, Order No. AA-4146B-TM, DECSYSTEM, Digital Equipment Corporation, 200 Forest Street, Marlboro, Massachusetts 01752.
9. *Data Base Management System, Programmer's Procedures Manual*, Order No. AA-4149B-TM, DECYSYSTEM, Digital Equipment Corporation, 200 Forest Street, Marlboro, Massachusetts 01752.
10. "CODASYL," Data Description Language Committee, *Journal of Development*, January 1978, Box 1808, Washington, D.C. 20043.

CHAPTER **9**

Data Base Design
(Physical Model)

In Part II we designed a conceptual and a logical model of a data base with "obvious" performance issues in mind. This chapter discusses the next two data base design steps from Figure 1.8. The first of the two steps is designing a physical model of a data base for the chosen data base management system. The second of the two steps is evaluating the physical model for performance.

9.1 TWO STEPS OF DATA BASE DESIGN (PHYSICAL MODEL)

The physical model is a framework of the data base to be stored on physical devices. Since a large percentage of data bases are used in an on-line environment, one has to be very concerned with "visible" performance. It is absolutely mandatory to evaluate the performance characteristics of the physical model before implementing the data base. Performance prediction is a multivariate analysis with the

267

physical model as a major variable. One should carry out a quantitative analysis of the physical model with average frequencies of occurrences of the groupings of the data elements, with expected auxiliary space estimates, and with expected time estimates for retrieving and maintaining the data.

The applications using the data base can be categorized into groups based on their importance to the enterprise, as well as on the usage pattern. Time estimates for these applications may be predicted. A "pencil and paper" method will be used for the estimation process. Any major flaws in the design may be detected, and the physical design of the data base can be evaluated before it is put into production. Performance estimation in the design phase should have full support from management because, once a data base is installed, it is extremely difficult, if not impossible, to redesign it. It is like an arrow that has left the bow.

A data base designer generally tries to optimize the physical model for space and time considerations. Trade-offs between space and time are found in almost all DBMSs, that is, a number of physical input/outputs can be eliminated if some "redundant" data is carried, or not carrying redundant data may save space but cost more time. But one should not get carried away with the space and time optimization and forget about the business requirements. It is possible that, from the business viewpoint, it is necessary to have multiple entry points into a data base, or to access a particular record type with more than one key. To provide this type of access, it may be necessary to invert the file on the keys, thereby posing some overhead on space and/or time. If so, that is the price that has to be paid for satisfying this particular business requirement.

Three major areas of expertise are needed by the designer of the physical model of a data base:

1. Knowledge of the DBMS functions.
2. Understanding of the characteristics of direct access devices.
3. Knowledge of the applications.

The first area where the physical model designer has to have expertise is knowledge of the DBMS, be it IMS, IDMS, ADABAS, IDS/II, DBMS-10/20, or TOTAL, to name just a few. The designer has to know how the DBMS performs its specific functions. Consider the example of DELETE. "Delete" means something to all of us. It means "get rid of something." Some systems may get rid of a record physically, that is, the space is freed and compacted. Other systems may only mark the record as "deleted" without claiming the space on disk, that is, the record is deleted only "logically." The second type of deletion may cause some problems in the long range as far as the disk space is concerned, as well as the time for fetching the desired records. Because of large unused space between the desired records, it may take longer to fetch the next record that is wanted. Knowledge of the DBMS to be used at the primitive function level is a necessity for the physical model designer.

The second area of expertise involves the characteristics of direct access devices. It is true that on many occasions we still think in terms of serial processing. When someone says "Get the next record," we expect the desired record to be physically close to the one we are working on. The thought that the "next" record may be three disk packs away may be disconcerting.

While designing the physical model of a data base, we need to worry about the physical aspects of the data base, that is, the record layout on disk, blocksizes, buffer sizes, and input/output characteristics, to name just a few examples. If these aspects are not considered in the physical model, the data base may collapse as a result of poor performance.

The third area is applications. The designer has to know the relationships of data elements and of entities referenced in the applications, that is, the external models. She/he must also know high volume transactions, and response time requirements for an on-line environment. It is necessary to know the major batch programs and critical turnaround time requirements for a batch environment.

In the next section, a set of general rules for designing a physical model to avoid gross mistakes is discussed. These rules are sufficient only for first-pass analysis; they do not recognize specific circumstances.

9.2 DESIGN A PHYSICAL MODEL OF A DATA BASE

A number of guidelines provided in this section are "universal," that is, they hold good irrespective of the DBMS used. To be specific, however, let us consider the following three data base management systems:

1. Information Management System (IMS), marketed by International Business Machines Corporation, supporting a hierarchical data model with some network and inverted file capabilities.

2. Data Base Management System-10/-20 (DBMS-10/20), marketed

by Digital Equipment Corporation for DECSYSTEM-10/-20, which uses a network data model with CODASYL specifications.

3. Adaptable Data Base System (ADABAS), marketed (in the U.S.A. and Canada) by Software AG of North America, which is a data base management system that uses file inversion.

9.2.1   Hierarchical Data Base Management Systems

We will consider guidelines for a DBMS that uses a hierarchical data model as its underlying structure. Most of the guidelines given below can be used for any DBMS with a hierarchical data model, for example, SYSTEM 2000, marketed by MRI Corporation and owned by Intel Corporation, and Mark IV, marketed by Informatics, Inc. In particular, we will place some emphasis on IBM's Information Management System (IMS); especially, the terminology used is from IMS. IMS is discussed in more detail in Chapter 8.

1. **Keep the hierarchical structure as simple as possible.** The hierarchy is defined in top-to-bottom and left-to-right order. The root is the dominant segment type. If secondary indexing capability is disregarded, access of any data base record takes place with the access of the root. The segments at the bottom and to the right of the hierarchy are the ones that are remote from the root. For this reason, the structure should be kept simple with fewer levels and less spread from left to right. The key issue here is not the number of segment types but the number of segment occurrences. A complex structure is usually an oversegmented structure. A result of oversegmentation is excessive DL/1 calls and accesses of segments, as well as longer reorganization times. An analysis should be performed to find alternatives to secondary indexing and logical relationships. Secondary indexing provides multiple key retrievals at the cost of updating secondary data sets. Logical relationships give network capabilities at the cost of updating logical pointers and possibly of having to access a number of physical data bases. The key issue in designing a physical model is considering alternative solutions.

2. **Do not sacrifice security and data independence because of too few segments.** If the same amount of data is stored in fewer segments, the amount per segment is relatively large. As a result of the segment level access, an application programmer may be

presented with data not required by the application. Fewer segments with the same amount of data affect security as well as data independence. The trade-off here is between too few and too many segments.

3. **Keep frequently accessed segments near the top of the hierarchy.** Since access to the data base records normally starts at the root level, data in the root segment is accessed faster than that in any other segment in the hierarchy. Ideally, most frequently accessed data should be kept at the root level. If that is not possible for security, privacy, or redundancy reasons, the next desirable level is the second level, as far left in the hierarchy as possible. This minimizes the probability of physical I/O when the segment is accessed from the root. One of the factors that increases the probability of physical I/O for accessing a segment from the root is the distance between them.

4. **Split segments in accordance with the key ranges.** In a hierarchical data model, if the segments are split according to the key ranges, access to the desired segment will probably be more selective and faster.

The answers to the following questions should also be considered n developing guidelines:

5. **What about a segment type whose relative frequency under its parent is 1?** One has to be suspicious about a segment of this type. The real question posed is why the segment is not included in the parent segment. Possible justifications for separation may be security, possibility of multiple occurrences of the segment, or no occurrences of the segment.

6. **What about a segment type whose prefix length is greater than its data length?** The prefix for every segment consists of pointers, physical as well as logical. If the prefix length is greater than the data length for a segment, it is advisable to consider merging the segment with its parent. If, for security reasons, the segment cannot be included in the parent segment and if the segment is not keyed, it may be possible to reduce the multiple occurrences of the segment to one occurrence only. If the segment with a longer length of prefix than of data is a root segment, it may be possible to merge the root segment with some second level segments to form a new root segment.

7. **When to use variable-length segments and when not to?** If a child segment is most likely to occur once or not at all, it is the

best candidate to be moved to the parent segment. The parent can be made a variable-length segment.

If a segment is most likely to grow in size after the initial insertion, it will be split and inserted in the data base. This may require two I/O operations for its retrieval. A segment that may grow in size after the initial insertion is not the best candidate for a variable-length segment.

8. **How to deal with different volatilities of the segments? How to separate segments with discrepancies in sizes and discrepancies in usage?** Problems of this nature may be resolved by using data set groups of a data base. A part of the data base may be stored as one data set group, whereas another part may be stored as another data set group. Different blocksizes and different free spaces may be specified for the data set groups. The segments that are accessed more frequently and together may be stored in one data set group. The segments to be accessed on-line may be separated from the segments to be accessed in batch. Data set groups may also be used to shorten the path to certain segments at the expense of others.

9. **When to split one physical data base into a number of physical data bases?** One physical data base of IMS is based on one hierarchical data model, that is, there is one root segment type per physical data base. If one physical data base is expected to become too big and there is a constraint (which most probably there will be in most data base environments on time availability for reorganization), or if because of high volatility there will be a need for frequent reorganizations, it may be advisable to split the physical data base.

But there is a trade-off between one physical data base and a number of physical data bases. The operational issues of backup and recovery become more complicated as the number of physical data bases increases. A costly process, as far as time is concerned, is opening and closing the data bases. As the number of physical data bases increases, the number of openings and closings increases too.

10. **How to provide alternative access paths besides the strict hierarchy?** Although IMS provides a hierarchical view to an application programmer, it offers a facility called "secondary indexing" that enables it to access a segment on its own without having to go through the strict hierarchy of a root and its dependents. IMS also provides a restricted network capability

called "logical relationships." Both these features, secondary indexing and logical relationships, have to be specified in the physical model of the data base.

10.1. **Secondary Indexing.** With secondary indexing, IMS data base records can be accessed on data elements other than the primary key.

The data element used as the entry point is called the "source segment." Secondary indexing enables the data base designer to invert the file. But secondary indexing should not be used for sequential processing. It is also not advisable to use secondary indexing on highly volatile source segments.

Extensive use of inverting data base records is made by System 2000, marketed by MRI Corporation and owned by Intel Corporation.

10.2. **Logical Relationships.** IMS provides many-to-many mapping with the help of logical relationships. This feature also helps to reduce the redundant data. The logical relationship must be specified in the physical data bases. The placement of the logical child in the physical data base may be critical from the viewpoint of performance; the logical child should be placed where the requests originate most frequently. Misplacement of the logical child may result in long logical twin chains, which may degrade the performance to a large extent because each access will probably result in an I/O.

Symbolic pointer and direct pointer have their benefits and drawbacks. An analysis should be performed to decide the types of pointers to be provided in the logical child segments. Unidirectional, physically paired bidirectional, and virtually paired bidirectional—each of the three methods has its benefits and drawbacks. Different trade-offs have to be made and decisions taken on an individual basis.

9.2.2 Network Data Base Management Systems

Here we discuss guidelines for a DBMS that uses a network data model as its underlying structure. In particular, we will emphasize the DBMS specified by CODASYL-DBTG, for example, DBMS-10/

20 for DECSYSTEM-10/-20 by Digital Equipment Corporation. The basic implementation steps of a physical data base are given below. These steps may be iterative.

1. **Diagram the data base structure.** As we saw in the preceding chapters, the diagramming technique for network data models was introduced by Charles Bachman. The boxes represent the record types, and an arrow between two boxes indicates the owner-member relationship and establishes a set type. The arrow strictly represents the logical relationship. The member record may or may not be close to the owner record. The owner and the member may have a set of storage and retrieval rules that are the same or are entirely different. The arrow does not imply the direction. It is possible that a member is retrieved first and the owner is retrieved afterwards, if the implementation has provided a way of accessing owner from member. Chapters 4 and 8 have detailed discussions of the set types supported by CODASYL-DBTG specifications.

2. **Apply the DBMS rules to the logical model in order to design the physical model as follows.**

    2.1. **Record Storage and Retrieval.** Decide the best way of accessing the records. Is it best to access them in a group or as an individual entry? Should they be calculated, that is should the records be accessed with some specific key values? Determine which record types must have the shortest access path. Analyze which record types should be CALC and which should be VIA SET.

    2.2. **Set Selection Rules.** This refers to the selection of the correct owner when inserting records into a set. What are the best criteria for establishing who the owner is? Should the system decide and fetch the record, or should there be a command in the application program that decides which record to fetch? Should the "automatic" or "manual" feature be provided?

    2.3. **Set Ordering.** This refers to how the records are inserted into the set. Should they be inserted in sorted sequence or a particular key, or should they be inserted in the beginning of the set or at the end of the set?

    2.4. **Set Processing.** If the DBMS provides optional pointers the designer has to know how the set will be processed This problem becomes less severe when the system auto matically provides the pointers. The designer has to decide on the combination of pointers of the types NEXT, PRIOR, OWNER, etc.

Sizing Calculations. Estimate the number of records in a set. Estimate the number of pages in a data base. Decide what type of clustering should be used for VIA SET for determining the page size.

3. **Finalize the record content.** Decide which data elements are contained in which records. The list of DOs and DON'Ts of data structuring provided below may be helpful in finalizing the record contents.

4. **Follow the DOs and DON'Ts of data structuring.**

   4.1. **DO: Structure Variable Data.** In the logical model, study the owner-member relationships. For a given owner there may be many member occurrences within a set, and it may be valid to keep the set type. But if, for a given owner, there is only one member occurrence, be suspicious about the set type. The member may be included in the owner as well.

   4.2. **DO: Recognize Trade-offs.** It is possible that the specific environment requires retrieval of some data in different contexts, for example, the EMPLOYEE record in Figure 9.1 may be retrieved based on PRIMARY SKILL or LOCA-TION or JOB CODE. Here the designer provides multiple retrieval capabilities at the cost of storing the employee data as a link, that is, establishing proper pointers between the three sets.

   4.3. **DO: Avoid Lengthy Sets.** There is no definition of a lengthy set. The designer has to impose these limits. Is a set lengthy when it has 50 members, or is it lengthy when

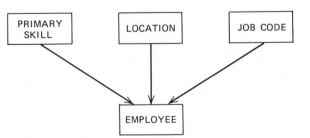

Figure 9.1 Trade-off is between multiple retrieval capability and time to store.

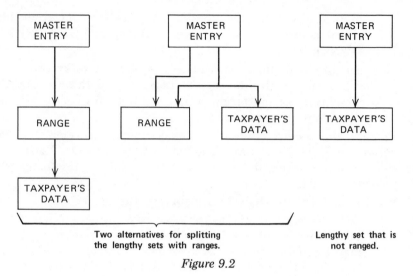

Two alternatives for splitting   Lengthy set that is
the lengthy sets with ranges.   not ranged.

Figure 9.2

it has 500 members? The answer also depends on whether the members are physically clustered or distributed. A lengthy set may be divided into a number of groups. It is advisable to build ranges of the keys, as in Figure 9.2.

4.4. **DO: Consider Pointer Arrays.** Pointers do take up space. Suppose that in a particular situation there is an owner record and some variables are associated with the owner. Let us assume that there are 500,000 owner records and four different sets. The volume of the substructure is very low, that is, out of 500,000 only 5 percent of the owner records need a substructure. In a case like this, consider to use pointer array where the pointer array is the member of a set. (See Figure 9.3.) As a result, the pointers are embedded in the pointer array instead of in the owner record. The pointers will not be present in the 500,000 occurrences of the owner records. They will be present only in 25,000 records of the pointer array. A majority of vendors do not supply pointer arrays.

4.5. **DO: Weigh Record Clustering versus Distribution.** A trade-off that the data base designer has to consider involves distributing the data. In a network environment, the smoother the distribution, the better is the performance of the data base. Consider an example where we have 5000 CUSTOMERS and 10,000 ACCOUNTS, and there are

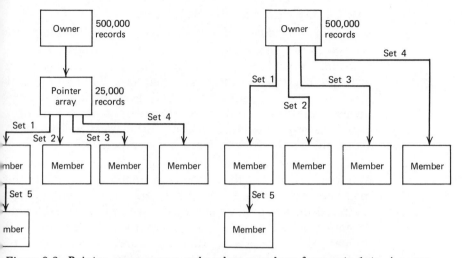

Figure 9.3 **Pointer array occurs only when members from sets 1 to 4 occur. More space is required without pointer array because the 500,000 owner records have to provide pointer space.**

five TYPES OF ACCOUNTS. (See Figure 9.4.) If the 10,000 ACCOUNTS are clustered with the five TYPES OF ACCOUNTS, the result is a skewed distribution. If, on the other hand, the 10,000 ACCOUNTS are clustered with the 5000 CUSTOMERS, the result is a smoother distribution. It is advisable to consider record clustering versus distribution.

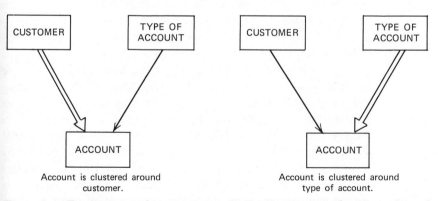

Figure 9.4 **For better performance smooth distribution is preferable to skewed distribution. The arrow, ⟹ indicates clustering.**

4.6.   DO: Use OWNER and PRIOR Pointers.

Members not clustered near owner. If the members are not clustered near the owners and the DBMS has the optional capability of OWNER pointers, this situation provides a good rationale for their use. Even though, at the time of design, no user has any need for accessing the owner from the member, most probably 3 or 6 months after the implementation some of the users will want to access the owner directly from the member.

Many members in a set. If the set is made up of several hundred members, the clustering may not store all the members on one page. If the hundreds of members are scattered on five or six pages of storage, it may be advisable to have OWNER pointers. As alternatives, the designer can increase the page size so that all records fit on a page, or he/she can give more buffer space to the application, so that all five or six pages are brought into memory simultaneously.

Processing considerations. If there are different processing considerations, it may be advisable to have PRIOR pointers. In one situation we may be interested in the newest invoices stored, whereas in another situation we may be interested in paying off the oldest invoices to avoid higher interest. If the invoices are the members of the set, PRIOR pointers will be helpful.

Deletion of records. PRIOR pointers are helpful also in the deletion process. If PRIOR pointers are not provided, the best way to get to the previous member record is most probably to go to the owner and use NEXT pointers. If PRIOR pointers are provided, the deletion process is often faster.

Don't overstructure. There may be a low ratio of owners to members; for example, for 100,000 INVOICES there are only 1000 BACK ORDERS. It may not be advisable to structure INVOICE and BACK ORDER as a set, as in Figure 9.5. It may be advisable to use the same invoice key for accessing both the INVOICES and the BACK ORDERS.

Don't sacrifice selectivity. In Figure 9.6 the three paths provide selectivity at the cost of space. With the single path in the same figure, the space used is less at the cost of time for acquiring some data.

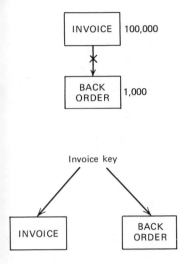

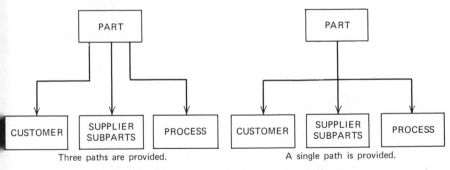

Figure 9.5 **For low ratio between owner and member, the same invoice key is used for accessing the invoice as well as the back order.**

Don't neglect pointer placement analysis. A data base usually consists of two types of records. One type is long duration, that is, the records stay in the data base for a relatively long time. The other type is short duration, that is, the records have a short life cycle. Data base records about CUSTOMERS, STUDENTS, and ACCOUNTS usually are of the long duration type, whereas records about INVOICES and ORDERS are of the short duration type. Short duration type records are usually the ones that have to be updated quite frequently. If pointers are placed in short duration type records, the pointers "go away" when the record is deleted, unlike the pointers in long duration type records. See Figure 9.7.

Figure 9.6 **Trade-off is between space and time.**

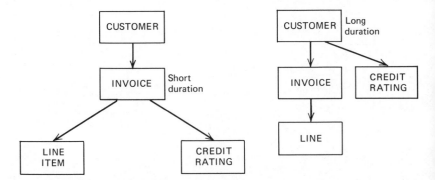

Figure 9.7 **Pointers placed in the short duration records need more maintenance than pointers placed in the long duration records.**

> *Don't overlook off-line processing.* Off-line processing
> may be a preferable alternative to on-line processing if
> data is voluminous. Historical and inventory data may be
> good candidates for off-line processing. Sorting in batch
> may not necessarily be the worst solution for certain
> problems!

9.2.3   Inverted File Data Base Management Systems

Most data files are organized with a primary key. The primary key
usually identifies the records uniquely. There may be other attributes
that serve as record identifiers but are not necessarily unique identifiers. These attributes are called secondary keys, and it may be desirable to locate the records that satisfy certain criteria regarding
these keys. There may be many records that have the same value
for a particular secondary key. Some data base management systems
do not distinguish between primary and secondary keys.

A good example is airline flight information. The attributes of
this file are flight number, departure date, departure city with airport,
departure time, destination city with airport, and arrival time. The
primary key is flight number and departure date combined. There is
only one record for a value of the flight number and departure date,
but there may be a number of records for the flights coming into
New York City. There may be a passenger who is interested in finding all the flights for three consecutive days where the destination
city is New York City and the departure city is San Francisco. A
specification of this type, about which records are desired that have
certain values of certain attributes, is called a "query." Data base

management systems that use file inversion are most probably best suited to an on-line query-oriented environment.

In a batch environment, if a question regarding some value of a secondary key is posed, it may be possible to scan the entire file for the records that satisfy the specific criterion. But in a query-oriented environment there is not as much time available for scanning the entire file. To speed up secondary key retrieval, therefore, an inverted list is created. An inverted list is a list of all records having a given value of some primary or secondary key.

The main questions to be answered in designing a physical model for inverted file data base management systems are posed below. We will use the terminology from ADABAS, discussed in Chapter 8.

I What are the considerations in regard to data duplication and data redundancy?

The main question to be answered here is when and how to duplicate data, as well as when and how to eliminate data redundancy. ADABAS techniques that pertain to the consideration of data duplication include the use of:

1. Multiple-value fields.
2. Periodic groups.
3. Multiple record types within a file.
4. Multiple files to store the data.

1. Multiple-Value Fields

Multiple-value fields may eliminate duplication. Consider the set of data items "Customer details" for a CUSTOMER repeated for one single item "Account number." With each CUSTOMER-ACCOUNT pair in a separate record, there is considerable duplication of data:

Customer details	Account number

Customer details	Account number

Customer details	Account number

If a multiple-value field is used for account number, these records for the same customer will compress into a single record:

Customer details	Account number	Account number	Account number

2. Periodic Groups

If we had a set of data items called "Account details" for an account, we could use a periodic group. The three records:

Customer number	Account details

Customer number	Account details

Customer number	Account details

could be compressed into a single record:

Customer number	Account details	Account details	Account details

When deciding the extent to which data duplication should be reduced, the high priority processing areas should be considered first. The aim is to keep all the fields required by a processing area in one record. Duplication of fields that are frequently updated should be avoided. As a general rule, however, duplication of short fields that are frequently accessed but rarely updated need not be removed. In fact, it is sometimes useful to build in this type of data duplication to assist performance.

3. Multiple Record Types within a File

Sometimes it is helpful to derive a record structure using multiple record types within a single file. Let the three records before splitting be:

Customer number	Customer details	Account details

Customer number	Customer details	Account details

Customer number	Customer details	Account details

Let us define a single file with two record types as:

Customer number	Customer details	E F C	Account details

Customer number	E F C	Customer details	Account details

(EFC: Empty field counter)

The record occurrences will be:

Customer number	Customer details	E F C

Customer number	E F C	Account details

Customer number	E F C	Account details

Customer number	E F C	Account details

} File 1

4. Multiple Files to Store the Data

The above situation could also be handled by splitting the data into two independent files. This requires duplicating the key item "customer number" only. The three records <u>before</u> splitting are:

Customer number	Customer details	Account details

Customer number	Customer details	Account details

Customer number	Customer details	Account details

<u>After</u> splitting the one file into two files, the records are:

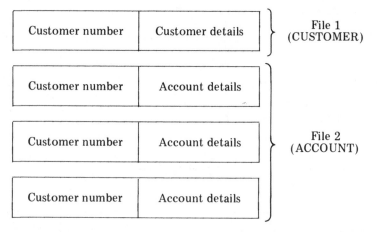

The question here is how many files should a data base consist of? In preceding chapters, the conceptual and the logical model for an inverted file data base management system consisted of a number of relations or "flat" files. The flat files in the physical model may be identical to the flat files in the logical model. Bigger numbers of "flat" files may result in shorter records, but at the same time considerable overhead may be incurred in switching files. This pertains largely to overhead in the programming effort.

Arguments in favor of multiple files are:

- Shorter records with fewer fields reduce I/O counts and elapsed time, since data blocks contain more records.

- The multiple files may result in more data independence and flexibility in extending data structures.

Arguments against multiple files are:

- Data may have to be retrieved from a number of files. This is somewhat less efficient in terms of I/O, CPU time, and programming development time.
- There may be a need to couple files to use search criteria from more than one file. There is a disk storage overhead for coupling and additional overhead in updating routines.

As a general rule, do not break out additional files unless doing so will improve the efficiency of a high priority processing area. It is unusual for a design to be optimum for all processing areas; therefore a compromise solution is normally the outcome of the design. The trade-off, however, should always favor the higher priority processing areas.

At this stage, after determining the layouts of the "flat" files, the physical records should be designed. The items to be considered are as follows.

II Which attributes should be inverted, that is, which fields should be defined as descriptors (keys)?

This is one of the basic questions to be answered for providing richness of the query facilities. But at the same time, each descriptor requires space for storage in the Associator inverted lists (as explained in Chapter 8) and processing time for updating. Descriptors should be defined, not just for convenience, but only where fully justified by retrieval requirements.

Guidelines for descriptor definition are:

- Descriptors that are always used together can be combined into a single superdescriptor. Retrieval can be achieved by specifying the combined value. By using one descriptor instead of two, space is saved in the Associator, and retrieval will be faster.
- If a descriptor is used for retrieval in combination with others and causes very little refinement in the records selected, it may be better not to have the field as a descriptor at all. The records selected on the basis of the other descriptors can be read to determine whether or not they satisfy this final criterion. Space is thereby saved in the Associator, and the

retrieval may be more efficient since there will be fewer search criteria and fewer inverted lists accessed. Also, updating overhead will be reduced.

- Descriptors should not be permitted to take values that are not used. In particular, the inclusion of null values must be avoided.

- Few-valued descriptors and descriptors that assume a particular value in most records correspond to long ISN (internal sequence number) lists in the Associator and are costly to retrieve. The best descriptors provide unique record identification.

- The selection of a descriptor when the inverted list itself may become a large data base should be avoided. A descriptor that will not "buy" much after the inversion should be avoided too. An example may be a file with "sex" as a descriptor. The descriptor can have only two values: "female" and "male." The corresponding inverted list is quite long and does not provide much benefit for unique selection.

- Descriptors that take a number of different values and have approximately uniform distribution as far as the number of records taking the specific values are concerned are good candidates for inversion. The main input for the decision-making process should be the needs of the enterprise for the queries involved.

III How many nondescriptor fields should be defined?

The number of fields defined in a record affects the CPU time needed for processing the commands.

- If two or more fields are always processed together, efficiency may be improved by defining them as a single field. Consider combining small contiguous fields.

- Do not store data that can be inexpensively derived. If the value of field Y is a simple function of field X, do not store field Y but derive its value by program, for example, Date of end of semester = Date of start of semester + 100 days.

IV How should the fields be ordered?

The order in which fields are defined in a record can affect the CPU time needed for processing.

- Define the most frequently used fields at the beginning of the record. Less CPU time is used in scanning the record to locate the data.
- Define fields in the sequence in which they are required by the major processing area.
- Group together fields that have a high possibility of being null and can be null suppressed.

V How much free space should be provided at the time of file loading? What consideration should be given to the file loading itself?

The free space provided at the time of loading affects not only disk space requirements but also CPU time, because of the number of records per block.

- For files with high update record activity, which causes records to grow in length, use larger free space. Conversely, for relatively static files, allot smaller free space.
- Have the physical sequence of records in the data storage correspond to the values of the descriptor field most heavily used for processing. Loading in this order reduces I/O counts, elapsed time, and CPU time in logical sequential processing.

VI How should the inverted list be organized and managed in storage?

If the inverted list itself is organized as a simple sequential file, the potential advantage of inversion is lost to a large extent. In large data bases, the inverted list itself may pose another file problem. In such a situation, a multilevel index should be provided. In most cases, for a given data base management system, the data base designer does not have too much choice as far as the organization of the index is concerned, since the organization and maintenance of the inverted list is under the control of the DBMS.

To reemphasize, the three areas where a data base designer needs expertise for performance estimation and tuning are:

1. Knowledge of the DBMS functions.
2. Understanding of the characteristics of direct access devices.
3. Knowledge of the applications.

9.3 EVALUATE THE PHYSICAL MODEL OF A DATA BASE

Evaluating the physical model prior to implementing the data base and writing any application code seems to be a desirable method of comparing design alternatives. In Section 9.2, we studied some trade-offs in the process of migration from the logical model to a physical model. As a result of trade-offs, there may be a number of alternative physical models that have to be evaluated. Two estimates that play a major role in the evaluation process are space and time. The emphasis here is on "desk checking."

The calculations made to answer the following questions often help in comparing the alternatives:

1. How many of each segment type or record type are there?
2. What is the average data base record size, and how large is the data base?

Since one of the factors affecting time is the number of physical I/Os necessary to carry out a CALL, it is necessary to know the probability that two segments or two records will be in different blocks or control intervals. With these probabilities and with the call patterns based on the applications, the designer is in a position to develop rough time estimates. We are not considering a data base that was loaded some time ago. Depending on its volatility, such a data base may consist of some fragmented space, some deleted parts of the data base records may still be occupying the physical space, and so on. The data base under consideration here is a newly loaded or a reorganized one. These basic facts about a data base also provide the usual side benefits of a programmed approach—consistent input, consistent output, and good documentation.

9.3.1 Space Estimates

A physical model can be evaluated only with detailed knowledge of a specific data base management system. Here we will consider IMS as the given DBMS. But the method of estimation of space, as well as of time, can be translated for most other DBMSs.

At this point in design, one is not concerned with precise calculation of total direct access storage device space. It is usually sufficient to deal only with segment storage. As a result, we will not compute any index storage needed by the access methods.

The following assumptions are made for the data base design analysis, which uses a "pencil and paper" method described below.

1. All data bases are as they were at initial load, or just after reorganization.
2. Segment sizes are small relative to blocksizes.
3. The child segment occurrence frequencies relative to the parents within a data base are independent random variables.
4. The segments are assumed to be of fixed length.
5. If not specified otherwise, the frequency distribution of a child segment under its parent is uniform.
6. Data base records with distinctly different patterns of segment occurrences are not treated. They should be modeled as separate cases.
7. The I/O estimates help the designer translate segment accesses into I/O. However, the translation of DL/1 CALLS into segment accesses has to be done with the help of the external models (called "logical" data bases in IMS) based on the internal model (called "physical" data bases in IMS).

The data base design analyzer will develop the space estimates and study the I/O characteristics. (See Figure 9.8). Knowing the I/O characteristics, the call patterns, and the unit path length (i.e., the number of instructions necessary to carry out a CALL) it should provide quantitative estimates of DL/1 (Data Language/1 is the data base control part and the Data Manipulation Language of IMS) performance.

The basic facts necessary for estimating the space are the answers to these questions:

1. What is the hierarchy? (In a CODASYL data base management system, it will be necessary to know the set constructs.)
2. What is the length of every segment type? Here we consider not only the data length but the space taken by pointers too. The pointers used may be physical or logical ones, for example, Physical Child First, Physical Child Last, Physical Twin Forwards, Logical Child First, Logical Child Last and Logical Parent. (In a CODASYL data base management system the pointers may be NEXT, PRIOR, OWNER, etc.)
3. What is the expected relative frequency of occurrence of every segment type relative to its parent? The length of a data base

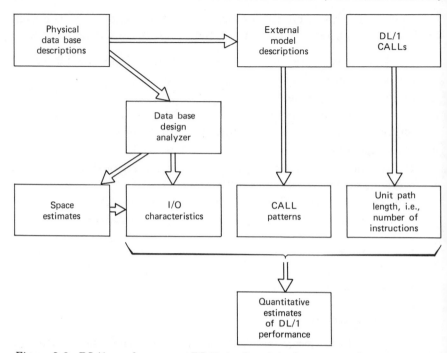

Figure 9.8 DL/1 performance. DL/1 is the data base control part and data manipulation language of IMS. The external model is called a "logical data base" in IMS.

record depends not only on the segment types in the data base but also (and mainly) on the segment occurrences. With the same reasoning, the distance between any two segment occurrences depends on the number of segment occurrences between them.

Using these factors, the designer can find:

1. The average physical data base record size in bytes.
2. The size of the data base.

IMS uses the hierarchical tree structure as its basic data model. A tree is composed of a number of "subtrees." Since the hierarchical tree structure is an "upside-down" tree, we will take the bottom-up approach. The subtree of a segment A (S_A) is defined as one occurrence of A and occurrences of all its dependents. The subtree size of

A (S_A) is then A's own length and the total of all the lengths of its dependents.

The space required on the direct access storage device is calculated in terms of SEGMENT BYTES, that is, the bytes occupied by the segments. SEGMENT BYTES is computed using the concept of a subtree.

In Figure 9.9, there are 2000 occurrences of segment A, and, for each occurrence of segment A, on an average 5 occurrences of segment B and 50 occurrences of segment C. With the bottom-up approach:

S_B (subtree of B) = 30, S_C (subtree of C) = 15,   and

S_A (subtree of A) = 1000

Figure 9.10 gives the subtree size of the isolated segment type X. The subtree size of any isolated segment type X is

$$S_x = L_x + (F_1 \times S_1) + (F_2 \times S_2) + \cdots + (F_N \times S_N)$$

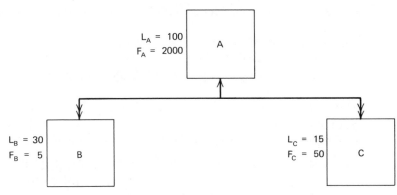

L = length of segment (including prefix)

F = relative frequency of occurrence of segment per occurrence of its parent

S = subtree size

    Subtree size of a segment is one occurrence of the segment and all occurrences of all its dependents.

Calculate from the bottom up.

$$S_B = 30$$
$$S_C = 15$$
$$S_A = 100 + (5 \times S_B) + (50 \times S_C)$$
$$= 1000$$

Figure 9.9 Estimation of the average physical data base record size.

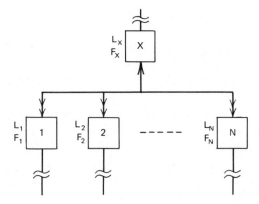

L = length of segment (including prefix)

F = relative frequency of occurrence of segment per occurrence of its parent

The subtree size of segment X is

$$S_X = L_X + (F_1 \times S_1) + (F_2 \times S_2) + \cdots + (F_N \times S_N)$$

Figure 9.10 **Determination of the subtree size of any isolated segment type X.**

The subtree size of the root is the same as the average physical data base record size. This leads the designer to the SEGMENT BYTES, that is, the number of bytes needed by the segments of the data base.

SEGMENT BYTES
= root subtree size
× frequency of occurrence of the root segment type

Estimate of the SEGMENT BYTES in Figure 9.9 = 1000 × 2000
= 2 million bytes.

The disk space to be used in bytes is dependent on the blocksize specified (BLK), the fraction of each block left free at load or reorganization time (FSW), the fraction of whole blocks left free at load time (FSB) or at reorganization time, and the end of block waste due to not splitting segments (W). (See Figure 9.11.)

As a result of FSW, FSB, and W, the effective blocksize is smaller than the specified blocksize.

Effective blocksize = [((1 − FSW) × BLK) − W] × (1 − FSB)

The bytes to be stored are SEGMENT BYTES. As a result of the effective blocksize being smaller than the blocksize assigned, the number of blocks necessary for storing the SEGMENT BYTES is bigger than anticipated. The BLOCK BYTES are obtained from the

DASD space to be used in bytes =
f(BLK, FSW, FSB, W)

BLK = blocksize (CI: control interval size
for VSAM)

FSW = free space within; fraction of each
block left free at load

FSB = free space blocks; fraction of whole
blocks left free at load

W = end of block waste due to not splitting segments

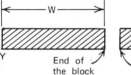

Y   End of   Beginning of
the block   another block

Figure 9.11 **W is the end of block waste. The segment with the length of the shaded areas does not fit at the end of the block. The distance between the point Y and the end of the block is W.**

SEGMENT BYTES by adjusting for free space and the unused space at the end of a block resulting from not splitting segments:

$$\text{BLOCK BYTES} = \text{SEGMENT BYTES} \times \frac{\text{blocksize}}{\text{effective blocksize}}$$

To find the distribution of W, two cases can be distinguished:

Case I. All the segments have the same length L in bytes.

Case II. The segments have different lengths L_X, where L_X is the length of segment X in bytes.

The essential information for space calculation is the physical hierarchical structure, that is, the parent-child relationships, the segment sizes, the data and the prefix, the segment frequencies relative to the parents, and any indexing relationships. The space computations are based on blocksize (control interval size for VSAM), free space, and data set grouping.

Case I. All the segments have the same length L in bytes.

BLK = block size

FSW = free space within block, the fraction of each block left free at load.

W = $(1 - \text{FSW}) \times \text{BLK mod.*}$ L

*mod. = "modulo." X mod. $Y = \begin{Bmatrix} 0 \\ n \end{Bmatrix}$, where n is the remainder of the division $X \div Y$ and $n < Y$.

Example 1.

L = 100 bytes
BLK = 4000 bytes
FSW = 10%, i.e., 400 bytes/block left free; at the initial load
    only 3600 bytes of each block will be used
W = (1 - 0.1) $\times$ 4000 mod. 100
  = 0

There is no end of block waste.

Case I
Example 2

L = 110 bytes
BLK = 4000 bytes
FSW = 10%
W = (1 - 0.1) $\times$ 4000 mod. 110
  = 80 bytes/block

Because of not splitting segments, 80 bytes/block will be wasted.

Case II. The segments have different lengths L_X, where L_X is
the length of segment X in bytes.

If simulation is carried out with the segments loaded in the blocks in
a hierarchical sequence, the exact waste of bytes can be calculated.
The simulation process would be extremely time consuming, however, and probably not worth the effort.
    The pessimistic average estimate of W per block is the length of
the longest segment in bytes - 1.
    The optimistic average estimate of W per block is the length of
the shortest segment in bytes - 1.

Case II
Example

FSW = 0.15
FSB = 0.10
BLK = 4096

Subtree size S_B = 30
Subtree size S_C = 15
Subtree size S_A = 100 + (5 $\times$ S_B) + (50 $\times$ S_C)
                  = 1000

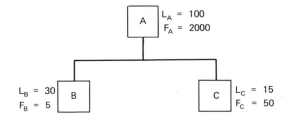

SEGMENT BYTES = $F_A \times S_A$ = 2,000,000
Estimated W = 99

$$\text{BLOCK BYTES} = \frac{2,000,000}{((1 - 0.15) \times 4096 - 99) \times 0.9} \times 4096$$

$$= 2,690,000$$

∴ DASD space is required for 2,690,000 bytes.

9.3.2 Time Estimates

In most data base management systems, one of the biggest time consumers in the execution of data base calls is physical I/O activity. In IMS every logical data base ("external model" in ANSI terminology) is composed of a physical data base or a number of physical data bases ("internal model(s)" in ANSI terminology). For a given application the access patterns can be estimated. Based on the access patterns, the sequence in which the segments are accessed is known. To access segment B from segment A, one needs to know all the segments that have to be touched on the way. One can estimate the number of I/Os necessary for accessing segment B from segment A if the probabilities of I/Os are known for all the intermediate segments that must be touched. If unit I/O time is known, it is possible to estimate the I/O time necessary for execution of the data base call when segment B has to be accessed from segment A.

The hierarchy of a physical data base, the length of every segment type, the expected frequency of occurrence of every segment type relative to its parent, and the sequence of segment accesses for a specific application can be used as input for finding the I/O activity necessary to access the required segments. The I/O activity needed to access the required segments also depends on the distance between the two desired segments, blocksize, buffer pool, and so on.

In DL/1 (which is composed of the data base controlling component of IMS and of Data Manipulation Language), the pointers are embedded in the segments. The accessing of segment B from segment

A is accomplished by using the pointers stored in the intermediate segments.

In HISAM data bases, the I/Os necessary for retrieving segment B from segment A can be calculated by summing the I/Os required for touching all the intermediate segments between A and B. There is no direct path between A and B, but the hierarchical order. For the direct access methods (HIDAM and HDAM), the possible pointers used may be physical child, physical twin, physical parent, logical child, logical twin, and logical parent. Since most of the segments related by logical relationships, which may be using logical child, logical twin, and logical parent pointers, are located in different physical records, the probability of I/O can be assumed to be 1 when using a logical relationship. An exception to this assumption may be made for any known physical relationships between the segments related logically.

The probability that the parent and the first occurrence of the child segment under the parent are not in the same block (called "control interval" for virtual storage access method: VSAM) is "PCIO" (physical child input/output). The assumption made here is that all occurrences of the child segment type are selected equally likely. The probability that a segment and its twin are not in the same block is "PTIO" (physical twin input/output). Finally, the probability that the segment and its parent are not in the same block is "PPIO" (physical parent input/output).

For an isolated parent-child relationship, as in Figure 9.12, the segment access paths between a segment of type A and a segment of type B are A to its first child B, B to its twin, and B to its parent A. The probability that segments A and B are in two different blocks depends on the distance between them, which is called the "SEGMENT DISTANCE." PCIO is dependent on the PC (physical child) bytes (SEGMENT DISTANCE) and the effective blocksize.

For HDAM overflow and for HIDAM:

$$PCIO_{A,B} = \min.\left(1, \frac{PC_{A,B}}{[((1 - FSW) \times BLK) - W] \times (1 - FSB)}\right)$$

For HISAM:

$$\text{Number of } I/O_{A,B} = \left(\sum_{X=A}^{Y=B} \text{probability } IO_{X,Y}\right) \times 100$$

for every intermediate segment between A and B in the hierarchy, if probability $IO_{X,Y}$ is calculated to two decimal places.

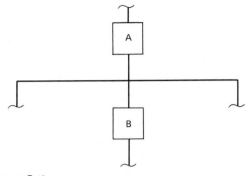

Segment Access Paths

- A to first B with PCF.
- B to next B with PTF.
- B to A with PP.

Segment distance from A to first B (i.e., from the end of A to the end of B):

$PC_{A,B}$ = length of B + all subtrees to left of B

$$PCIO_{A,B} = \min.\left(1, \frac{PC_{A,B}}{[((1 - FSW) \times BLK) - W] \times (1 - FSB)}\right)$$

$PCIO_{A,B}$ = 1 if A and B are in two different data set groups

where FSW = percentage of free space within block, W = end of block waste

BLK = blocksize (control interval for VSAM),

FSB = percentage of whole blocks left free at load time

Figure 9.12

In Figure 9.12, the segment distance between A and its immediate physical twin is the subtree size of segment A. The physical twin (PT) distance for segment A is the subtree size of A.

$$\text{PTIO for segment type A} = \min.\left(1, \frac{S_A}{\text{effective blocksize}}\right)$$

$$PTIO_A = \min.\left(1, \frac{\text{subtree size of segment A}}{[((1 - FSW) \times BLK) - W] \times (1 - FSB)}\right)$$

where FSW = percentage of free space within a block,
      W = end of block waste
      BLK = blocksize (control interval for VSAM)
      FSB = percentage of whole blocks left free at load time
For HDAM overflow and HIDAM:

$$PTIO_A = \min.\left(1, \frac{S_A}{[((1 - FSW) \times BLK) - W] \times (1 - FSB)}\right)$$

For HISAM:

$$\text{Number of I/O}_A = \left(\frac{S_A}{(1 - FSW) \times BLK}\right) \times 100$$

if

$$\frac{S_A}{[((1 - FSW) \times BLK) - W] \times (1 - FSB)}$$

is calculated to two decimal places.

The following assumptions are made in using the PTIO_A to estimate the number of I/Os required for reaching the desired segment from the twin chain:

1. Every twin segment is equally likely to be selected.
2. The desired segment has an unknown position in the twin chain.
3. The expected number of segments to be touched before reaching the desired segment of the twin chain is equal to one-half the average number of segment occurrences in the twin chain.

In Figure 9.13, the segment distance between any B and its parent A is dependent on B's length, all the subtrees of the siblings before B (from the hierarchical order), and all the subtrees left to B (also from the hierarchical order). The PP (physical parent) distance is to be calculated for the segment Bi, that is, the distance between Bi and A.

$$PP_{Bi, A} = L_{Bi} \text{ (i.e., } B_i\text{'s own length in bytes)}$$
$$+ \text{ (subtree of the sibling } B_1 \text{)}$$
$$+ \text{ (subtree of the sibling } B_2 \text{)} + \cdots$$
$$+ \text{ (subtree of the sibling } B_{i-1} \text{)}$$
$$+ \text{ all the subtrees to the left of B}$$

For the sake of simplicity we will assume that Bi is the middle segment of all the occurrences of B. For any occurrence of B:

$$PP_{B, A} = L_B + \left(\frac{f_B}{2} \times S_B\right) + \text{ all the subtrees to the left of B}$$

$$PPIO_{B, A} = \min. \left(1, \frac{PP_{B,A}}{[((1 - FSW) \times BLK) - W] \times (1 - FSB)}\right)$$

PCIO, PTIO, and PPIO are valid for HDAM if both segments, that is, the "from and to," are in overflow. The factors affecting the I/O activity for HDAM are byte limit, data base record size, block-

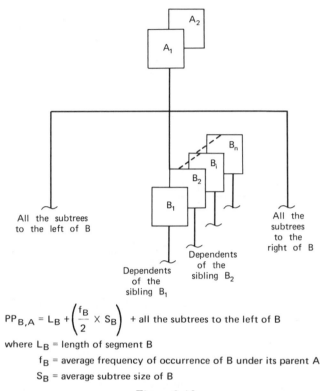

$$PP_{B,A} = L_B + \left(\frac{f_B}{2} \times S_B\right) + \text{all the subtrees to the left of B}$$

where L_B = length of segment B

f_B = average frequency of occurrence of B under its parent A

S_B = average subtree size of B

Figure 9.13

size (control interval size for VSAM), number of root anchor points per block, and number of roots that may be placed in a block, that is, the ratio of number of roots to number of blocks in the root addressable area. Because of the unique aspects of HDAM, it is necessary to calculate the average number of I/Os for retrieval of the root, average number of synonyms that must be read to retrieve an HDAM root, and probability of overflow of a given segment occurrence.

A DL/1 CALL can be exploded into a number of segment calls. In Figure 9.14, a DL/1 CALL is to retrieve a specific Z for a specific Y when positioned at a specific X:

$$\text{Number of I/Os} = \left[PCIO_{X,Y} + \left(PTIO_Y \times \left(\frac{f_Y}{2} - 1\right)\right)\right]$$

$$+ \left[PCIO_{Y,Z} + \left(PTIO_Z \times \left(\frac{f_Z}{2} - 1\right)\right)\right] \times 100,$$

if PCIO and PTIO are adjusted to two decimal places.

Figure 9.15 is an example of the calculations of PCIO and PTIO.

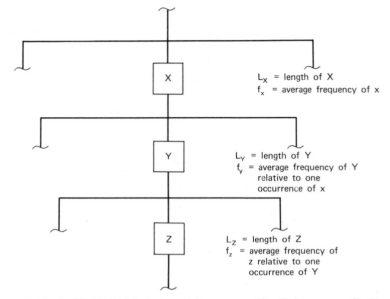

L_X = length of X
f_x = average frequency of x

L_Y = length of Y
f_y = average frequency of Y
relative to one
occurrence of x

L_Z = length of Z
f_z = average frequency of
z relative to one
occurrence of Y

Figure 9.14 A DL/1 CALL is to retrieve a specific Z for a specific Y when positioned on X.

9.3.3 Data Base Applications

In estimating the time requirements for the data base applications, the major batch programs, the high volume transactions, and the transactions with critical response time specifications should be studied. The objective of the analysis is to estimate the average CPU time and the I/O time required for processing a transaction or for executing a specific CALL from the batch program. The primary objective of the analysis in the design phase is to locate the transactions that use the CPU and I/O time the most and to provide a comparison of the design alternatives for better performance. In our paper and pencil method, the CPU time and I/O time are estimated for a stand-alone, noncontention environment.

The analysis should be done for one CALL at a time; for example, for DL/1 two of the CALLs are GU (Get Unique) and GN (Get Next). The CALL should be exploded to the segment or to the record level. In the case of DL/1, the segments, the logical records, and the I/O activities are used for calculating the estimates.

With the help of input such as the external models, the internal model, the access patterns for transactions, the I/O probabilities, the unit times for the possible data base calls (which have to be provided

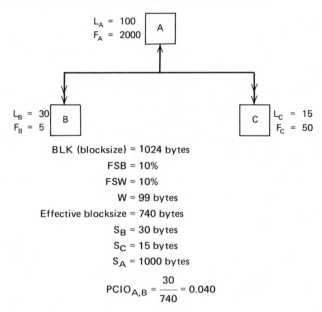

BLK (blocksize) = 1024 bytes

FSB = 10%

FSW = 10%

W = 99 bytes

Effective blocksize = 740 bytes

S_B = 30 bytes

S_C = 15 bytes

S_A = 1000 bytes

$$PCIO_{A,B} = \frac{30}{740} = 0.040$$

that is, if B is accessed from A, out of 100 times most probably 4 times I/Os will be required.

$$PCIO_{A,C} = \frac{15 + 5 \times 30}{740} = 0.223$$

that is, if C is accessed from A, out of 100 times most probably 23 times I/Os will be required.

$$PTIO_A = \min. \left(1, \frac{1000}{740}\right) = 1$$

$$PTIO_B = \min. \left(1, \frac{30}{740}\right) = 0.040$$

$$PTIO_C = \min. \left(1, \frac{15}{740}\right) = 0.020$$

Figure 9.15

by the vendor of the DBMS used), and the unit times for the I/O, it is possible to estimate the CPU time and the I/O time required for the specific transactions.

The estimation process at the level explained in this section requires a knowledge of the data base management system at the pointer level and some familiarity with data base internals. At the internal model level, it is hardly possible to estimate performance in general. Therefore a representative data base management system, IMS, was taken as an example.

REFERENCES

1. *The IMS Data Base/Application Design Review*, Esther L. Dechow and Don C. Lundberg, Technical Bulletin, October 1977, Order No. G320-6009, IBM Palo Alto Systems Center, Palo Alto, California.

2. *The IMS Data Base/Application Design Review—Errata*, E. M. Gearhart, Technical Bulletin, January 1978, Order No. G320-6012, IBM Palo Alto Systems Center, Palo Alto, California.

3. "Analysis and Performance of Inverted Data Base Structures," Alfonso F. Cardenas (IBM Research Laboratory, San Jose, California), *Communications of the ACM*, Vol. 18, No. 5 (May 1975).

4. *The CODASYL Approach to Data Base Management*, T. William Olle, A Wiley-Interscience Publication, John Wiley & Sons, 1978.

5. *The Art of Computer Programming*, Vol. 3; *Sorting and Searching*, Donald E. Knuth, Addison-Wesley Publishing Company, 1973.

6. *Computer Data Base Organization*, James Martin, Prentice-Hall, 1977.

7. *Database Design*, Gio Wiederhold, McGraw-Hill Book Company, 1977.

8. *Pointers in Simple Hierarchical Structured Data*, Sakti P. Ghosh, IBM Research Paper RJ 1775.

9. *Analysis of Data Base Design for Performance*, R. G. Brown, SHARE XLV, Vol. II.

10. DBPROTOTYPE/II, Order No. G320-1535, SH20-1391, IBM Data Processing Division, 1133 Westchester Avenue, White Plains, New York 10604.

11. *ADABAS Design Guide*, Software AG of North America, Inc., Reston International Center, 11800 Sunrise Valley Drive, Reston, Virginia 22091.

12. *Data Base Management System, Administrator's Procedures Manual*, Order No. AA-4146B-TM, DELSYSTEM, Digital Equipment Corporation, 200 Forest Street, Marlboro, Massachusetts 01752.

13. *Data Base Management System, Programmer's Procedures Manual*, Order No. AA-4149B-TM, DECSYSTEM, Digital Equipment Corporation, 200 Forest Street, Marlboro, Massachusetts 01752.

Performance
Issues

Once the physical design is evaluated, it can be implemented. The structure of the physical design, the specifications of the access methods, and several details about retrieving, updating, adding, and deleting the data have to be supplied to the data base management system. Some of the existing data files will be converted and integrated into the physical data base. A number of performance issues need to be considered in the implementation phase.

The day-to-day chores will be performed on the implemented data base. Since software as well as hardware may fail, it is absolutely necessary to have established recovery and backup procedures in every data base environment. The best physical design in the world cannot provide consistently good performance for a volatile data base despite the self-reorganizing features of some data base management systems. Most DBMS packages provide reorganization routines, and the physical design of the data base must be evaluated with the possible reorganization in mind. There is also a need for continuous and long-term monitoring of service delivered by the data base environment. The data collected from these tools can be used for performance tuning. It is also mandatory to provide a certain measure of security and privacy, which will vary from environment to environment, even at the cost of some performance.

10.1 IMPLEMENTATION

10.1.1 Physical Creation

Usually it is not the best implementation strategy to store the data regarding the entire enterprise in one gigantic data base. Rather, it is advisable to describe the conceptually separate units of the enterprise in separate data bases. At the same time it may be advisable to provide "linkages" between these separate physical data bases. The actual storage of data in auxiliary storage with the physical design as the framework is called a "physical data base" in IMS terminology. As we saw in Chapter 8, however, ADABAS supports a number of files, and these files can be related to each other via a "coupling" feature. It is realistic to store the data regarding the entire enterprise in several physical data bases with a corresponding physical design underlying each physical data base. The existence of a number of physical data bases should not be the concern of the application programmers. The DBMS is the "black box" that supports the logical view or external model seen by the application programmer.

Two basic issues that need considerable attention are the options to be provided in the physical implementation and the physical placement of the data bases. One may go to the extreme of saying, "Show me a poorly performing data base, and you will find a poorly placed data base."

Almost every DBMS lets the data base implementor choose a number of combinations from a spectrum of possible options. The major issue here is which combination to pick to meet the desired performance level. The implementor faces almost the same dilemma as does a child in a candy store with limited money in his/her pocket.

We saw a number of alternatives for physical data structures in Chapter 9. Other options are available in splitting a data base into a number of data bases or parts. Should the volatile part of the data base be separated from the nonvolatile part? Also, should any free space be provided at the time of initial loading or at the time of reorganization of a data base, and, if so, how much, and how should it be distributed? Free space provided may degrade performance today but be helpful for performance 6 months from now. How big should be the blocksize (control interval size for VSAM), and how big the logical record length? A large blocksize enhances the probability of finding two segments or two records in the same block. But what if the application does not require the two segments or two records to be in the same block? Then it will just take longer for a channel to transfer the big block of data without gaining any benefit from it.

How large should the buffers be and how many should exist? Buffers take away storage from real memory. One of the major issues in designing the physical structure of the data base is pointers, which use storage. As a result of using pointers, the distance between segments or records widens. But at the same time faster access from one record to another record is provided. If the implementor does not select the pointers, most DBMSs provide default pointers and sometimes, with the defaults, some surprises.

Most DBMSs provide a number of access methods to choose from. For some DBMSs one access method has to be selected for the entire data base, whereas for others different methods may be chosen for accessing different parts of the data base. Should the records of a data base be accessed sequentially or with the help of an index or directly, using some hashing algorithm? For some applications it may be advisable to access the records sequentially; for others, directly. The pointers to be chosen to reside in the data base records depend on the access method chosen. Although most DBMSs provide some kind of software with which the organization and access method can be changed, this change may be quite time consuming. In the data base environment, there is nothing better than getting things right the first time.

Another option that has to be considered is whether any compaction technique should be used. With some DBMSs and with some access methods, when a data base record is deleted, it is deleted logically and not physically. If the activity of deletion of data base records is heavy, a considerable part of the space on auxiliary storage may be unused. This unused space may widen the distance between the active data base records, resulting in longer time for retrieval. The question to be answered is whether compaction should be done on a daily basis during the third shift, on a weekly basis, or on a monthly basis or should be postponed until performance becomes unacceptable as a result of a "disorganized" data base.

Another basic issue that affects the performance of a data base is the placement. Most of the data is stored on auxiliary storage. Methods for giving fast response include combinations of the following:

1. Storing frequently referenced data on fast devices.
2. Positioning data so that lengthy seeks are avoided where possible.
3. Selection of address and search schemes that require few seeks, preferably only one per retrieval.
4. Use of multiple operations in parallel.

In space allocation and placement, it should be considered whether to separate index and data and put them on separate volumes. Before placing a data base on a device, an analysis of device and channel activity for other data processing should be made. It should be determined which applications or transactions refer to the data base and to part of the data base concurrently. It should also not be forgotten that a voluminous data base, if not required to be kept on-line, may be stored on magnetic tape(s).

10.1.2 Conversion and Integration

One of the biggest cost factors of the data base environment is the conversion of data from the existing data files to a data base. In most environments, the data to be converted will exist in different formats scattered across a number of data files. There will be a considerable redundancy in the stored data. To move the scattered data to a central data base, a number of application programs will have to be written. It will not be easy to justify the considerable programmer time required to write these programs.

The programs to be written for the conversion are not trivial. They have to access a large number of data files, with redundant data. Only part of the data files are extracted in certain situations. Time is needed to understand the conversion "from" and "to," and writing the application code, testing and revising it, and coordinating a number of programs is not a trivial job. Management of an enterprise has to be aware of the fact that acquisition of a DBMS is not the end but rather the beginning of a commitment.

Another major issue that should not be forgotten during the process of conversion and integration is that the data has to be validated and then the data base must be populated. Errors in the data conversion will have long lasting effects.

As a result, conversion to a data base is not a one-time shot. The conversion process is incremental. The enterprise and its various disciplines have to function during the process of conversion on the existing data files. The enterprise cannot shut its doors during the time period, which may extend over months, of conversion from data files to a data base. Application programs and the data manipulated by them will be transferred gradually to the data base as new application programs for the data base are written.

Most DBMSs do not provide a general purpose software to convert the existing data files to a data base, although some load utilities and aids are provided. The major obstacle in providing a tool for conversion is nonuniformity of data files in different environments. Most enterprises have developed data files tailored to their needs. Some research is being done in this area, however, and one of the results is EXPRESS: A Data EXtraction, Processing and REStructuring System. (See reference 1 in the list at the end of the chapter.) EXPRESS can access and restructure data from multiple files and produce multiple restructured files in a single run.

In most environments, it may be advisable to redesign the existing applications to be able to take advantage of the data base approach. In some environments, however, it may be advisable to let the existing applications alone and use the data base approach for new applications. But wherever conversion and integration is undertaken, it should work only on a small part of the functions of the enterprise. As with every project, there is a learning curve involved, and the most important and visible applications should not be the guinea pigs! To make any conversion project successful, standards should be adhered to strictly. But at the same time the standards should be easy to adhere to and adequate.

Any conversion and integration project is made up of two parts. One part is the data file conversion, and the other is the application program conversion. In the conversion phase, it may be necessary to maintain the same data in conventional data files for current operation of the business and in the data base for future use. This puts almost a double load on the maintenance staff. In most environments, it will be necessary to rewrite the application programs for the data base environment. Moreover, the application programs for a data base require different program writing habits than do the programs for a conventional environment. As a result there is a need for retraining on the part of application programmers.

10.2 OPERATIONS

10.2.1 Backup and Recovery

Once a data base is implemented, one of the major concerns of management is keeping it up and available to users. The major components of a data base environment are the operating system, data base management system, application programs, transactions for an on-line environment, hardware, and users. In a data base environment, damage to the data base has to be taken more seriously than in the conventional data file environment. In the latter environment, if one data file is damaged, there may be ways of reconstructing the damaged data because of its probable multiple appearance in various data files. In a data base environment, however, there may be a chain reaction in a number of places in the data base as a result of damage to data in one place. The following steps should be considered for backup and recovery.

STEP 1.   Detecting the error that damaged the data base. At what time did the error take place? Which part of the data base was damaged? What or who triggered the error? The application program, the transaction, the logical and the physical terminal in an on-line environment, or the user?

STEP 2.   Tracing all the activity against the data base that took place between the occurrence of the damage and the correction of the damage.

STEP 3.   Restoring the data base to the most recent error-free stage and running all the activity detected in step 2.

In addition to these three steps, it may be wise on the part of management to establish a mechanism that will not let an error, as detected above, happen. "Prevention is better than cure" holds for the data base environment too.

To recover to the error-free stage, a backup copy of the "healthy" (i.e., undamaged) data base at a certain point in time has to be kept. In addition, a log of all the activities that took place against the data base after that point in time must be maintained. Merging the backup copy of the data base and all the activities against it should result in an accurate indication of the current state.

Most DBMSs provide a facility, called "logging," that records all the activities against the data base on a "log tape" or on an exchangeable disk. As the reader can imagine, a lot of information will be stored on the log tape, and the installation will need a number of log tapes.

The main components of the information stored on a log tape in a transaction-oriented environment may be:

1. **Transaction Record (Input and Output).** This component includes transaction identification, such as user identification, logical terminal identification, time of day, and date; input

message, such as type of transaction to be processed and input message of the transaction; and output message, such as whether the transaction was completed successfully and list of blocks read.

2. **Before Images.** Whenever a change is made to the data base, the DBMS can write a copy of what the block, segment, page, or record looked like before the change. When a failure occurs, the DBMS can remove changes by writing these "before" copies (usually called "before images") back into the data base. This kind of restoration "rolls back" the data base from one point in time to an earlier point.

3. **After Images.** In a manner similar to writing before images, the DBMS can write copies that show the changes made. Thus, if a data base is damaged, these copies can be added to a backup copy of the data base. This kind of restoration "rolls forward" the data base from a point in time when it is known to be correct to a later time.

Before step 2, the access control mechanisms have to check whether the user is authorized to request the changes. If she/he is not authorized, the transaction should be interrupted without making any changes to the data base record. Log tapes may be used for auditing. They may also be used for checking the integrity of data in the data base by inspecting the before and after images for given transactions.

Checkpoints. If backing out is necessary for certain transactions or application programs because of the detection of an error, it may be quite time consuming to start the transaction or the application program from the beginning. To be able to start at certain points in the execution, "checkpoints" may be taken. In case of a possible backout, it may be possible to go back to the latest checkpoint instead of all the way to the beginning of the execution.

In on-line environments, checkpointing may be cumbersome because of concurrent processes. All the processes have to be made "inactive" before taking a checkpoint. In some environments where all the processes cannot be made inactive, checkpointing is done on individual processes separately. These checkpoints have to be synchronized at the time of recovery.

Checkpointing results in a degrading of performance. There is a trade-off between the number of checkpoints and the time interval between two checkpoints; the higher the number of checkpoints, the greater is the degradation of performance but the easier the recovery. If the time interval between two checkpoints is long, the degradation of performance is less at the cost of more difficult recovery.

The timing of checkpoints may depend on a number of factors:

1. An operator should issue a checkpoint command.
2. The system should automatically take a checkpoint after a certain time interval; the time interval may vary during the day. At the "peak" load the time span between two checkpoints may be smaller than for a "sluggish" load.
3. A checkpoint should be taken by the system after a certain number of changes to the data base.
4. A checkpoint should be taken by the system after a certain number of records are written out to the log tape or after a certain number of transactions have been processed.

In some environments, if these backup facilities are not sufficient, two identical copies of the data base should be maintained. The updating by the system has to be such that the two copies are identical.

The log tape or the journal is a way of backing up to an error-free stage of the data base if a recovery has to take place. The recovery process starts at the point where an error is discovered. The detection of the error (i.e., "What went wrong?") and the determination of the error source (i.e., "Who did it?") may be time consuming and may require considerable manual intervention.

If there is a system crash, the time period of incorrect operation is usually small. But if there is error detection on the basis of incorrect output, there may be a long time interval between occurrence and detection of error. In the latter case, considerable detective work may be necessary to restore the data base to an error-free stage.

Unfortunately, errors usually take place in groups. What happens if the log tape itself cannot be read properly? This means that a backup of a backup has to be provided. In most environments, however, multiple errors occur because proper attention is not paid to single errors. It is the data base administrator's responsibility to provide adequate backup and recovery procedures and see to it that they are followed.

10.2.2 Reorganization

In most data base environments, it will be necessary from time to time to clean up the data base. After the initial loading or after the reloading of the data base, there will be unused space between the valid records as a result of a deletion of some records. There will also be some fragmentation of space. Inserted records will not necessarily be stored in the logical sequence, and this may result in the creation of long chains. The fetch or sequential processing time may become excessive. Most DBMSs provide reorganization routines to rearrange the untidy data base in order to reclaim space occupied by deleted data and to move records from overflow areas to free space in prime data areas. The basic activities involved in the reorganization of a data base are copying the old data base onto another device, excluding records marked "deleted"; reblocking the valid records; and reloading them. One side effect of reorganization is that it provides a backup copy of the data base.

At the time of reorganization, it may also be possible to rearrange records so that, for most of them, their physical sequence is the same as their logical sequence. It may also be possible to rearrange the records so that the more frequently accessed ones are stored on a high speed medium, whereas the rarely accessed records are stored on a slower speed medium.

In the case of a sequentially organized data base, reorganization means taking the old data base and the transaction log file and combining the two into a new data base, omitting any data base records marked "deleted" on the transaction log file. In the case of an indexed sequentially organized data base, reorganization means taking the entire data base from the prime and overflow areas and reloading the data base without any records in the overflow areas. In the case of a directly organized data base, reorganization means moving the records from the overflow areas physically closer to the records from the prime area with the same synonyms. This will also recover space lost because of fragmentation. With most DBMSs, the access methods with direct organization reclaim space used by the deleted segments or records on an ongoing basis. As a result, reorganization is probably needed much less frequently for a data base using direct organization than for one with sequential or indexed sequential organization.

Ideally, reorganization should be under direct control of the DBMS on a continuous basis. As records are deleted, the space should be reclaimed automatically. The DBMS should be monitoring the changes to different sectors of the data base, and after a certain threshold of changes and insertions is reached, reorganization should take place for the corresponding sectors.

In most data base environments, although certain organization methods reclaim deleted space on a continuous basis, reorganization of the data base is a major effort. The frequency of reorganization varies from environment to environment. The major causes of frequent reorganizations may be heavy activity of insertions and deletions of data base records, failure to provide sufficient free space for later insertions at the time of initial loading or reloading of the data base, incorrect selection of the organization and access methods, and incorrect selection of storage media.

Reorganization should take place when the overflow area exceeds a certain percentage of utilization and the average daily increase in the overflow area reaches a certain percentage. These percentages vary from environment to environment. The DBMSs provide statistics about the utilization and increase of the overflow area.

The major impact of reorganization on users is the "downtime" or unavailability of the data base. Here the DBA has two choices: either reorganize the data base on a continuous basis at the cost of some unavailability of the data base to the users, or reach the stage, without any reorganization, where more and more hardware has to be added to keep the same performance requirements. In some cases, more hardware is the only choice.

10.2.3 Restructuring

It is conceivable that in a dynamic environment, after a data base has been in operations phase for some time, the usage pattern of the data base has changed relative to the initial design and anticipation. The priorities of data base applications, transactions, and performance requirements have changed. The basic entities and relationships between them may not have deviated drastically, but the way in which the entities and their relationships are modeled may need restructuring. Besides the changes to the original structure, it is also possible that the data base needs expansion, not relative to the volume of data but relative to the addition of new record types, new data elements, and so on.

Implementing changes at the logical model and at the internal (physical) model levels is called "restructuring." Changing the access control and data base procedures may be categorized as restructuring too. The basic difference between reorganization and restructuring may be stated through the following analogy. Reorganization is something like "spring cleaning" a house, with the restoring of misplaced items like clothes, books, toys, and tools to their proper preassigned places and the throwing away of accumulated junk. Restructuring on the other hand, is like expanding a house with an attic or a basement for a family that has grown bigger, providing new passages between some rooms, and so on. Reorganization basically does not affect the existing applications or procedures, whereas restructuring may affect them.

Let us distinguish between three types of restructuring changes: procedural changes, physical level (internal model) changes, and logical level changes.

1. **Procedural Changes**

    Backup and Recovery. Any changes to the procedures will affect the operations staff only.

    Access Control. If, for some business reason, any of the access control procedures relative to security, privacy, or integrity is changed, the users will be affected. If any of the access controls to be changed is anchored in applications, the applications must be changed.

2. **Physical Level Changes**

    Hardware Configuration or Data Base Placement Changes. It may be possible that statistics from performance monitoring indicates that the hardware configuration relative to channels and direct access storage devices (DASDs) should be restructured to minimize contention. It may also be possible that, for better performance, a data base has to be split into two or more data bases. The placement of the data bases must be reconsidered. Changes of this nature do not affect the existing applications as far as modification is concerned.

    Reconfiguration of pointers. Before a data base can be implemented, specification of pointers used is presented to the DBMS with the internal model. (In IMS the physical and logical pointers are specified at the physical data base description level; for CODASYL systems NEXT, PRIOR, and other pointers to be used by the DBMS have to be specified at this level.) If a change in the pointer structure, adding or subtracting some pointers, is justified by performance statistics, the change should be conveyed to the DBMS. Most DBMSs provide utility routines for reconfiguring the pointers. The data base descriptions of the physical data base are changed, and the actual physical data base is unloaded and then reloaded with the new set of pointers. Existing applications do not need any modification if the pointers are not used explicitly.

    Changing Blocksizes, Buffer Pool Sizes, Prime Areas, Overflow

Areas. Most of these changes may be considered as reorganization changes.

Changing the Attributes for Inversion. Based on the latest requirements for searching data base records, it may be necessary to change the set of attributes for inversion. Ideally, this change should not affect the existing applications.

Changing the Randomizing (also called "Hashing") Algorithm. The hashing algorithm may have been based on the key distribution of data base records at the time of implementation. The key distribution will probably change as time passes. A modified algorithm should not affect the existing applications.

3. Logical Level Changes

All of the following changes at the logical level may affect the existing applications:

Adding or deleting data elements in existing segments or records.

Combining a number of records or segments into one, or splitting one record or segment into a number of records or segments.

Changing the relationships between records, sets, or segments, for example, owner-member, parent-child.

Changing the roles of data elements as keys or nonkeys.

Restructuring may require modifying the internal model, logical model, and contents of the data base. It may also necessitate reassigning the contents of the data base to different devices and media. Considerable time may be consumed in rewriting and recompiling applications and in debugging the new applications. It is advisable to dedicate the whole data base for restructuring if the contents of the data base as far as pointers or data are to be changed.

In most installations, restructuring is a major effort similar to the initial loading. Most DBMSs today do not provide a utility for a major restructuring. Most of them provide a set of simple utilities for loading a data base from a dump, whereas the dump consists of data in blocks without any underlying structure. The application programs written for loading the initial data base may not be used for reloading the data base for the new structure.

Restructuring is a big project as far as machine time and involvement on the part of data base professionals are concerned. It should not be done on a production data base without a duplicate copy. The time to be spent on restructuring should be outweighed by the benefits resulting from data base change.

10.2.4 Performance Monitoring and Tuning

In a data base environment, continuous, long-term measurements are necessary to understand the service provided by a DBMS. The performance monitor should provide a detailed as well as a bottom line picture of the demand on the data base service, the service provided, the resource consumption in the delivery of that service, and any resource overcommitments. The monitor should be inexpensive to operate and should create concise reports on a few pages. Voluminous reports are not reviewed on a daily basis.

Performance tuning of a data base is done successfully only when detailed knowledge of the performance of the existing system is gained. A number of useful statistics can be collected on the data base activity. The major questions in performance evaluation are what data to collect, when and how much to collect, and how to analyze it.

Let us consider an on-line environment. In an environment where performance is seen chiefly in terms of response time in seconds to users at terminals, degradation of performance is highly visible.

Hundreds of factors determine the performance of transactions within an on-line system. Most data base and data communications packages are complex software packages, and the large number of performance-related factors present are due mostly to the high function nature of the products and the large number of user options that can be specified for the system.

Examples of these performance-related factors are data base structure, number of different segment types or record types, relationships between a number of physical data bases, pointer selection, size of buffer pools for data bases, and physical and logical data base descriptions. Performance-related factors for teleprocessing are transaction classes, transaction mixes and volumes, transaction format blocks, number of transaction processing regions, and size and execution time of transaction processing programs, to name a few. Most of these performance factors could be more accurately classified as performance tuning factors, that is, given adequate resources to perform the job required (even though we have not yet determined what resources we need), we need only to understand the real meaning and effect of these factors, apply knowledge of the application, and evaluate possible trade-offs.

This is not meant to minimize the importance of the performance tuning activity. It is very important that installations which are dependent on a data base and/or teleprocessing system have people who understand the factors and their effects, the relationships between these factors, and the trade-offs involved. This usually requires detailed knowledge of the DBMS and the teleprocessing interface, since many of the factors, relationships, and effects are undocumented, misdocumented, or ignored in the manuals provided. However, once the performance factors are understood, the system can, given adequate amounts of central processing unit (CPU) power, main storage space, direct access storage device (DASD) space, channels, teleprocessing lines, and terminals, be tuned to do the work required of it. However, the purpose of performance prediction is to determine system performance capabilities, not by building the whole system and tuning it to a suitable level, but rather by determining beforehand what the "adequate resources" are that will be required (how large a CPU, how many channels, how much DASD), and, given these adequate resources, what kind of performance results can reasonably be expected. We would like to restrict ourselves to the "central" system, ignoring the teleprocessing lines and line delays (which can be analyzed separately).

To determine what "reasonable results" are, it would be useful if we could reduce the hundreds of interacting factors to a few general, major determinants of transaction performance. The selection of the following factors can be partially justified by the fact that they tie into many of the detailed performance factors and affect the major performance factors strongly:

1. **Transaction Rates** (as seen by the DBMS). It is obvious that the transaction rate is a major determinant. Note that the DBMS transaction rate may be higher than the rate of transactions from the user to the system (as when one user transaction causes multiple DBMS transactions to be scheduled). Also, the relative transaction rates of different transactions (i.e., the transaction mix) can be important, particularly if the resource usages of different transactions are very different, for example, one transaction type issues 10 times more DBMS CALLS than all the others. Such a "different" nonhomogeneous transaction not only can result in poor performance for itself, but also can adversely affect other transactions in the system to a degree far out of proportion to its own high resource usage.

2. **Transaction Processing Program Loading and Scheduling.** Generally, the longest single time component of a transaction is the time taken to load the program. Also, the largest single "piece" of CPU time consumed, if all DBMS CALLS are counted as

separate pieces, is the time used to schedule a transaction into a transaction processing region. In particular, the I/O time to locate the proper directory entry by scanning one or more partitioned data set directories and to read the program into storage often accounts for more than 50% of a transaction's total transit time through the system. Also, program loading by multiple transaction processing regions from a few common program libraries may cause channel contention problems.

The DBMS transaction processing preload facilities are the most commonly used means of reducing or eliminating program load and overload. However, this is effective only for very highly active transaction processing programs, and depends on the availability of adequate real main storage (since page faulting one's way through a program may be more costly than program loading). Also, the operating systems page reuse algorithms (e.g., Multiprogramming with Virtual Storage: MVS) may defeat the desired effect of preloading.

3. **Data Base CALLs Issued per Transaction.** For all but the most trivial transactions, this is the major determinant of the CPU consumption of a transaction. Generally, the complexity of the data base CALLs and of the data base structures, and the type of CALLs (e.g., CALLs that scan the data base), are less important than the sheer volume of CALLs issued (except as they affect point 4 below). This is mostly due to the fixed overheads of data base CALLs, including interregion communication and CALL analysis. Generally, many of the trade-offs in the design and implementation of transactions and systems are made to minimize the number of data base CALLs and the number of I/O operations per CALL (point 4 below). Also, the number of data base CALLs estimated in the design phase of system implementation is usually low (often by a factor of 2).

4. **Physical I/O Operations per Data Base CALL.** This affects both the transaction elapsed time and the CPU time, since the issuing and processing of I/Os by the DBMS and the operating system consumes a significant amount of CPU time. Generally, reduction of physical I/O operations is the major factor in data base design for performance, affecting the choice of access methods, data base structure, data base CALL types used, and use of relationships between the data base structures. On the other hand, attempts to severely reduce this quantity may greatly increase the complexity of the application programming involved.

5. **System Interactions with Other Tasks.** The other tasks processed on a system [e.g., batch jobs, time sharing operations (TSOs)] may also seriously affect data base performance. This is probably the most difficult area to assess and estimate, particularly if data base transaction processing is not clearly identified as the most important work being done on the system. The most common way of handling this performance determinant is to ignore it, rationalizing that data base work is clearly the most important work in the system and as such will be given the highest system priority, and thus its performance will not be degraded by other applications. However, the assumption that the DBMS, having the highest priority, will get the resources it needs is not always correct. This is particularly important to consider when there is contention for a highly used system resource, such as the CPU, real storage pages, a system channel, or a DASD device. Generally, contention for common system resources must be closely considered whenever a common resource is heavily used. For example, a CPU more than 70% busy, a block multiplexor channel more than 35% busy, a selector channel more than 50% busy, or a device more than 50% busy would be considered to be heavily used. Even after a potential problem has been identified, it may not be clear how to evaluate its effects.

6. **Input Queue.** The number of transactions on the input queue is a good indicator of the DBMS's responsiveness. If there is no queue buildup, the response time probably cannot be made significantly better except by reducing the I/O activity. Response time worsens as the queue builds up. A benchmark transaction may be developed, entered, and clocked at various levels of queues to determine the relationship between the queue length and the response time.

In an on-line environment the components of response time and the servicing component are:

Transaction Activity	Servicing Component
Teleprocessing line time	Systems control program
Queuing	DBMS
Scheduling	DBMS and systems control program
Application processing code	DBMS and systems control program

Transaction Activity	Servicing Component
Application terminal output	DBMS and systems control program
Termination	DBMS and systems control program

Thus the major response time components are the systems control program (SCP), DBMS, and application programs. The response time is affected by hardware configuration, terminal network, and data base design. The classical I/O approach to performance is based on the assumption that response time increases in an exponential fashion as the I/O rate increases in a linear fashion.

To understand the performance of the existing system and to be able to tune it to the desired level of responsiveness, statistics on the following factors may be collected:

1. **CPU, Channel, and Device Utilizations.** The information will indicate whether any of these major components affecting the performance of the data base are posing bottleneck problems. Statistics on these are normally provided by the operating system. A detailed analysis should be performed for the peak time utilizations.

2. **Memory Usage.** Paging rates and swapping rates (in a virtual system environment) are good indicators of whether enough real memory is available. The buffer pool can be expanded with more memory, resulting in fewer physical I/Os. Periodic "snapshots" should be taken to indicate the usage.

3. **Transaction Statistics.** The major source of information for the transaction statistics is the log tape. Analysis of the log tapes by vendor-supplied or user-written programs can provide information on:

Transaction rates and transaction rate distribution.

Transaction response times.

Transaction priorities and classes.

Number of data base calls per transaction.

CPU time used by transaction processing program per transaction.

4. **Distribution of Data Base Contents.** The absolute number of occurrences of owners and members or parents and children in the entire data base, as well as the relative frequency of occurrences, will be helpful in expanding or restructuring the data base. Statistics on space used by pointers, by data, by variable-length records, by prime data areas, and by overflows will be helpful for tuning the data base. Statistics on free space will be of assistance in reorganization.

5. **Statistics on Usage of Data Base Contents.** This information will be useful in reorganizing and restructuring the data base on the basis of the frequently used data items and the rarely used data items.

6. **Usage of Application Modules and DBMS Procedures.** Since the longest single time component of a transaction is the time taken to load the program, it will be better to keep the most frequently used programs, as well as the DBMS procedures, in memory.

7. **Usage of the Data Base by People.** People are one of the major determinants of the effective usage of the data base system. Statistics on the error rate in usage may indicate whether any training is necessary for the persons using the data base system.

8. **Statistics Collected by the Monitor for Data Base and Tele-processing.** This tool is by far the most important source of performance information for tuning a data base. It provides detailed information on the internal operations of the DBMS, but does impose some monitoring overhead on the measured system. Almost all the important performance information is contained somewhere in its reports (e.g., IMS/VS DB/DC Monitor), including:

> Buffer pool statistics.
> Region utilizations.
> I/O times and I/O waits.
> Program load time.
> Data base CALLs by program.
> Activity by data base.
> Transaction counts and rates.
> Schedulings per transaction.
> I/Os per data base call.
> Data base calls per transaction.

Data base calls by call type.

Deadlock and enqueue data.

10.2.5 Security in the Data Base Environment

The issue of data security is crucial in the era of the centralized data base. We use the term "data security" to mean protection of the data in the data base against unauthorized or accidental disclosure, alteration, or destruction.

Historically, the prime incentive for data security was the protection of critical business records. Recently, however, the importance gained by the social issue of privacy has forced organizations to protect their personal records from any unauthorized disclosure. Access to sensitive data must be controlled. This means that the security issue extends beyond the data stored in the data base and beyond the data processing department. It extends to all levels of management, and therefore they must be involved in establishing and maintaining data security.

Realizing that perfect security is unattainable, the objective of a data security program is to minimize the risk and probability of loss and disclosure to the lowest affordable level and also to be able to implement a full recovery program if a loss occurs.

With increasingly reliable hardware and software, it is people who may breach the security, either intentionally or unintentionally. Let us try to classify into three different groups the people who will have direct contact with the data base.

Users. This group of people decides on an application requirement. As a result of the application requirement and its justification, the entities, the relationships between the entities, and so on are integrated into the data base design and the stored data base. The data base administrator's staff, together with the users, determines the origin of each piece of data. The originator of data determines accessibility and types of access to the data. To provide integrity of data, there must be only one department responsible for the accuracy of a particular piece of data. Once the authorized use of the data is determined by the originator of the data, the data base administrator's staff can control the data usage according to the originator's intention. Access to the data can be a combination of the following:

- *Partial Retrieval Only.* The authorized user can see only a specific part of the data and cannot change it.

- *Retrieval of All Types of Records.* The authorized user can see the entire data base but cannot change it.
- *Insertion of Certain Types of Records.* The authorized user can insert only certain types of records to the data base and cannot change any existing ones.
- *Insertion of All Types of Records.* The authorized user can insert all types of records to the data base but cannot change the existing ones.
- *Deletion of Certain Types of Records.* The users can see only certain types of records, which they can delete too.
- *Deletion of All Types of Records.*
- *Updating of Certain Types of Records.*
- *Updating of All Types of Records.*

This list is by no means an exhaustive one, but it gives an idea of the kind of checking required of a data base management system to determine whether a user who wants to access data from the data base is authorized to do so. For this purpose, the DBA has to provide the users with some way of identifying themselves to the DBMS.

Identification, verification and authorization. Before accessing the data base, the user has to identify to the DBMS who he/she is. One method to accomplish this in an on-line environment is by using a sign-on number coupled with a confidential password. The DBMS will check the user profile supplied by the DBA and will let the user perform only the actions for which he/she is authorized. The user profile, which can consist of the user sign-on number with his/her authorization, confidential password, and so on, can be conveniently stored in a data dictionary. Security can be implemented on the physical locations of the terminals, that is, terminals located within an area can perform limited operations.

If the user cannot provide satisfactory identification and authentication, the DBMS should sign off the user with a message and keep a log of such instances, consisting of the terminal number, the day, the time of the day, the supplied sign-on number, and so on. There should be at least one person on the DBA's staff who is responsible for keeping track of such potential threats to security.

For a detailed treatment of user identification, the reader is encouraged to read selected references from the bibliography at the end of the chapter.

Programmers. A high percentage of disclosure, alteration, and destruction is done by programmers. Before we discuss embezzelment by programmers, let us distinguish between:

1. Application programmers.
2. Systems programmers.
3. Operators.

There should be a clear distinction in responsibilities between these three groups.

1. *An application programmer* writes only application programs, not systems programs. An application programmer has the same type of access to the data base as any other user using the application program, that is, the application programmer has to use the sign-on procedures and the passwords.
2. *The systems programmers* make changes only to the systems code. A systems programmer may not write or run any application programs.
3. *An operator* can run but not write application programs. An operator may not change the systems code.

A librarian on the DBA's staff provides the following security protections:

- Changes to application programs can be made only by the application programmers. These changes must go through and must be recorded by the librarian.
- The librarian keeps only the latest version of the application program. This prevents the possibility of floating versions of an application program.
- The librarian has to back up the latest versions of all application programs and store them off-site to protect against a major disaster like fire or flood.
- The librarian can request an operator to delete or load any programs.

Operations Staff. Frequently the accidental destruction of data is the result of untrained operators, or it may be due to insufficient guidelines for running the applications or to procedures too complex for the operator to follow. It is a wise technique to remove as many responsibilities from an operator as possible and to put those responsibilities in the application programs. Usually a new employee is given the job of computer operator as a beginning assignment. As a result, there is frequent turnover. Therefore it is risky to ask an operator to take care of backup tapes, to decide what action should be taken in case of a job failure, and the like.

The following precautions should be taken by the operations staff in order to avoid any security problems due to operational errors:

A complete log should be kept of all the activities and of any errors. The error messages should be clearly stated. The system should also print on the log the run times of all the jobs. The log can be generated by the system off-line.

Important decisions should not be left to the operators.

An operator should not have any access to the source listings of the application programs.

Operator embezzlement. An operator desiring to breach security may manipulate data or application programs. To prevent fraud of this type, the following precautions should be taken:

An operator should not write any application programs.

Console printouts should be checked every day by a DBA staff member for all the activity on the data base.

The application source programs should be kept *only* in a library and run *only* when the librarian requests them.

There should be at least two people in the computer room.

Critical forms such as checks should be locked away.

Program errors. A vast majority of accidental destruction of data is caused by program errors. Program errors or "bugs" often do not surface until some combination of circumstances takes place for which the application program was not tested. Program bugs are often the result of flaws in design, errors in program logic, errors in coding, incomplete definitions, or inadequately tested programs.

Certain precautionary steps can be taken to provide reliable application programs. Principles of structured programming can enable an application programmer to write more reliable code, and code walk-throughs can help him/her to detect any errors in the logic of the program. Fictitious data for testing the program logic should be developed by some other person than the coder. The following checkpoints should be made before sending a program into production:

1. Does the program have validity checking of input data? Most data values in real life, such as account numbers, transaction amounts, and invoice amounts, have reasonable ranges. If the calculated invoice amount does not fall in the reasonable range, the program should take proper action.

2. Does the program run successfully in extreme situations, such as the processing of one transaction only? What happens if the first or the last transaction is in error? Remember an analogy: statistically, most airplane accidents occur while taking off or while landing.

3. Does the program provide a log of record counts, card counts, transaction counts, and so on? An unreasonably high or low number of records, cards, or transactions may indicate errors.

4. Has the program been tested by someone other than the programmer? Quite often the programmer who writes the programs is not the best person to detect the program bugs.

5. Are the programs simple to read and documented in an understandable manner? (*Note:* Usually the programmer and the maintainer are different people. A well documented program facilitates reconstruction of lost data.)

6. Do program error actions explain what the precise error is and the operator/user action necessary for correction?

To check all the items above, the DBA's staff should be able to borrow competent people who have application programming background. To obtain the maximum benefit, the DBA and other management should not participate in code walk-throughs or the like.

Physical Security. Not long ago computer facilities were considered showcases of prestige for the company. Recently the trend has been in the other direction, in that in many installations the computers receive less visibility. One of the major reasons for providing maximum physical security is to prevent loss due to a disaster like fire. Special precautions against fire are:

1. Most computer room fires start in areas adjacent to the computer room and then spread to the computer area. The site for the computers should be chosen with this fact in mind.

2. Smoking should not be allowed in the computer room. No exceptions should be granted.

3. Clearly marked fire extinguishers should be placed in conveniently located areas.

4. The emergency power-off switch should be clearly marked and easily accessible.

5. Safety exits for people should not be blocked.

6. Fire drills should be conducted from time to time.

7. Important records should be stored in fireproof vaults.
8. Fire alarm systems must notify the computer room and an attended remote location of every defect.
9. Updated source program copies should be stored off the computer room premises, preferably in a different building.
10. Data necessary to reconstruct the data base should be stored off-site.

For security measures against water, vandalism, and sabotage the reader is referred to the bibliography at the end of the chapter.

10.2.6 Privacy in the Data Base Environment

Privacy is the right of an individual to determine what type of information can be stored and when and how, about him/her and what type can be transferred for other purposes than the one for which the information was collected originally. The individual about whom the information will be collected is the sole "owner" of that information.

Privacy—or rather the lack of it—has become a matter of public concern. According to the Privacy Act of 1974, federal agencies, the state, and federally financed institutions must not use certain types of information about people illegally; for example, the social security number is not supposed to be used for identification purposes. Extension of the privacy act with further legislation may occur in the foreseeable future. This legislation will make major changes in the way we process information today. Legislation will also specify civil and criminal sanctions for violations of the individual's right to privacy.

Legislation will definitely provide for fines and imprisonment for executives and administrators who do not take "reasonable" precautions to safeguard the privacy of information. The word "reasonable" will be interpreted more precisely by the courts once the legislation has been passed. The following safeguards are recommended by the legislative committee:

There must be no personal data record-keeping systems whose very existence is secret.

There must be a way for an individual to find out what information about him/her is recorded and how it is used.

There must be a way for an individual to prevent information about him/her obtained for one purpose from being used or made available for other purposes without his/her consent.

There must be a way for an individual to correct or amend a record of identifiable information about him/her.

Any organization creating, maintaining, or disseminating records of identifiable personal data must assure the reliability of that data for its intended use and *must take precautions to prevent misuse of the data.*

Privacy is more an ethical and social issue than an information processing one. Information processing systems are normally established to process and protect the data, not the sources of the data. The privacy issue will have far reaching effects on the way future information processing systems will function.

Privacy versus Security. The term "privacy" is often confused with the term "security," but the two words have different meanings. Information privacy includes the right of individuals to know that recorded personal information about them is accurate, pertinent, complete, up to date, and reasonably secure from unauthorized access, either accidental or intentional.

Moreover, according to the definition of privacy an individual has the right to control information that can readily be identified as applying to her or him.

As a result of the discussion above, it becomes clear that the data base administrator and management have to make the protection of privacy an organizational objective. The best time for the DBA and management to solve any privacy problems or to prevent problems of this type from happening is during data base design.

What Is Private? Once information about people (e.g., their credit records, financial positions, criminal records, addresses, purchases with credit cards, tax information, medical information) is collected, the distinction between what information should be public and what information should remain confidential is not always clearly stated. This decision requires ethical, moral, and legal judgments that administrators may be ill prepared or reluctant to make. But the question remains, which an administrator and executive must answer, whether the organization provides maximum protection for the personal information within its systems.

Does the Organization Have Privacy Problems?   The data base administrator should supply answers to the following questions:

What concern has there been for the individual and his/her personal privacy as the information systems were developed?

What were the priorities concerning privacy?

What are they now?

What other systems can access information within the data base system?

If the enterprise is storing any information regarding the individuals in the system, does a single individual have a chance to examine, update, refute, or generally know what the record contains about him/her?

If the answer to any of these questions is "I don't know," the organization probably has an information privacy problem. Moreover, the data base administrator and the management are responsible for invasion of privacy by not taking proper care of the private information stored in the data base, as explained below.

The information privacy problem can involve one or a combination of the following:

• Erroneous or misleading information.
• Accidental disclosure or modification of information.
• Intentional infiltration of an information system.
• Loss of data.

This list makes it clear that security and privacy issues are interwoven. The last three items are security problems. This means that, if security measures are not in place, lack of privacy is probably not far off, and if a reasonable policy for protecting private information is not established, security is at stake.

Erroneous or misleading information.   Generally, people have a tendency to trust anything that is printed. But it must be understood that, when erroneous information is passed through the computer, it will still be erroneous. Inadequately tested programs, last minute conversions of data to computer-readable media, information collected from hearsay, and insufficiently controlled information systems can all contribute to misleading information about individuals. Inaccurate information about individuals can result in lawsuits!

Accidental disclosure. Negligence is the biggest enemy of information systems. The best technological measures and most sophisticated systems are of no value if a careless administrator leaves a sensitive report on an unattended desk.

Intentional infiltration of an information system. Certain types of data stored in a data base may offer financial incentives and as such become the targets of potential intruders. The data base administrator must identify and categorize this type of information in the data base and establish measures to prevent any intrusion.

Loss of data. The loss of data due to natural occurrences (e.g., floods, tornadoes, earthquakes), malfunctions of mechanical equipment (e.g., power failures, air-conditioning problems,) or acts of violence (e.g., civil disturbances, malicious acts of disgruntled employees) can range in magnitude from minor, inconvenient disturbances or interruptions in operations to major disasters that may break down a total organization. As far as loss of data is concerned, the data base administrator has to differentiate between the CONFIDENTIALITY of data and the CRITICALITY of data. Criticality of data is based on the length of time an organization can survive if it loses that information.

The answers to the following questions will assist the data base administrator and management in establishing a specific plan to avoid the invasion of privacy:

What should be done?
Who should do it?
How will one know when—and if—it is done correctly?

STEP 1. Check the information processed
In many installations, more information is collected than necessary. In a requirement analysis study made before designing a data base, it is advisable to answer the following questions with the help of the user organizations:

What data is being collected?
Who needs this data?
Why do they need it?
When do they need it?

Are all new items of data collection and all new uses of data being cleared through the proper level of management?

These questions show that management must take an active interest in the privacy issue and support the data base administrator in carrying out the duties involved. An efficient and important tool for storing this type of information is a data dictionary, discussed in Chapter 3. The questions above are crucial for any management information system. The goals of information privacy must be consistent with the optimum management information system. When extraneous information is not introduced during the data base design, two main advantages result:

1. Elimination of many unnecessary threats to information privacy.
2. Potential cost avoidance as a result of having only an "optimum" information system.

STEP 2.   Identify personal, critical, and proprietary data.
Processed either manually or automatically by machines, the data used by an organization generally falls within three general categories:

Personal, for example, certain medical and criminal history information.

Proprietary, for example, research and development data or copyrighted or patented information.

Critical, for example, accounts receivable or airline reservation information.

Personal data and proprietary data are both confidential in nature. Critical data may be the basic necessity for the existence of the organization. If the data is not critical, proprietary, or personal, why collect it?

To be able to take an effective action, the following questions must be answered:

How complex should the information classification structure be (i.e., how many levels of security are required)?

What guidelines are available to assess the value of information?

What are the legal and social responsibilities regarding information privacy?

How much protection is required for each kind of information?

Senior management, including the organization's counsel, must be prepared to accept the responsibility for answering these questions.

STEP 3. Investigate susceptibility to damage and risks.
Mangement should assess the risk of exposure of personal information in the data processing system. It should also study whether the risk can be reduced by increasing the security protection.

Making an assessment of this type is not an easy task. The best way to solve the problem is to make a list of all possible exposures and to try to estimate the value of the information, that is, how much it will cost to reconstruct any loss of information. In this process the DBA will be aware of the effectiveness of the safeguards currently implemented. The information systems executive, together with the data base administrator, should evaluate new technological security systems on comparable software systems, similar access control systems, and similar encryption techniques.

STEP 4. Determine the budget for information privacy.
To implement any security and privacy measures, a specific budget must be set aside. The cost of implementing and operating a security and privacy program must be estimated. The budget should reflect the value of information security and privacy to the organization. In general, the higher the value, the more one should be willing to adequately secure—thus budget properly. It should also be determined what percentage of the cost should be billed to the information systems users.

STEP 5. Organize for information privacy.
Depending on the size, the number of functions supported, and the criticality of the data base, one person, either half time or full time, should support the privacy and security program. The job description of such an individual could look like:

1. Research state-of-the-art security technology.
2. Classify information according to its use.
3. Authorize, after concurring with the data base administrator and senior management, specific individuals to access confidential and critical resources; for example, only a pair of specific operators can run certain information-sensitive application programs, a specific operator has the responsibility for a critical resource such as a specific disk.
4. Ensure that all new information systems are designed with information privacy controls in mind.

5. Administer a program of education to assure the proper collection, handling, processing, dissemination, storage, and disposal of information.
6. Execute periodic technical and financial audits.
7. Investigate security and privacy breaches, and enforce policy and procedures.
8. Test all procedures that are enacted to ensure operability.

STEP 6. Establish individual accountability.
To establish the guidelines for data access, the data base administrator has to be told:

Who has the need to know, the need to change, and the right to expunge information?

When do these persons need to know?

Have these individuals received security clearances?

In addition, the personnel department must inform the DBA of all personnel transfers or terminations so that the authorization entries can be deleted.

STEP 7. Implement technological safeguards, and create a privacy-conscious environment.
The plans developed for the privacy area should be implemented. Since the implementation of a privacy and security plan will need systems and people resources, the data base administrator should consider the following:

- What is the priority of information privacy objectives in relation to other organization objectives (e.g., production, efficiency, other projects)?
- How will the implementation of an information system security and privacy program affect user information system development plans and vice versa?
- How much and what kind of vendor support will be required to implement new technology?
- What additional resources (e.g., people, computer time) will be required during the implementation?
- Who is responsible for periodically communicating project status and plans to the information system user community?
- Where is the implementation plan?

- How will the plan be monitored and tested on a continuous basis?

The best developed plan is of no value unless management through all levels makes full commitment to its implementation and control throughout time.

- The information privacy problem should be addressed in organization policies.
- The substantive procedures should be well documented, understood by all concerned parties, and enforced.
- The education program should be expanded to include courses in the privacy area.
- Individuals having information privacy responsibilities should be evaluated accordingly.

REFERENCES

1. EXPRESS: A Data Extraction, Processing, and REStructuring System," N. C. Shu, B. C. Housel, R. W. Taylor, S. P. Ghosh, and V. Y. Lum, *ACM Transactions on Database Systems*, Vol. 2, No. 2 (June 1977), 134–174.

2. *Data Base Systems: A Practical Reference*, Ian R. Palmer, Q. E. D. Information Sciences, Inc., Wellesley, Massachusetts, 1978.

3. *Data Base Systems Design, Implementation, and Management*, Ronald G. Ross, AMACOM, a division of American Management Associations, 135 West 50th Street, New York, New York 10020.

4. *Database Design*, Gio Wiederhold, McGraw-Hill Book Company, 1977.

5. *An Introduction to Database Systems*, 2nd ed., C. J. Date, The Systems Programming Series, Addison-Wesley Publishing Company, 1977.

6. *Data Base Management Systems*, edited by Donald A. Jardine, North-Holland and American Elsevier, 1974.

7. *Managing IMS Performance via IMS Control Block and Buffer Pool Statistics*, David A. Schramm, Technical Bulletin, Order No. GG22-9013, IBM Washington Systems Center, January 1978.

8. *The Codasyl Approach to Data Base Management*, T. William Olle, a Wiley-Interscience Publication, John Wiley & Sons, 1978.

9. *Computer Security Management*, Dennis Van Tassel, Prentice-Hall, 1972.

10. *Security, Accuracy, and Privacy in Computer Systems*, James Martin, Prentice-Hall, 1973.

11. *Data Security and Data Processing*, Vols. 1, 2, and 3, G320-1370, G320-1371, and G320-1372. IBM Corporation, Data Processing Division, 1133 Westchester Avenue, White Plains, New York 10604.

12. *Guidelines for Automatic Data Processing Physical Security and Risk Management*, FIPS PUB 31, U.S. Department of Commerce, National Bureau of Standards, Washington, D.C. 20234.

13. *The Database Administrator*, John K. Lyon, A Wiley-Interscience Publication, John Wiley & Sons, 1976.

14. "Two Men Arrested on Bribery Attempt," *Illinois State Register*, Friday, November 11, 1972, p. 16.

15. "Recovery Techniques for Database Systems," J. S. M. Verhofstad, *ACM Computing Surveys*, Vol. 10, No. 2 (June 1978).

Designing a Data Base for a Banking Environment

"Popular Bank"-Case Study 1

The list of reports in pictorial format shown in Figure A.0 presents the information needs of a hypothetical "Popular Bank." The reports and transactions are shown in Figures A.1 to A.7. Design a data base for the "Popular Bank" as follows:

I   Design a conceptual model of a data base (refer to Chapters 1, 2, 3, 4, and 5).

    I.1   Study the environment, and document assumptions for it (Chapters 1 and 2).

    I.2   Determine the data elements referenced in every report individually (Chapter 3).

    I.3   Determine the relationships between the data elements, such as identifiying the primary key data elements and the nonkey data elements (Chapters 4 and 5).

    I.4   Develop third normal form relations for each set of data elements. Where this is not possible for individual reports, merge data from reports to establish third normal form relations (Chapter 5).

    I.5   Draw a conceptual model on the basis of the third normal form relations (Chapter 5).

II   Design a logical model of a data base (refer to Chapters 4, 5, and 6).

335

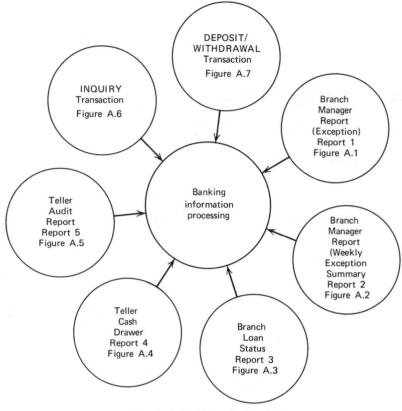

Figure A.0 **"Popular Bank"**

II.1 Draw a logical model based on the conceptual model above for a data base management system, using:

1. A relational data model.
2. A hierarchical data model.
3. A network data model.

II.2 Draw external models for the reports in Figures A.1 to A.5, INQUIRY Transaction, and DEPOSIT/WITHDRAWAL Transaction on the basis of the logical model above.

III Design a physical model of a data base (refer to Chapters 7, 8, and 9).

III.1 Draw an internal model (also called a physical model) on the basis of the logical model from step II.1.

IV   Evaluate the physical model of a data base (refer to chapters 7, 8, 9 and Appendix C on statistics).

IV.1   Develop space estimates for the internal model above (as in step III.1). Develop input/output probabilities for the internal model above (as in step III.1)

IV.2   Draw external models for the reports in Figures A.1 to A.5, Inquiry Transaction, and DEPOSIT/WITHDRAWAL Transaction on the basis of the internal model above.

IV.3   Develop time estimates for the external models as in step IV.2.

STEP I   DESIGN A CONCEPTUAL MODEL OF A DATA BASE
(refer to Chapters 1, 2, 3, 4, and 5).

STEP I.1   Study the environment and document assumptions for it
(refer to Chapters 1 and 2).

"Popular Bank" has a number of branches scattered throughout the city and the suburbs. A customer may walk into any branch and open an account. The customer is assigned a customer identification number (CID number) with the first account at the bank. The customer may open a number of accounts at the bank, but his/her CID number is not changed. The bank maintains checking accounts (accounts on which the customer may write personal checks), savings accounts (for which passbooks are required, and interest is given by the bank), loan accounts (customers must return the loans with interest), and mortgage accounts (customers must make regular payments with interest).

Branch Manager Report (Exception) (Figure A.1)

Every branch has a branch manager. At a certain point in time a branch has only one branch manager. A Branch Manager Report (Exception) is printed for the branch manager on a daily basis. The report consists of exceptional transactions only; for example, an automatic loan account called "Checking Plus" is overdrawn, or a savings account exceeds the balance of $100,000, which is the maximum amount insured by the Federal Deposit Insurance Company.

Branch Manager Report (Weekly Exception Summary) (Figure A.2)

Another type of report for the branch manager is the Weekly Exception Summary. This report is not based on individual accounts but is a summary. These two reports may be considered as batch reports.

DATE: January 11, 1980

Popular Bank
Branch Manager Report (Exception)

BRANCH—NO (Branch Number): 1234
BRANCH—NAME: Downtown Branch
BRANCH—ADDR (Branch Address):1 First Street, New York, N.Y. 10001
MGR—NAME (Manager's Name) :J. J. Smith

Report for: January 10, 1980

CUST—NAME (Customer Name)	CID (Customer Identification Number)	ACCT—TYPE (Account Type)	ACCT—NO (Account Number)	AMOUNT (Involved)	X—DATE (Date of Transaction)	X—TIME (Time of Transaction)	X—TYPE (Trans. Code)	REASON—CODE	ACTION—CODE	REMARKS
Prof. Higgins	123456789	Checking	653210	268.50	1/10/80	10:15:20	Check withdraw	Checking overdrawn	Automatic loan	Notify customer Tel. 555—1234
Zalaf, Amir	345678901	Savings	12345—1	10,000.00	1/10/80	15:02:10	Check deposit	Savings exceed 100,000 limit	No deposit	Send back check and inform customer

Figure A.1

REPORT 2

DATE: JANUARY 14, 1980

Popular Bank

Branch Manager Report   (Weekly Exception Summary)

BRANCH—NO (Branch Number): 1234

BRANCH—NAME: Downtown Branch

BRANCH—ADDR (Branch Address): 1 First Street, New York, N.Y. 10001

MGR—NAME (Manager's Name): J. J. Smith

DSTRPT (Date Report Started): January 9, 1980

DENDRPT (Date Report Ended): January 13, 1980

REASON— CODE	NO—X—TOTAL (Total Number of Transactions Involved)	NO—ACCTS—TOTAL (Total Number of Accounts Involved)	AMT—TOTAL (Total Dollar Amount Involved)
Checking overdrawn	2072	1572	170,900.00
Checking overdrawn unavailable funds	650	560	100,000.00
Savings exceed 100,000 limit	24	20	2,150,000.00

Figure A.2

Branch Loan Status (Figure A.3)

The branch manager also receives a Branch Loan Status. This report helps the branch manager to keep track of the loans given at the branch. It also serves as a source of new ideas for making loans at the branch attractive.

Teller Cash Drawer (Figure A.4)

The bank employs a number of tellers who cash checks and make deposits and withdrawals for the customers. The tellers are rotated

DATE: January 11, 1980

Popular Bank

Branch Loan Status

BRANCH—NO (Branch Number): 1234
BRANCH—NAME: Downtown Branch
BRANCH—ADDR (Branch Address): 1 First Street, New York, N.Y. 10001

MGR—NAME (Manager's Name): J. J. Smith

LOAN—NO (Loan Number)	LOAN—TYPE	LOAN—ASSGND (Loan Assigned)	TOTAL—LOAN—COLLECTED (Total Loan Collected)	TOTAL—LOAN—TO—BE—COLLECTED (Including Interest)	INTEREST (Total Interest Received, i.e., profit)
1234	Car loan	4000	1000	3350	200
2389	Mortgage	45,500	5000	70,000	4550

Figure A.3

among the branches, but it is assumed that once a teller is sent to a branch he/she will stay at that branch the whole day. A cash drawer is recorded every day for every teller. It keeps track of all the money flow for that day, for that teller, and at that branch. Teller Cash Drawer may be considered as a batch application.

Teller Audit Report (Figure A.5)

The tellers are audited periodically, as well as for specific reasons. Every teller has a unique identification number called a teller num-

Report 4

Teller Cash Drawer   DATE: January 11, 1980

TELLER—NO (Teller Number): 6789

DATE: January 11, 1980

TELLER—NAME: XYZ

BRANCH—NO (Branch Number): 1234

BRANCH—NAME: Downtown Branch

BRANCH—ADDR (Branch Address): 1 First Street, New York, N.Y. 10001

Total cash on hand start of day:	775.00
Plus total cash received during day:	5243.39
Less total cash dispensed during day:	4976.97
Final cash on hand end of day:	1041.42

Number of checks received drawn on us:	752
Number of checks received drawn on others	337

Total number of checks received: 1089

Dollar amount of checks received drawn on us:	$ 73,272.21 ⎱ deposits made
Dollar amount of checks received drawn on others:	35,369.76 ⎰ by customers

---

Total dollar amount of checks received: 108,641.97

Number of checks dispensed	972 ⎱ withdrawals made
Dollar amount of checks dispensed	$ 76,197.60 ⎰ by customers

Summary:

Final cash on hand:	1,041.42
Plus dollar amount of checks received:	108,641.97
Cash and checks for the day:	109,683.39
Less dollar amount of checks dispensed:	76,197.60
(certified checks, money orders)	33,485.79
Less initial cash on hand (start of day):	775.00
Net cash flow for day:	32,710.79

Figure A.4

341

REPORT 5

Popular Bank   DATE: January 11, 1980

Teller Audit Report

TELLER—NO (Teller Number): 6789
TELLER—NAME: XYZ
BRANCH—NO (Branch Number): 1234
BRANCH—NAME: Downtown Branch
BRANCH—ADDR (Branch Address): 1 First Street, New York, N.Y. 10001

Date audit started: January 2, 1980
Date audit ended: January 4, 1980
Reason code for audit: Regular audit

Total number of transactions by type processed:
Type 1: 100 (Deposit)
Type 2: 150 (Withdrawal)

Largest dollar amount involved for each transaction type:
Type 1: 5000 (Deposit)
Type 2: 2552 (Withdrawal)

Figure A.5

ber. Based on experience and on previous audit records, a teller may withdraw only up to a certain amount of money for a customer. If the customer wants to withdraw more money than the specific teller's maximum allowable upper limit, the teller has to request another teller who can withdraw the amount to do so. The Teller Audit Report, which could be considered as a batch report, is sent to the central audit location for the bank.

Inquiry Transaction (Figure A.6)

It may happen occasionally that a customer walks into a branch and wants to deposit or withdraw a certain amount of money. Or he/she may want to know the balance of a specific account. The customer may not be able to provide the customer identification number (CID) or the account number(s). In such a situation the teller should be able to provide the information needed by the customer. This on-line transaction is only an INQUIRY Transaction; it does not deposit or withdraw any money from any of the accounts but only provides information about the status of the accounts.

Popular Bank

Inquiry Transaction   DATE: January 11, 1980

Input consists of:

(Customer name and birth date) or CID number
Transaction type (i.e., INQUIRY)

Output consists of:

CID number
Customer information (e.g., name, date of birth, address, telephone number)

Account number, account type (e.g., savings),
special type (e.g., time deposit), account balance

Loan number, loan balance (all loans given to the customer will be displayed)

(All accounts of a specific customer will be displayed.)

The assumption made here is that the customer name
and the customer date of birth uniquely identify the
customer, that is, the customer identification number
(CID number). If the teller does not know the customer,
the teller has to uniquely identify her/him by asking
the address, telephone number, and so on.

Figure A.6

Deposit/Withdrawal Transaction (Figure A.7)

These are two types of transactions. Type 1 is DEPOSIT, and Type 2
is WITHDRAWAL. These two are on-line transactions.

After studying the environment, the following assumptions
may be made.

Assumptions about the Environment of "Popular Bank"

1. The customer identification number (CID number) is unique.
2. Account numbers are allotted bankwide, that is, the account
   numbers are unique. The account number uniquely identifies the account type, the branch in which the particular account was opened, and the customer's name, that is, the same
   account number will not be given to two or more accounts.
   The account number also uniquely identifies the customer.
3. Teller numbers are unique.

Popular Bank

Deposit/Withdrawal   Transaction   DATE: January 11, 1980

BRANCH—NO (Branch Number): 1234

BRANCH—NAME: Downtown Branch

BRANCH—ADDR (Branch Address): 1 First Street, New York, N.Y. 10001

DEPOSIT   Transaction (type 1)   OR

WITHDRAWAL   Transaction (type 2)

Input consists of:

Branch number

Teller number

Transaction type

Account number

CID number (CID: customer identification number)

Amount

Output consists of:

Branch number   (Date of transaction and time of transaction

Teller number   are implied, that is, on a given day and at a
                                    specific unit of time only one transaction can

Transaction type   take place.)

Account number

Type of account

Balance

Passbook line number (will be there only if the passbook is there)

Figure A.7

4. A teller can be assigned to different branches on different days, but once assigned to a branch he/she works there the whole day.

5. The account number, with transaction date and transaction time, uniquely identifies the transaction.

6. The action to be taken and the remarks to be registered for an exception are dependent on the reason code and on the account number, that is, on the customer for whom an exceptional action has to be taken.

7. Branch number, together with reason code, the date of start of report, and the date of end of report, uniquely identifies

the total number of transactions for the weekly exception summary.

8. The loan number uniquely identifies the specific loan. The loan number is different from the account number. Account and loan are two separate entities.

9. A customer can have many account numbers at the same branch.

10. A passbook is provided only for savings accounts.

11. "Transaction type" and "transaction code" are synonymous.

12. An INQUIRY Transaction is only an information retrieval transaction.

13. If the teller worked in several branches during the audit period, a report for each branch will be printed. For each audit period for a given teller, there is only one reason code for the audit. Only the count of transactions and the largest dollar amount handled by teller being audited are taken into consideration.

14. The Exception Report and Weekly Exception Summary are for the branch where the account is kept. The reason is that the branch manager where the transaction was made is not too concerned if the account in another branch is overdrawn or if savings exceeds a certain limit. The branch manager is interested, however, if these things happen to his/her bank's accounts, even if the transaction triggering them takes place elsewhere.

15. Two types of transactions are recorded. Type 1 is the DEPOSIT Transaction, and Type 2 is the WITHDRAWAL Transaction. An INQUIRY Transaction is not recorded.

16. At a given point in time a branch has only one branch manager.

STEP I.2 Determine the data elements referenced in every report individually (refer to Chapter 3).

Examine every report individually, and build a cross-reference table showing the data elements and the reports where the information is referred to as in Table 1.

A list of all data elements referenced in the reports from Table 1 in alphabetical order is:

ACCT-NO   The account number uniquely identifies the particular account.

ACCT-TYPE
: The account type can be checking, savings, etc.

ACTION-CODE
: The action code specifies the action to be taken in exceptions: for example, if the checking plus account is overdrawn, give automatic loan not to exceed the total loan given by a particular amount.

AMOUNT
: The amount involved in a particular transaction.

AMT-RECD-OTHER
: Dollar amount of checks received drawn on others.

AMT-RECD-TOTAL
: Total dollar amount of checks received.

AMT-RECD-US
: Dollar amount of checks received drawn on us.

AMT-TOTAL
: Dollar amount involved (total) in Weekly Exception Summary of the Branch Manager's Report.

AUDIT-REASON
: Reason code for audit in the Teller Audit Report.

BALANCE
: Balance of an account; either is asked for by a customer in an INQUIRY transaction or is the result of a DEPOSIT or a WITHDRAWAL transaction.

BRANCH-ADDR
: The address of the branch.

BRANCH-NAME
: The name of the branch.

BRANCH-NO
: The number of the branch.

CASH-DISPENSED
: Total cash dispensed during day; referred to in Teller Cash Drawer.

CASH-RECD
: Total cash received during day; referred to in Teller Cash Drawer.

CHECKS-DISPENSED-TOTAL   Number of checks dispensed; referred to in Teller Cash Drawer.

CHECKS-RECD-OTHER   Number of checks received drawn on other banks; referred to in Teller Cash Drawer.

CHECKS-RECD-TOTAL   Total number of checks received.

CHECKS-RECD-US   Number of checks received drawn on us; referred to in Teller Cash Drawer.

CID   Customer identification number.

COH-EOD   Cash on hand at end of day.

COH-SOD   Cash on hand at start of day.

CUST-DOB   Customer date of birth.

CUST-ADDR   Customer address.

CUST-NAME   Customer name.

CUST-TEL-NO   Customer telephone number.

DATE   A business day. Every teller has a cash drawer report on a business day. A Teller Audit Report for a day or a group of days may be prepared. DATE is synonymous with X-DATE: transaction date.

DENDRPT   Date of end of report for the branch manager's Weekly Exception Summary.

DSTRPT   Date of start of report for the branch manager's Weekly Exception Summary.

INTEREST   Interest paid by the customer on a loan; referred to in Branch Loan Status Report.

LARGEST-AMT-TYPE1   Largest amount of money for transaction type 1, which is depositing money.

LARGEST-AMT-TYPE2	Largest amount of money for transaction type 2, which is withdrawing money.
LOAN-ASSGND	Amount of money assigned as a loan.
LOAN-NO	Referred to in Branch Loan Status Report.
LOAN-TYPE	Mortgage loan, installment loan; referred to in Branch Loan Status Report.
MGR-NAME	Branch manager's name; the assumption is that there is only one branch manager per branch at a given point in time.
NET-FLOW	Net flow of money in Teller Cash Drawer.
NO-ACCTS-TOTAL	Exceptions took place on this number of accounts in a week.
NO-X-TOTAL	Total number of transactions that took place in a week; referred to in branch manager's Weekly Exception Summary.
NO-X-TYPE1	Number of transactions of type 1, i.e., depositing of money performed by a specific teller; referred to in Teller Audit Report.
NO-X-TYPE2	Number of transactions of type 2, i.e., withdrawals performed by a specific teller; referred to in Teller Audit Report.
PASSBOOK-LINE-NO	The passbook-line number is provided only for savings

passbooks; referred to in DEPOSIT/WITHDRAWAL Transaction. The passbook-line number is provided at the time when the transaction is processed.

REASON-CODE   Reason code for the exception at execution of a transaction; referred to in the Branch Manager Exception Report and the Weekly Exception Summary.

REMARKS   Any information provided to take care of an exception as a result of a transaction; referred to in the Branch Manager Exception Report.

TELLER-NO   The teller number uniquely identifies the teller.

TELLER-NAME   The teller name is uniquely identified by the teller number.

TOTAL-LOAN-COLLECTED   Total amount collected from an assigned loan.

TOTAL-LOAN-TO-BE-COLLECTED   Total amount collected from the loan.

X-DATE   The day on which the transaction took place.

X-NO   The number of the transaction.

X-TIME   The unit of time at which a transaction took place.

X-TYPE   The type of transaction. There are two types of transactions: type 1 is depositing money, and type 2 is withdrawing money.

Table 1. Cross-Reference Table between Data Elements and Reports

	Reports						
Data Elements	Branch Manager Report (Exception)	Branch Manager Report (Weekly Exception Summary)	Branch Loan Status	Teller Cash Drawer	Teller Audit Report	Inquiry Transaction	Deposit/ Withdrawal Transaction
BRANCH-NO	X	X	X	X	X		X
BRANCH-NAME	X	X	X	X	X		X
BRANCH-ADDR	X	X	X	X	X		X
MGR-NAME	X	X	X				
ACCOUNT-NO	X					X	X
ACCT-TYPE	X					X	X
CID	X					X	
CUST-NAME	X					X	
CUST-ADDR						X	
CUST-TEL-NO						X	
X-DATE	X						X
X-TIME	X						X
X-TYPE	X						X

	Reports						
Data Elements	Branch Manager Report (Exception)	Branch Manager Report (Weekly Exception Summary)	Branch Loan Status	Teller Cash Drawer	Teller Audit Report	Inquiry Transaction	Deposit/ Withdrawal Transaction
X-NO							X
AMOUNT	X						X
REASON-CODE	X	X					
ACTION-CODE	X						
REMARKS	X	X					
DSTRPT		X					
DENDRPT		X					
NO-X-TOTAL		X					
NO-ACCTS-TOTAL		X					
AMT-TOTAL		X					
LOAN-NO			X				
LOAN-TYPE			X				
LOAN-ASSGND			X				

Cross-Reference Table between Data Elements and Reports *(Continued)*

Data Elements	Reports						
	Branch Manager Report (Exception)	Branch Manager Report (Weekly Exception Summary)	Branch Loan Status	Teller Cash Drawer	Teller Audit Report	Inquiry Transaction	Deposit/ Withdrawal Transaction
TOTAL-LOAN-COLLECTED			X				
TOTAL-LOAN-TO-BE-COLLECTED			X				
INTEREST			X				
TELLER-NO				X	X		X
TELLER-NAME				X	X		
DATE				X			
COH-SOD				X			
COH-EOD				X			
CASH-RECD				X			
CASH-DISPENSED				X			

	Col 1	Col 2	Col 3	Col 4
CHECKS-RECD-US				X
CHECKS-RECD-OTHER				X
CHECKS-RECD-TOTAL				X
AMT-RECD-US				X
AMT-RECD-OTHER				X
AMT-RECD-TOTAL				X
CHECKS-DISPENSED-TOTAL				X
NET-FLOW				X
AUDIT-REASON			X	
NO-X-TYPE 1			X	
NO-X-TYPE 2			X	
LARGEST-AMT-TYPE 1			X	
LARGEST-AMT-TYPE 2			X	
BALANCE	X	X		
CUST-DOB		X		
PASSBOOK-LINE-NO	X			

STEPS I.3 and I.4   (refer to Chapters 4 and 5)

I.3   Determine the relationships between the data elements, such as identifying the primary key data elements and the nonkey data elements.

I.4   Develop third normal form relations for each set of data elements. Where this is not possible for individual reports, merge data from reports to establish third normal form relations.

Branch Manager Report (Exception)

The data elements representing the entities of this report are:

> BRANCH-NO, BRANCH-NAME, BRANCH-ADDR, MGR-NAME, ACCT-NO, ACCT-TYPE, CID, CUST-NAME, X-DATE, X-TIME, X-TYPE, AMOUNT, REASON-CODE, ACTION-CODE, REMARKS

The relationships between the data elements are:

1. BRANCH-NO ◄——► BRANCH-NAME, BRANCH-ADDR, MGR-NAME. For a given BRANCH-NO there is only one BRANCH-NAME and BRANCH-ADDR (branch address), and also only one MGR-NAME (manager name). This is a one-to-one mapping, represented as ◄——► or as $\overset{one}{\underset{one}{\rightleftarrows}}$.

2. ACCT-NO ◄◄——► ACCT-TYPE. For a given ACCT-NO (account number) there is only one ACCT-TYPE (account type). But there may be many accounts of the same type. This is a one-to-many mapping, represented as ◄◄——► or as $\overset{one}{\underset{many}{\rightleftarrows}}$.

3. CID ◄◄——► CUST-NAME. A given CID (customer identification number) uniquely identifies the CUST-NAME (customer name). But there may be many customers with the same name. This is also a one-to-many mapping.

4. ACCT-NO*X-DATE*X-TIME ◄◄——► X-TYPE, AMOUNT. The ACCT-NO (account number) with X-DATE (transaction date) and X-TIME (transaction time) uniquely identify the transaction. The X-TYPE (transaction type), and the AMOUNT are uniquely determined.

5. ACCT-NO*REASON-CODE ◄◄─► ACTION-CODE, REMARKS. The action to be taken (ACTION-CODE) and the REMARKS to be registered for an exception are dependent on the REASON-CODE and on the ACCT-NO (account number), that is, on the customer for whom an exceptional action has to be taken.

The third normal form relations for the Branch Manager Report (Exception) are represented in Figure A.8.

```
1  BRANCH-NO ◄───► BRANCH-NAME, BRANCH-ADDR,
                   MGR-NAME
2  ACCT-NO ◄◄─►    ACCT-TYPE
3  CID ◄◄─►        CUST-NAME
4  ACCT-NO*X-DATE*X-TIME ◄◄─► X-TYPE, AMOUNT
5  ACCT-NO*REASON-CODE ◄◄─►   ACTION-CODE, REMARKS
```

Figure A.8

Branch Manager Report (Weekly Exception Summary)

The data elements representing the entities of this report are:

```
BRANCH-NO, BRANCH-NAME, BRANCH-ADDR,
MGR-NAME, REASON-CODE, DSTRPT,
DENDRPT, NO-X-TOTAL, NO-ACCTS-TOTAL,
AMT-TOTAL
```

The relationships between the data elements are represented as the third normal form relations in Figure A.9.

```
6  BRANCH-NO ◄───► BRANCH-NAME, BRANCH-ADDR,
                   MGR-NAME
7  BRANCH-NO*REASON-CODE*DSTRPT*DENDRPT
   ◄◄─► NO-X-TOTAL, NO-ACCTS-TOTAL,
        AMT-TOTAL
```

Figure A.9

Branch Loan Status

The data elements representing the entities of this report are:

> BRANCH-NO, BRANCH-NAME, BRANCH-ADDR,
> MGR-NAME, LOAN-NO, LOAN-TYPE, LOAN-ASSGND,
> TOTAL-LOAN-COLLECTED, TOTAL-LOAN-TO-BE-COLLECTED,
> INTEREST

The relationships between the data elements are represented as the third normal form relations in Figure A.10.

> 8 BRANCH-NO ◄──► BRANCH-NAME, BRANCH-ADDR,
> MGR-NAME
> 9 LOAN-NO ◄──► LOAN-TYPE, LOAN-ASSGND,
> TOTAL-LOAN-COLLECTED,
> TOTAL-LOAN-TO-BE-COLLECTED,
> INTEREST

Figure A.10

Teller Cash Drawer

The data elements representing the entities of this report are:

> BRANCH-NO, BRANCH-NAME, BRANCH-ADDR,
> TELLER-NO, TELLER-NAME, DATE,
> COH-SOD, COH-EOD, CASH-RECD, CASH-DISPENSED,
> CHECKS-RECD-US, CHECKS-RECD-OTHER, CHECKS-
> RECD-TOTAL, AMT-RECD-US, AMT-RECD-OTHER,
> AMT-RECD-TOTAL, CHECKS-DISPENSED-TOTAL,
> NET-FLOW

The relationships between the data elements are represented as the third normal form relations in Figure A.11.

```
10  BRANCH-NO  ←→  BRANCH-NAME, BRANCH-ADDR
11  TELLER-NO  ←←→  TELLER-NAME
12  BRANCH-NO*TELLER-NO*DATE  ←←→  COH-SOD,
    COH-EOD, CASH-RECD, CASH-DISPENSED,
    CHECKS-RECD-US, CHECKS-RECD-OTHER,
    CHECKS-RECD-TOTAL, AMT-RECD-US, AMT-RECD-OTHER,
    AMT-RECD-TOTAL, CHECKS-DISPENSED-TOTAL,
    NET-FLOW
```

Figure A.11

Teller Audit Report

The data elements representing the entities of this report are:

```
BRANCH-NO, BRANCH-NAME, BRANCH-ADDR,
TELLER-NO, TELLER-NAME, DATE, AUDIT-REASON,
NO-X-TYPE1, NO-X-TYPE2, LARGEST-AMT-TYPE1,
LARGEST-AMT-TYPE2
```

The relationships between the data elements are represented as the third normal form relations in Figure A.12.

```
13  BRANCH-NO  ←→  BRANCH-NAME, BRANCH-ADDR
14  TELLER-NO  ←←→  TELLER-NAME
15  BRANCH-NO*TELLER-NO*DATE  ←←→  AUDIT-REASON,
    NO-X-TYPE1, NO-X-TYPE2, LARGEST-AMT-TYPE1,
    LARGEST-AMT-TYPE2
```

Figure A.12

INQUIRY Transaction

The data elements representing the entities of this report are:

> ACCT-NO, ACCT-TYPE, BALANCE, CID, CUST-NAME,
> CUST-ADDR, CUST-TEL-NO, CUST-DOB

The relationships between the data elements are represented as the third normal form relations in Figure A.13.

> 16 ACCT-NO ◄◄──► ACCT-TYPE, BALANCE
> 17 CID ◄◄──► CUST-NAME, CUST-ADDR,
>   CUST-TEL-NO
> 18 CUST-NAME*CUST-DOB ◄──► CID

Figure A.13

DEPOSIT/WITHDRAWAL Transaction

The data elements representing the entities of this report are:

> ACCT-NO, ACCT-TYPE, BALANCE,
> BRANCH-NO, BRANCH-NAME, BRANCH-ADDR,
> X-DATE, X-TIME, X-TYPE, X-NO,
> AMOUNT, TELLER-NO, PASSBOOK-LINE-NO

The relationships between the data elements are represented as the third normal form relations in Figure A.14.

> 19 ACCT-NO ◄◄──► ACCT-TYPE, BALANCE
> 20 BRANCH-NO ◄──► BRANCH-NAME, BRANCH-ADDR
> 21 ACCT-NO*X-DATE*X-TIME ◄◄──► X-TYPE,
>   X-NO, AMOUNT, TELLER-NO,
>   PASSBOOK-LINE-NO

Figure A.14

The merging of the third normal relations results in the entities BRANCH, TELLER, CUSTOMER, LOAN, and ACCOUNT. The relationships between the entities result in the entities DRAWER, AUDIT, TRANSACTION, EXCEPTION, and EXCEPTION SUMMARY. The entities and the relationships between them are represented in the total set as follows:

I. BRANCH: BRANCH-NO ◄──► BRANCH-NAME,
            BRANCH-ADDR,
            MGR-NAME

II. TELLER: TELLER-NO ◄◄──► TELLER-NAME

III. CUSTOMER: CID ◄◄──► CUST-NAME, CUST-DOB,
                CUST-TEL-NO, CUST-ADDR,
                BRANCH-NO

CUST-NAME and CUST-DOB are underlined because they participate as part of a primary key in some other relations.

Included as a nonkey attribute is also BRANCH-NO for establishing the connection between the customer identification number (CID) and the branch where the account is kept.

IV. LOAN: LOAN-NO ◄◄──► LOAN-TYPE, LOAN-
           ASSGND, INTEREST, TOTAL-LOAN-
           COLLECTED, TOTAL-LOAN-TO-BE-
           COLLECTED, BRANCH-NO, CID

Included as two nonkey attributes are also BRANCH-NO and CID for establishing the connection between the loan and the branch where the loan was assigned and the customer (CID) to whom the loan was given.

V. ACCOUNT: ACCOUNT-NO ◄◄──► ACCT-TYPE,
             BALANCE, CID, BRANCH-NO

Included as two nonkey attributes are also CID and BRANCH-NO for establishing the connection between the account and the branch where the account is kept and the customer (CID) for whom the account was opened.

VI. DRAWER: TELLER-NO*BRANCH-NO*DATE ◄◄──►
             COH-SOD, COH-EOD, CASH-RECD,
             CASH-DISPENSED, CHECKS-RECD-US,

		CHECKS-RECD-OTHER, CHECKS-RECD-TOTAL, AMT-RECD-US, AMT-RECD-OTHER, AMT-RECD-TOTAL, CHECKS-DISPENSED-TOTAL, NET-FLOW
VII.	AUDIT:	BRANCH-NO*TELLER-NO*DATE ◄◄—► AUDIT-REASON, NO-X-TYPE1, NO-X-TYPE2, LARGEST-AMT-TYPE1, LARGEST-AMT-TYPE2
VIII.	TRANSACTION:	ACCT-NO*X-DATE*X-TIME ◄◄—► X-TYPE, X-NO, AMOUNT, PASSBOOK-LINE-NO, TELLER-NO, CID, BRANCH-NO TELLER-NO is underlined as a nonkey attribute because it participates as part of a primary key in another relation. CID and BRANCH-NO are included as nonkey attributes for establishing the connection between the transaction performed and the customer for whom the transaction took place and the branch where the transaction was executed.
IX.	EXCEPTION:	ACCT-NO*REASON-CODE ◄◄—► ACTION-CODE, REMARKS
X.	EXCEPTION SUMMARY:	BRANCH-NO*REASON-CODE* DSTRPT*DENDRPT ◄◄—► NO-X-TOTAL, NO-ACCTS-TOTAL, AMT-TOTAL

STEP I.5   Draw a conceptual model on the basis of the third normal form relations from step I.4 (refer to Chapter 5).

Figure A.15 represents the conceptual model based on the total set of third normal form relations I to X. The squares containing the roman numerals represent the numbered third normal form relations from the total set. The DATE, TIME, and REASON-CODE participate in the third normal form relations as part of the primary keys but are not represented as entities anywhere. To show the participation of DATE, TIME, and REASON-CODE in the primary keys we have drawn squares for them at level 1. Relations VI, VII, VIII, IX, and X represent relationships between the entities from level 1. Relation VIII in TRANSACTION represents the relationships between the entities TIME, DATE, ACCT, and TELLER.

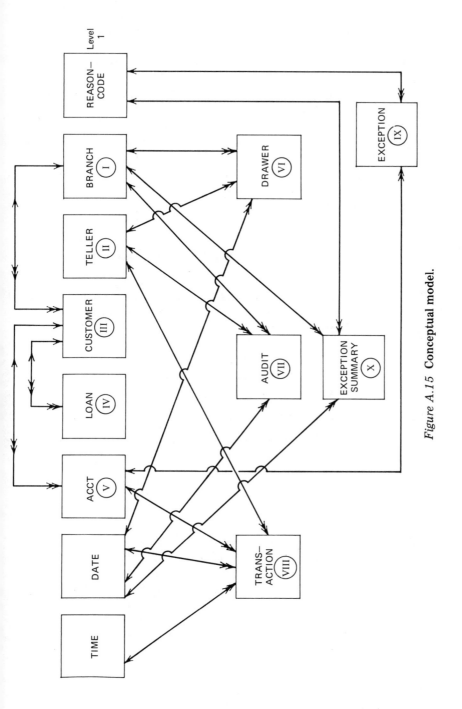

Figure A.15 Conceptual model.

The arrows drawn on the top of level 1 represent the relationships between ACCT and CUSTOMER, between LOAN and CUSTOMER, and between CUSTOMER and BRANCH, that is, a customer may have many accounts but a given account is assigned to a specific customer, a customer may have many loans but a given loan is assigned to a specific customer, and a branch has many customers, but a specific customer opens the first account at a branch [i.e., is assigned a customer identification number (CID) at the branch]. The arrows on the top of level 1 are introduced after the conceptual model for the total set of third normal form relations has been drawn. The relationships on the top of level 1 are fundamental to the enterprise and are not evident in the total set of third normal form relations based on the reports under consideration.

STEP II   DESIGN A LOGICAL MODEL OF A DATA BASE (refer to Chapters 4, 5, and 6).

STEP II.1   Draw a logical model based on the conceptual model from step I.5 above for a data base management system, using:

    1.   A relational data model.
    2.   A hierarchical data model.
    3.   A network data model.

STEP II.1.1   Mapping to a relational data model

The tables represented will be relations I to X, for example, *Relation I:*

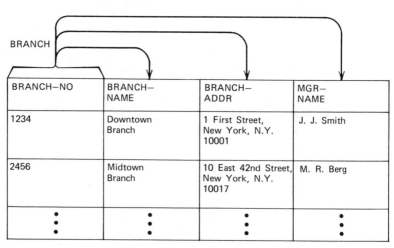

BRANCH—NO	BRANCH—NAME	BRANCH—ADDR	MGR—NAME
1234	Downtown Branch	1 First Street, New York, N.Y. 10001	J. J. Smith
2456	Midtown Branch	10 East 42nd Street, New York, N.Y. 10017	M. R. Berg
⋮	⋮	⋮	⋮

STEP II.1.2   Mapping to a hierarchical data model
A   Derive a hierarchical data model without regard for a particular DBMS.

A.1   Eliminate transitivity.

No transitivity exists in the conceptual model of Figure A.15.

A.2   Derive parent-child relationships.

In the conceptual model of Figure A.15 the created entities TIME, DATE, and REASON-CODE do not have to exist in their own right. These entities may be integrated into the relations referring to them.

The conceptual model in Figure A.15 can be transferred into Figure A.16 (after removal of the boxes TIME, DATE, and REASON-CODE).

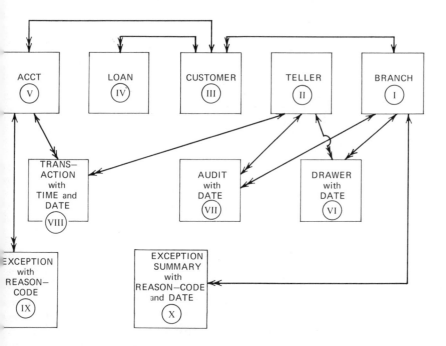

Figure A.16   The modified conceptual model after removal of the boxes TIME, DATE, and REASON-CODE from Figure A.15.

A.3   Resolve multiple parentage.

In performing step A.2, we resolved the problem of multiple parentage with the number of parents three or more. Figure A.16, redrawn in two hierarchical trees, is shown in Figure A.17. Some boxes, such as DRAWER, AUDIT, and TRANSACTION, have two parents each. We will not resolve multiple parentage with two parents for consideration of logical relationships with IMS.

B   Modify the model to eliminate conflicts with the rules of the DBMS to be used.

In the logical model of Figure A.17, none of the conditions imposed by IMS is violated; hence no modifications are required.

C   Refine the modified model according to some "obvious" performance considerations.

D   Simplify key names.

In Figure A.17 the segment type EXCEPTION with REASON-CODE (relation IX) and the segment type EXCEPTION SUMMARY with REASON-CODE and DATE (relation X) take place as a result of TRANSACTION with TIME and DATE (relation VIII.) Integrating the boxes with relations IX and X with the box with relation VIII results in the logical model shown in Figure A.18 for IMS.

Two other versions of logical models are given in Figures A.19 and A.20 for IMS.

E   Add intrinsic requirements.

In Figures A.18, A.19, and A.20 there should be a possibility of accessing the customer information with CUST-NAME and CUST-DOB (date of birth). The primary key for CUSTOMER is CID (customer identification number). Accessing the segment with a secondary key, for example, CUST-NAME and CUST-DOB as in an INQUIRY TRANSACTION, is called a secondary indexing capability.

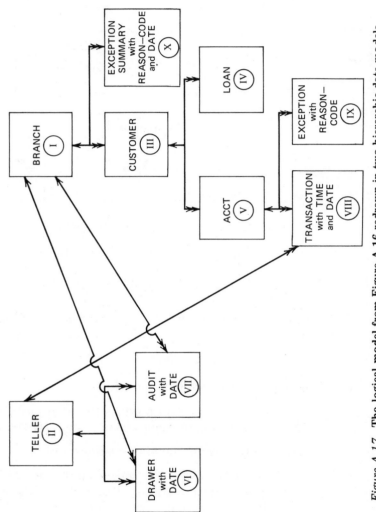

Figure A.17 The logical model from Figure A.16 redrawn in two hierarchic data models.

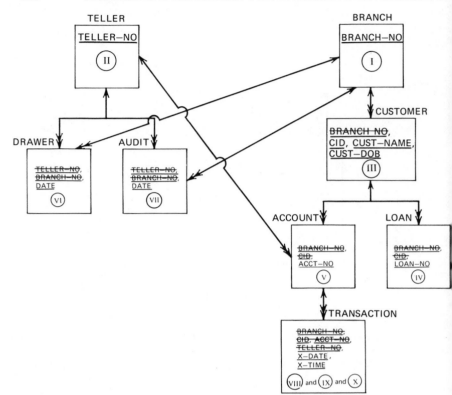

Figure A.18   One version of the refined logical hierarchical model from Figure A.17.

STEP II.1.3   Mapping to a network data model

A   Derive a network data model without regard for a particular data base management system (DBMS).

A.1   Derive owner-member relationships

After removing the boxes TIME and DATE, and after integrating REASON-CODE with the transaction, the conceptual model in Figure A.15 can be transferred to Figure A.21. If the REASON-CODE is not integrated with the transaction, the logical model appears as in Figure A.21*a*.

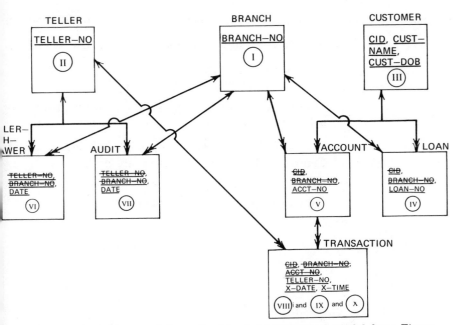

Figure A.19 One version of the refined logical hierarchical model from Figure A.17.

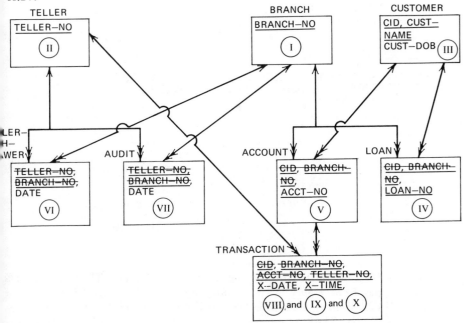

Figure A.20 One version of the refined logical hierarchical model from Figure A.17.

A.2   Resolve any violations of unique ownership.

There are no violations of unique ownership in the set types of Figure A.21.

B   Modify the model to eliminate conflicts with the rules of the DBMS to be used.

The CODASYL DBMS supports the set types of Figure A.21. No modifications are necessary.

C   Refine the modified model according to some "obvious" performance considerations.

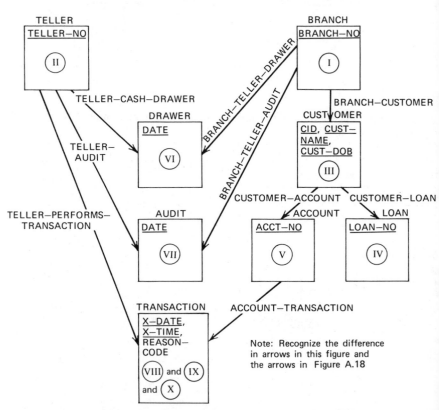

Figure A.21   One version of the logical network model.   TIME and DATE record types from Figure A.15 are integrated with the corresponding record types. DATE is integrated with DRAWER (VI), AUDIT (VII), and TRANS-ACTION (VIII). TIME is integrated with TRANSACTION (VIII). REASON-CODE, EXCEPTION SUMMARY (X), and EXCEPTION (IX) are integrated with TRANSACTION (VIII).

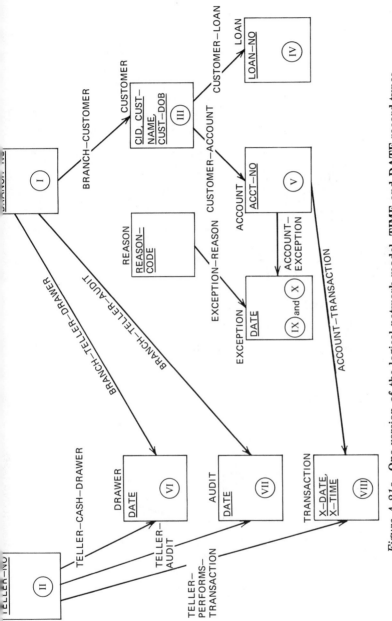

Figure A.21a One version of the logical network model. TIME and DATE record types from Figure A.15 are integrated with the corresponding record types as in Figure A.21. The difference between this figure and Figure A.21 is that EXCEPTION (IX) and EXCEPTION SUMMARY (X) form a record type EXCEPTION and REASON-CODE is a separate record type.

369

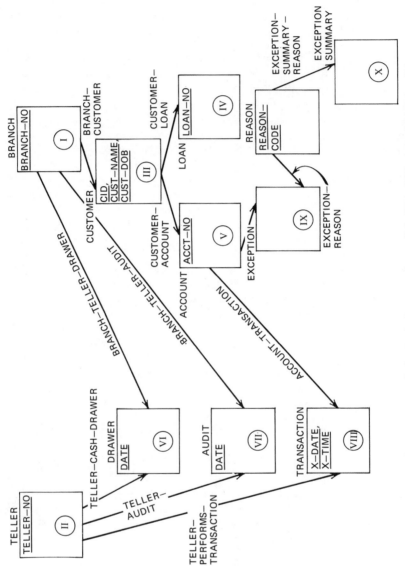

Figure A.21b One version of the logical network model. The difference between this figure and Figure A.21a is that EXCEPTION and EXCEPTION SUMMARY are two separate record types.

370

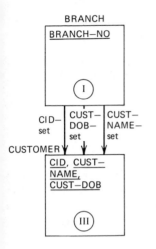

Figure A.21c Two record types, BRANCH and CUSTOMER, from Figure A.21*b* are involved in three set types. One set type between BRANCH and CUSTOMER is based on the CID number. One set type between BRANCH and CUSTOMER is based on CUST-DOB. And one set type between BRANCH and CUSTOMER is based on CUST-NAME.

D   Simplify key names.

Integrating the EXCEPTION and EXCEPTION SUMMARY in the TRANSACTION record type results in Figure A.21.

The key names have been simplified too. Figure A.21*a* shows the EXCEPTION and EXCEPTION SUMMARY as a separate record type not integrated with the TRANSACTION record type.

Figure A.21*b* shows the EXCEPTION and EXCEPTION SUMMARY as separate record types.

E   Add relationships that exist but have not surfaced between data in the logical model so far.

We would like to access the customer information based not only on CID but also on CUST-NAME and CUST-DOB (date of birth). To obtain a facility of that nature, three sorted sets between BRANCH and CUSTOMER must be provided. Each set has to be provided with its own key. See Figure A.21*c*, with only two record types, BRANCH and CUS-TOMER, taken from Figure A.21*b*.

STEP III   DESIGN A PHYSICAL MODEL OF A DATA BASE
(refer to Chapters 7, 8, and 9.)*

*In this section and section IV for designing a physical model and evaluating it, we will be considering IBM's IMS as the given data base management system.

STEP III.1   Draw an internal model (also called a "physical" model) on the basis of the logical model from step II.1.

Let us consider the following segment (or record) types: BRANCH, CUSTOMER, LOAN, ACCOUNT, TRANSACTION, TELLER, TELLER-CASHDRAWER, and AUDIT. The segment sizes are estimated as follows.

Segment Sizes

An estimate of field size is made, and each field is assigned to a segment. The field and the segment sizes are entered into the data dictionary. It is assumed that, on average, three pointers are stored in every segment, that is, 12 bytes have to be added to each segment.

Segment	Field	Length (bytes)
BRANCH	BRANCH-NO	4
	BRANCH-NAME	25
	BRANCH-ADDR	55
	MGR-NAME	25
		109
CUSTOMER	CID	9
	CUST-NAME	25
	CUST-DOB	6
	CUST-ADDR	55
	CUST-TEL-NO	10
		105
LOAN	LOAN-NO	17
	LOAN-ASSGND	12
	LOAN-TYPE	2
	INTEREST	12
	TOTAL-LOAN-COLLECTED	12
	TOTAL-LOAN-TO-BE-COLLECTED	12
		67
ACCOUNT	ACCT-NO	17
	ACCT-TYPE	2
	BALANCE	12
		31
TRANSACTION	AMOUNT	12
	ACTION-CODE	2
	PASSBOOK-LINE-NO	15
	REASON-CODE	2
	X-DATE	6

Segment	Field	Length (bytes)
	X-NO	10
	X-TIME	4
	X-TYPE	2
	REMARKS	50
	BRANCH-NO	4
	TELLER-NO	4
		111
TELLER	TELLER-NO	5
	TELLER-NAME	25
		30
TELLER–CASH–DRAWER	AMT-RECD-OTHER	12
	AMT-RECD-US	12
	AMT-RECD-TOTAL	12
	CASH-DISPENSED	12
	CASH-RECD	12
	CHECKS-DISPENSED-TOTAL	5
	CHECKS-RECD-OTHER	5
	CHECKS-RECD-US	5
	CHECKS-RECD-TOTAL	6
	COH-EOD	12
	COH-SOD	12
	NET-FLOW	12
	BRANCH-NO	4
	DATE	6
		127
AUDIT	DATE	12
	AUDIT-REAS	2
	BRANCH-NO	4
	LARGEST-AMT-TYPE 1	12
	LARGEST-AMT-TYPE 2	12
	NO-X-TYPE 1	7
	NO-X-TYPE 2	7
		56

The following assumptions are made regarding segment frequencies:

1. There are 100 branch offices.
2. Each branch serves an average of 1000 customers.
3. Each branch employs an average of 10 tellers.
4. Each customer has an average of two accounts and one loan. Transactions for a loan are kept together with the loan information.

5. Detail information (i.e., transactions, Teller Cash Drawer, and Teller Audit Report) is retained for a current period of 2 months and then archived.
6. There is an average of 100 transactions for each account in the 2-month period.
7. Each teller works an average of 50 days during each 2-month period.
8. Each teller is audited once every 4 months, that is, the average frequency of audits per teller for the 2-month period is 0.5.

These descriptions are an explanation of the frequencies that appear on versions 1 to 3, as in Figures A.22, A.23, and A.24.

The versions of a logical model in Figures A.18, A.19, and A.20 are reflected with the respective lengths (L) and average frequencies (F) relative to the parents in Figures A.22, A.23, and A.24. Note the difference between Figures A.19 and A.23, and A.20 and A.24. A dummy segment type ACCT-TRAN has been introduced between ACCOUNT and TRANSACTION. ACCT-TRAN is a physical child of ACCOUNT and a physical parent of TRANSACTION.

To calculate the space and time estimates, we will use a blocksize

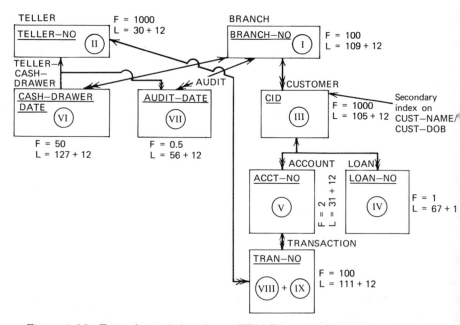

Figure A.22 Two physical data bases TELLER and BRANCH for IBM's IMS. There are three logical relationships interconnecting the two physical data bases.

of 4096 bytes (4 × 1024, i.e., 4K) with FSB (free space blocks) and FSW (free space within a block) values of 10% each.

The version in Figure A.22 represents two physical data bases: TELLER and BRANCH. There are three logical relationships interconnecting the two physical data bases:

1. TELLER-CASH-DRAWER is a logical relationship between TELLER and BRANCH, TELLER being the physical parent and BRANCH the logical parent.
2. AUDIT is a logical relationship between TELLER and BRANCH, TELLER being the physical parent and BRANCH the logical parent.
3. TRANSACTION has ACCOUNT as its physical parent and TELLER as its logical parent.

The version in Figure A.23 represents three physical data bases: TELLER, BRANCH, and CUSTOMER. There are five logical relationships interconnecting the three physical data bases:

1. TELLER-CASH-DRAWER is a logical relationship between TELLER and BRANCH, TELLER being the physical parent and BRANCH the logical parent.
2. AUDIT is a logical relationship between TELLER and BRANCH, TELLER being the physical parent and BRANCH the logical parent.
3. ACCOUNT is a logical relationship between BRANCH and CUSTOMER, CUSTOMER being the physical parent and BRANCH the logical parent.
4. LOAN is a logical relationship between CUSTOMER and BRANCH, CUSTOMER being the physical parent and BRANCH the logical parent.
5. TRANSACTION is a logical relationship between ACCT-TRAN and TELLER, ACCT-TRAN being the physical parent and TELLER the logical parent.

The version in Figure A.24 represents three physical data bases: TELLER, BRANCH, and CUSTOMER. There are five logical relationships interconnecting the three physical data bases.

1. TELLER-CASH-DRAWER is a logical relationship between TELLER and BRANCH, TELLER being the physical parent and BRANCH the logical parent.

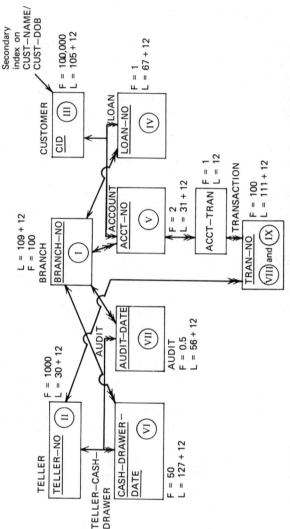

Figure A.23 Three physical data bases TELLER, BRANCH, and CUSTOMER for IBM's IMS. There are five logical relationships interconnecting the three physical data bases.

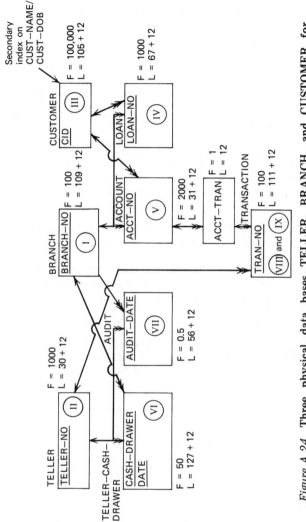

Figure A.24 Three physical data bases TELLER, BRANCH, and CUSTOMER for IBM's IMS. There are five logical relationships interconnecting the three physical data bases. Note the difference in the hierarchies of BRANCH and CUSTOMER between this figure and Figure A.23.

2. AUDIT is a logical relationship between TELLER and BRANCH, TELLER being the physical parent and BRANCH the logical parent.

3. ACCOUNT is a logical relationship between BRANCH and CUSTOMER, BRANCH being the physical parent and CUSTOMER the logical parent.

4. LOAN is a logical relationship between BRANCH and CUSTOMER, BRANCH being the physical parent and CUSTOMER the logical parent.

5. TRANSACTION is a logical relationship with ACCT-TRAN as the physical parent and TELLER as the logical parent.

We will now compare the three different versions of the banking data base shown in Figures A.22, A.23, and A.24. To determine the most effective view, we will take the approach of estimating data base size and times for the important transactions.

STEP IV EVALUATE THE PHYSICAL MODEL OF A DATA BASE
(refer to Chapters 7, 8, and 9, and Appendix C on statistics)

STEP IV.1 Develop space estimates for the internal model above (as in step III.1). Develop input/output probabilities for the internal model above (as in step III.1).

STEP IV.2 Draw external models for the reports in Figures A.1 to A.5, INQUIRY Transaction, and DEPOSIT/WITHDRAWAL Transaction on the basis of the internal model, as in step III.1. (*Exercise for the reader.*)

STEP IV.3 Develop time estimates for the external models, as in step IV.2. (*Exercise for the reader.*)

STEP IV.1. Version from Figure A.22

Space Estimates: BLK = 4096, FSB = 0.1, FSW = 0.1

1. TELLER data base
$S_{TELLER-CASH-DRAWER}$ (i.e., subtree size) = 139 bytes
S_{AUDIT} = 68 bytes
S_{TELLER} = 42 + 50 $\times$ 139 + 0.5 $\times$ 68 bytes
= 7026 bytes
SEGMENT BYTES = 7026 $\times$ 1000
Wasted space (W)/block = the biggest segment size 139 (TELLER-CASH-DRAWER segment) - 1
= 138 bytes

Effective blocksize:

Effective blocksize $= [((1 - FSW) \times BLK) - W] \times (1 - FSB)$
(bytes)
$= [((1 - 0.1) \times 4096) - 138] \times 0.9$
$= 3193$ bytes

BLOCK BYTES:

$$BLOCK\ BYTES = SEGMENT\ BYTES \times \frac{blocksize}{effective\ blocksize}$$

$$= 7026000 \times \frac{4096}{3193}$$

$$= 9,012,996\ bytes$$

2. BRANCH data base

$S_{TRANSACTION} = 123$ bytes
$S_{ACCOUNT} = 43 + 100 \times 123 = 12343$ bytes
$S_{LOAN} = 79$ bytes
$S_{CUSTOMER} = 117 + (2 \times 12343) + 79$
$= 24882$ bytes
$S_{BRANCH} = 121 + 1000 \times 24882$
$= 24,882,121$ bytes

SEGMENT BYTES $= 24,882, 121 \times 100$ bytes

Wasted space (W)/block = the biggest segment size 123 (TRANS-
ACTION segment) $- 1$
$= 122$ bytes

Effective blocksize $= (0.9 \times 4096 - 122) \times 0.9$
$= 3207.9$ bytes

BLOCK BYTES:

$$BLOCK\ BYTES = 2,488,212,100 \times \frac{4096}{3207.9}$$

$$= 3,177,068,100\ bytes$$

Input/Output Probabilities (Version from Figure A.22)

1. Teller data base

$PCIO_{TELLER, TELLER-CASH-DRAWER}$

$$= min. \left(1, \frac{\text{Length of TELLER-CASH-DRAWER + all subtrees to left of TELLER-CASH-DRAWER}}{3193} \right)$$

$$= min. \left(1, \frac{139}{3193} \right) = 0.0435$$

$$PCIO_{TELLER, AUDIT} = min. \left(1, \frac{68 + 50 \times 139}{3193} \right)$$

$$= 1$$

$$PTIO_{\text{TELLER-CASH-DRAWER}} = \min.\left(1, \frac{139}{3193}\right)$$
$$= 0.0435$$

$$PTIO_{\text{AUDIT}} = \min.\left(1, \frac{68}{3193}\right)$$
$$= 0.0213$$

$$PPIO_{\text{TELLER-CASH-DRAWER,TELLER}} = \min.\left(1, \frac{139 + 25 \times 139}{3193}\right)$$
$$= 1$$

$$PPIO_{\text{AUDIT,TELLER}} = \min.\left(1, \frac{68 + 0.025 \times 68 + 50 \times 139}{3193}\right)$$
$$= 1$$

2. BRANCH data base

$$PCIO_{\text{BRANCH,CUSTOMER}} = \min.\left(1, \frac{117}{3208}\right)$$
$$= 0.0365$$

$$PTIO_{\text{CUSTOMER}} = \min.\left(1, \frac{24,882}{3208}\right)$$
$$= 1$$

$$PPIO_{\text{CUSTOMER,BRANCH}} = \min.\left(1, \frac{117 + 500 \times 24,882}{3208}\right)$$
$$= 1$$

$$PCIO_{\text{CUSTOMER,ACCOUNT}} = \min.\left(1, \frac{43}{3208}\right)$$
$$= 0.0134$$

$$PTIO_{\text{ACCOUNT}} = \min.\left(1, \frac{12343}{3208}\right)$$
$$= 1$$

$$PCIO_{\text{CUSTOMER,LOAN}} = \min.\left(1, \frac{79 + 2 \times 12343}{3208}\right)$$
$$= 1$$

$$PTIO_{\text{LOAN}} = \min.\left(1, \frac{79}{3208}\right)$$
$$= 0.0246$$

$$PCIO_{\text{ACCOUNT,TRANSACTION}} = \min.\left(1, \frac{123}{3208}\right)$$
$$= 0.0383$$

$$PTIO_{TRANSACTION} = min. \left(1, \frac{123}{3208}\right)$$
$$= 0.0383$$
$$PPIO_{TRANSACTION,ACCOUNT} = min. \left(1, \frac{123 + 50 \times 123}{3208}\right)$$
$$= 1$$
$$PTIO_{BRANCH} = min. \left(1, \frac{24,882,121}{3208}\right)$$
$$= 1$$

STEP IV.1   Version from Figure A.23

Space Estimates: BLK = 4096, FSB = 0.1, FSW = 0.1

1. TELLER data base
$S_{TELLER-CASH-DRAWER}$ (i.e., subtree size) = 139 bytes
S_{AUDIT} = 68 bytes
S_{TELLER} = 42 + 50 × 139 + 0.5 × 68 bytes
        = 7026 bytes
SEGMENT BYTES = 7026 × 1000
Wasted space (W)/block = the biggest segment size 139 (TELLER-
                      CASH-DRAWER) - 1
                      = 138 (same as in version from Figure
                      A.22)
Effective blocksize:
Effective blocksize = 3193 bytes
BLOCK BYTES:
BLOCK BYTES = 9,012,996 bytes
2. BRANCH data base
S_{BRANCH} = 121 bytes
SEGMENT BYTES = 121 × 100 = 12100 bytes
Average waste space (W)/block: since there is only one segment
type with length 121 bytes, W = 121 - 1 = 120 bytes.
Effective blocksize:
Effective blocksize = (0.9 × 4096 - 120) × (0.9)
                  = 3209 bytes

BLOCK BYTES:

$$BLOCK\ BYTES = 12,100 \times \frac{4096}{3209}$$
$$= 15,444\ bytes$$

3. CUSTOMER data base

$S_{\text{TRANSACTION}} = 123$ bytes

$S_{\text{ACCT-TRAN}} = 12 + 100 \times 123$ bytes
$= 12{,}312$ bytes

$S_{\text{ACCOUNT}} = 43 + 1 \times 12312$
$= 12{,}355$ bytes

$S_{\text{LOAN}} = 79$ bytes

$S_{\text{CUSTOMER}} = 117 + 2 \times 12{,}355 + 79$
$= 24{,}906$ bytes

SEGMENT BYTES $= 24{,}906 \times 100{,}000$ bytes

Wasted space (W)/block = the biggest segment size 123 (TRANS-
ACTION segment type) $- 1 = 122$ bytes

Effective blocksize:

Effective blocksize $= (0.9 \times 4096 - 122) \times 0.9$
$= 3208$ bytes

BLOCK BYTES:

$$\text{BLOCK BYTES} = \text{SEGMENT BYTES} \times \frac{4096}{3208}$$

$$= 2{,}490{,}600{,}000 \times \frac{4096}{3028}$$

$$= 3{,}180{,}018{,}000 \text{ bytes}$$

Input/Output Probabilities (Version from Figure A.23)

1. TELLER data base (refer to the version from Figure A.22)

$\text{PCIO}_{\text{TELLER, TELLER-CASH-DRAWER}} = 0.0435$

$\text{PCIO}_{\text{TELLER, AUDIT}} = 1$

$\text{PTIO}_{\text{TELLER-CASH-DRAWER}} = 0.0435$

$\text{PTIO}_{\text{AUDIT}} = 0.0213$

$\text{PPIO}_{\text{TELLER-CASH-DRAWER, TELLER}} = 1$

$\text{PPIO}_{\text{AUDIT, TELLER}} = 1$

2. BRANCH data base

$$\text{PTIO}_{\text{BRANCH}} = \min. \left(1, \frac{121}{3209}\right)$$
$$= 0.0377$$

3. CUSTOMER data base

$$\text{PCIO}_{\text{CUSTOMER, ACCOUNT}} = \min. \left(1, \frac{43}{3208}\right)$$
$$= 0.0134$$

$$\text{PTIO}_{\text{ACCOUNT}} = \min. \left(1, \frac{12{,}355}{3208}\right)$$
$$= 1$$

$$\text{PCIO}_{\text{ACCOUNT, ACCT-TRAN}} = \min.\left(1, \frac{12}{3208}\right)$$
$$= 0.0037$$

$$\text{PTIO}_{\text{ACCT-TRAN}} = \min.\left(1, \frac{12,312}{3208}\right)$$
$$= 1$$

$$\text{PCIO}_{\text{ACCT-TRAN, TRANSACTION}} = \min.\left(1, \frac{123}{3208}\right)$$
$$= 0.0383$$

$$\text{PTIO}_{\text{TRANSACTION}} = \min.\left(1, \frac{123}{3208}\right)$$
$$= 0.0383$$

$$\text{PCIO}_{\text{CUSTOMER, LOAN}} = \min.\left(1, \frac{79 + 12,355 \times 2}{3208}\right)$$
$$= 1$$

$$\text{PTIO}_{\text{LOAN}} = \min.\left(1, \frac{79}{3208}\right)$$
$$= 0.0246$$

STEP IV.1   Version from Figure A.24

Space Estimates: BLK = 4096, FSB = 0.1, FSW = 0.1

1. TELLER data base
   $S_{\text{TELLER-CASH-DRAWER}}$ = 139 bytes
   S_{AUDIT} = 68 bytes
   S_{TELLER} = 42 + 50 $\times$ 139 + 0.5 $\times$ 68 bytes
          = 7026 bytes
   SEGMENT BYTES = 7026 $\times$ 1000 bytes
   Wasted space (W)/block = the biggest segment size 139 (TELLER-
                   CASH-DRAWER segment type) – 1
                   = 138 bytes
   Effective blocksize:
   Effective blocksize = 3193 bytes (refer to version from Figure A.22)
   BLOCK BYTES:
   BLOCK BYTES = 9,012,996 bytes (refer to version from Figure A.22)
2. BRANCH data base
   $S_{\text{TRANSACTION}}$ = 123 bytes
   $S_{\text{ACCT-TRAN}}$ = 12 + 100 $\times$ 123
               = 12,312 bytes

$S_{ACCOUNT}$ = 43 + 12312
     = 12,355 bytes
S_{LOAN} = 79 bytes
S_{BRANCH} = 121 + 2000 × 12355 + 1000 × 79
     = 24,789,121 bytes
SEGMENT BYTES = 24,789,121 × 100 bytes
Wasted space (W)/block = the biggest segment size 123 (TRANS-
     ACTION segment type) – 1
     = 122 bytes
Effective blocksize:
Effective blocksize = (0.9 × 4096 – 122) × 0.9
     = 3207.9 bytes
BLOCK BYTES:

BLOCK BYTES = 24,789,121 × $\dfrac{4096}{3207.9}$
     = 31,651,934 bytes

3. CUSTOMER data base
$S_{CUSTOMER}$ = 117 bytes
SEGMENT BYTES = 117 × 100,000
Wasted space (W)/block = 117 – 1 = 116 bytes
Effective blocksize:
Effective blocksize = (0.9 × 4096 – 116) × 0.9
     = 3213 bytes
BLOCK BYTES:

BLOCK BYTES = 117 × 100,000 × $\dfrac{4096}{3213}$
     = 14,915,406 bytes

Input/Output Probabilities (Version from Figure A.24)

1. TELLER data base (refer to version from Figure A.22)
$PCIO_{TELLER, TELLER-CASH-DRAWER}$ = 0.0435
$PCIO_{TELLER, AUDIT}$ = 1
$PTIO_{TELLER-CASH-DRAWER}$ = 0.0435
$PTIO_{AUDIT}$ = 0.0213
$PPIO_{TELLER-CASH-DRAWER, TELLER}$ = 1
$PPIO_{AUDIT, TELLER}$ = 1
2. BRANCH data base

$PCIO_{BRANCH, ACCOUNT}$ = min. $\left(1, \dfrac{43}{3208}\right)$
     = 0.0134

$$\text{PTIO}_{\text{BRANCH}} = \text{min.} \left(1, \frac{24{,}789{,}121}{3208}\right)$$
$$= 1$$

$$\text{PCIO}_{\text{BRANCH,LOAN}} = \text{min.} \left(1, \frac{79 + 12{,}355 \times 2000}{3208}\right)$$
$$= 1$$

$$\text{PTIO}_{\text{ACCOUNT}} = \text{min.} \left(1, \frac{12{,}355}{3208}\right)$$
$$= 1$$

$$\text{PTIO}_{\text{LOAN}} = \text{min.} \left(1, \frac{79}{3208}\right)$$
$$= 0.0246$$

$$\text{PCIO}_{\text{ACCOUNT,ACCT-TRAN}} = \text{min.} \left(1, \frac{12}{3208}\right)$$
$$= 0.0037$$

$$\text{PTIO}_{\text{ACCT-TRAN}} = \text{min.} \left(1, \frac{12{,}312}{3208}\right)$$
$$= 1$$

$$\text{PCIO}_{\text{ACCT-TRAN,TRANSACTION}} = \text{min.} \left(1, \frac{123}{3208}\right)$$
$$= 0.0383$$

$$\text{PTIO}_{\text{TRANSACTION}} = \text{min.} \left(1, \frac{123}{3208}\right)$$
$$= 0.0383$$

3. CUSTOMER data

$$\text{PTIO}_{\text{CUSTOMER}} = \text{min.} \left(1, \frac{117}{3213}\right)$$
$$= 0.0364$$

Designing a Data Base for a University Environment

"The University"-Case Study 2

The list of reports in pictorial format shown in Figure B.0 presents the information needs of a hypothetical university. The reports are shown in Figures B.1 to B.8. Design a data base for "The University" as follows:

I   Design a conceptual model of a data base (refer to Chapters 1, 2, 3, 4, and 5).

   I.1   Study the environment, and document assumptions for it (Chapters 1 and 2).

   I.2   Determine the data elements referenced in every report individually (Chapter 3).

   I.3   Determine the relationships between the data elements, such as identifying the primary key data elements and the nonkey data elements (Chapters 4 and 5).

   I.4   Develop third normal form relations for each set of data elements. Where this is not possible for individual reports, merge data from reports to establish third normal form relations (Chapter 5).

   I.5   Draw a conceptual model on the basis of the third normal form relations (Chapter 5).

II   Design a logical model of a data base (refer to Chapters 4, 5, and 6).

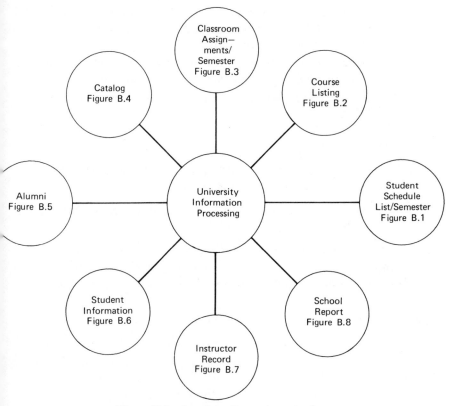

Figure B.0 **A university environment.**

II.1 Draw a logical model based on the conceptual model above for a data base management system, using:

1. A relational data model.
2. A hierarchical data model.
3. A network data model.

II.2 Draw external models for the reports in Figures B.1 to B.8 on the basis of the logical model above.

III Design a physical model of a data base (refer to Chapters 7, 8, and 9). (Exercise for the reader.)

III.1 Draw an internal model (also called a physical model) on the basis of the logical model from step II.1.

IV Evaluate the physical model of a data base (refer to Chapters 7, 8, and 9 and Appendix C on statistics). (Exercise for the reader.)

IV.1   Develop space estimates for the internal model above (as in step III.1). Develop input/output probabilities for the internal model above (as in step III.1).

IV.2   Draw external models for the reports in Figures B.1 to B.8 on the basis of the internal model above.

IV.3   Develop time estimates for the external models as in step IV.2.

STEP I DESIGN A CONCEPTUAL MODEL OF A DATA BASE
(refer to Chapters 1, 2, 3, 4, and 5).

STEP I.1   Study the environment and document assumptions for it. (refer to Chapters 1 and 2).

The university has a number of campuses. Undergraduate courses are taught during the day, and graduate courses are taught evenings. A data base should be designed for the following applications.

Student Schedule List/Semester (Figure B.1)

A student registers for a number of courses every semester. The student may choose the number of credits for which she/he wants to be registered. Before the start of the semester the student receives a list of the courses for which he/she has registered. In addition to the course numbers, the course titles, the instructors' names, the number of credits registered for, the campus where each course will be taught and also the day, time, building, and room number are provided.

Course Listing (Instructor's Copy) (Figure B.2)

This is a list of all the students who have registered for a particular course. The instructor provides grades at the end of the semester.

Classroom Assignments/Semester (Figure B.3)

This report is for administrative purposes. The administrative people have a list of the classrooms and their corresponding capacities. This enables them to assign the classrooms with larger capacities to the courses with bigger enrollments.

Student Schedule List/Semester

DATE: SEPTEMBER 7, 1979

SEMESTER: FALL 1979:   SEPTEMBER 10, 1979
TO DECEMBER 22, 1979

SCHOOL: STATE UNIVERSITY
STUDENT: 123456789
NAME: JOHN F. SMITH
STATUS: UNDERGRADUATE
MAJOR: COMPUTER SCIENCE
MINOR: GYMNASTICS
FACULTY–
ADVISOR: JOSEPH A. CORRIGAN

NO–COURSE	COURSE–TITLE	NAME–INSTR	CREDITS	CAMPUS	DAY–TIME	BLDG–NO–ROOM
CS601	INTRO TO COMP SCIENCE	A.B. ADAMS	3	WHITE PLAINS	W6–8 P.M.	AL201
CS605	INFO STRUCT ALGORITHMS	J.S. FINK	3	BROOKLYN	TH8–10 A.M.	MAIN 605

Figure B.1 **Every registered student at the school receives the report at the beginning of every semester. It is a confirmation of the courses for which the student has registered.**

389

Course Listing (Instructor's Copy)

DATE: SEPTEMBER 9, 1979

SEMESTER:	FALL 1979: SEPTEMBER 10, 1979 TO DECEMBER 22, 1979
SCHOOL:	STATE UNIVERSITY
DEPT:	ELECTRICAL ENGINEERING
NO–COURSE:	CS601
COURSE–TITLE:	INTRO TO COMP SCIENCE
NAME–INSTR:	A.B. ADAMS
CAMPUS:	WHITE PLAINS
BLDG–NO–ROOM:	AL201
DAY–TIME:	W6–8 P.M.
PREREQ: (Prerequisite Courses)	NONE

NO–STUDENT	NAME–STUDENT	DEGREE–SOUGHT	GRADE
123456789	JOHN F. SMITH	B.S.	
897654321	FRANK H. FRAN	M.S.	
967831201	JANE F. BUNDY	M.S.	
⋮	⋮	⋮	

TOTAL–STUDENTS–COURSE = 35

Figure B.2 The Course Listing is printed for every course to be taught at the school. A copy is sent to the corresponding instructor.

Catalog (Figure B.4)

A Catalog is printed before the start of every semester. It lists the name of the department offering the course, the course number and title, the maximum credits a student can enroll for, the course description, and the prerequisite courses.

Alumni (Figure B.5)

Information about alumni will be kept up to date. The information will be mainly used for fund raising purposes.

Classroom Assignments/Semester

SEMESTER: FALL 1979, SEPTEMBER 10, 1979
TO DECEMBER 22, 1979

NO–COURSE	COURSE–TITLE	NAME–INSTR	CAMPUS	DAY–TIME	BLDG–NO–ROOM
CS601	INTRO TO COMP SCIENCE	A.B. ADAMS	WHITE PLAINS	W6–8 P.M.	AL201
CS605	INFO STRUCT & ALGORITHMS	J.S. FINK	BROOKLYN	THU8–10 A.M.	MAIN 605
CS623	SWITCHING & DIGITAL SYSTEMS	A.M. JONES	LONG ISLAND	TU6–8 P.M.	MAIN 238
PH500	FIELDS & WAVES	A.B. ADAMS	BROOKLYN	THU 8–10 A.M.	ACCT 389
⋮	⋮	⋮	⋮	⋮	⋮

Figure B.3 **This report is for administrative purposes. Since introductory courses usually have larger enrollments than advanced courses, the bigger classrooms should be assigned to the introductory courses. The administrative people have a list of the classrooms and their corresponding capacities.**

Catalog

DATE: AUGUST 18, 1979

DEPT (Department): ELECTRICAL ENGINEERING

NO–COURSE: CS601

COURSE–TITLE: INTRO TO COMP SCIENCE

MAX–CREDITS (Maximum–Credits): 3

COURSE–DESCR (Course Description): THIS IS AN INTRODUCTORY COURSE IN COMPUTER SCIENCE

TOPICS: ---

OBJECTIVES: ---

PREREQ (Prerequisite Courses): NONE

Figure B.4 **A Catalog is printed at the beginning of every semester.**

Alumni

NO–STUDENT	NAME–STUDENT	ADDR–STUDENT–BUS (Student's Business Address)
238912411	JAY R. KEIL	205 EAST 42 STREET, NEW YORK, N.Y. 10017
364123889	MAUREEN F. SULLIVAN	19 WATER STREET, NEW YORK, N.Y. 10001
⋮	⋮	⋮

ADDR–STUDENT–RES (Student's Residential Address)	NO–TEL–BUS	NO–TEL–RES
15 MAIN STREET, LARCHMONT, N.Y.	(212) 411–2342	(914) 654–1489
241 HIGHLAND STREET, RYE, N.Y.	(212) 895–1245	(914) 894–3412
⋮	⋮	⋮

DEGREE–REC (Degrees Received)	DEGREE–DATE	NAME–EMPLOYER
B.S.	APRIL 15, 1950	AMC CORPORATION
M.S.	JANUARY 5, 1976	PQR INC.
⋮	⋮	⋮

ADDR–EMPLOYER	JOB–TITLE
205 EAST 42 STREET, NEW YORK, N.Y. 10017	SENIOR DESIGNER
19 WATER STREET, NEW YORK, N.Y. 10001	VICE PRESIDENT MARKETING
⋮	⋮

Figure B.5   The information about alumni is kept up to date.

Student Information (Figure B.6)

At the end of every semester the courses finished by the student and the corresponding credits will be added to the student's record.

Instructor Record (Figure B.7)

Information will be kept for every instructor. In case an instructor becomes unable to teach a course, the Instructor Records can be checked for candidates who can take over the course with minimum preparation and schedule conflicts.

Student Information   (To Be Updated Every Semester)

NO—STUDENT:	967831201
NAME—STUDENT:	JANE F. BUNDY
ADDR—STUDENT—BUS: (Business)	44 EAST 86 STREET, NEW YORK, N.Y. 10028
ADDR—EMPLOYER:	44 EAST 86 STREET, NEW YORK, N.Y. 10028
ADDR—STUDENT—RES: (Residence)	5 BOSTON POST ROAD, RYE, N.Y. 10580
NO—TEL—BUSINESS:	212—345—4412
NO—TEL—RES: (Residence)	914—684—1242
NEXT—OF—KIN:	JOHN J. BUNDY
FACULTY—ADVISOR:	ABRAHAM S. GOLDSTEIN
CREDITS—EARNED—HERE:	24
CREDITS—TRANSFERRED:	9
TOTAL—CREDITS:	33
NO—COURSE—FINISHED—SEMESTER:	NERVOUS SYSTEM IN MAMMALS, SPRING 1978
GRADE:	A
NO—COURSE—FINISHED—SEMESTER:	ORGANIC CHEMISTRY I, FALL 1977
GRADE:	B

Figure B.6 **At the end of every semester the courses finished by the student are added to the corresponding record.**

School Report (Figure B.8)

This report gives information about all the departments of the school, such as Electrical Engineering, Computer Science, Physics, and Business Administration.

Assumptions about the Environment of the "University"

The purpose of stating the assumptions is not to solve the environment's problems regarding these assumptions but rather to reflect the assumptions in our conceptual model.

1. Every semester starts on a specific day and ends on a specific day.

NAME—INSTR: A.B. ADAMS

SEMESTER: FALL 1979

COURSE(S)—TAUGHT	STUDENTS'—COMMENTS
CS601	INFORMATIVE, COMPETENT INSTRUCTOR
PH500	EXCELLENT
⋮	⋮

CS601	COURSE—CAN—TEACH
CS622	COURSE—CAN—TEACH
CS625	COURSE—CAN—TEACH
PH500	COURSE—CAN—TEACH
CS777	COURSE—CAN—BACKUP
CS897	COURSE—CAN—BACKUP
⋮	⋮

Figure B.7   The information will be kept for every instructor. In case an in-structor becomes unable to teach a course, the Instructor Records can be checked for candidates who can teach the course with minimum preparation and conflicts.

School Report

DATE: SEPTEMBER 19, 1979

DIRECTOR:	A.B. BRIGHT
NO—TEL—DIRECTOR:	
(Director's Telephone Number):	212—845—1243
⎧ DEPT:	COMPUTER SCIENCE
⎨ TOTAL—STUDENTS—DEPT (Number of	
⎩ Students Registered in the Department):	150
⎧ DEPT:	PHYSICS
⎩ TOTAL—STUDENTS—DEPT:	120
⋮	⋮
TOTAL—STUDENTS—SCHOOL:	11,523

Figure B.8   School report for all the departments of the school.

394

2. The student number uniquely identifies the student, that is, the name of the student, the address of the student, the status (whether undergraduate or graduate), the major discipline, the minor discipline, and so on.

3. Every student is assigned to a faculty advisor.

4. A student can register for a number of courses in a semester.

5. The same course (e.g., CS601) can be taught in different semesters with different course titles. It can also be taught by different instructors. In two different semesters it can be taught on different campuses. The course schedules can be different, and the courses can be taught in different buildings.

6. If multiple offerings of a course are given, the course number will be made unique by means of a section number; for example, CS601.1 and CS601.2 are two offerings of the same course, CS601.

7. A student has the freedom to register for fewer credits for a given course in a given semester (e.g., auditors are permitted).

8. An offered course is taken by a number of students.

9. The Course Listing (instructor's copy) has a blank column for GRADE at the beginning of the course. The instructor enters the grade achieved by the student at the end of the semester and submits the listing to the administration office.

10. The Catalog lists the courses offered in a specific semester.

11. A student enrolling for a course in a specific semester can register for the maximum number of credits.

12. A course offered in the catalog may have more than one prerequisite course, which students have to finish successfully before registering for the desired course.

13. Alumni information is kept up to date for mailing purposes, such as informing the alumni about special program courses offered and fund raising.

14. The Student Information will be updated at the end of every semester. A student can receive credits for a limited number of courses taken at a different school.

15. At the end of every semester the students' comments about the course will be entered on the Instructor Record.

16. An instructor may not be listed as "CAN-TEACH" or "CAN-BACKUP" unless he/she has taught the course in question at least once.

STEP I.2   Determine the data elements referenced in every report individually (refer to Chapter 3).

Examine every report individually and build a cross-reference table showing the data elements and the reports where the information is referred to as in Table 1.

A list of all the data elements referenced in the reports from Table 1 in alphabetical order is:

ADDR-EMPLOYER	Address of the employer of the student, either a current student or an alumnus.
ADDR-STUDENT-BUS	Address of the student's business; it could be the same as ADDR-EMPLOYER or different.
ADDR-STUDENT-RES	Address of the student's residence.
BLDG-NO-ROOM	Building number and room number where the course will be taught.
CAMPUS	Campus where the course will be taught.
COURSE-CAN-BACKUP	The instructor can "back up" the course.
COURSE-CAN-TEACH	The instructor can teach the course.
COURSE-DESCR	Course description.
COURSE-TITLE	Course title.
CREDITS	Credits for which the student has registered.
CREDITS-EARNED-HERE	Credits earned at this school by the student.
CREDITS-TRANSFERRED	Credits transferred from another school.
DAY-TIME	Which day and what time the course will be taught.
DEGREE-DATE	Date on which the student received a degree.
DEGREE-REC	Degree received by the student.
DEGREE-SOUGHT	Degree toward which the student is earning credits.
DENDSEM	Date of end of semester.
DEPT	Department of the school.
DIRECTOR	Director's name.

DSTRTSEM	Date of start of semester.
FACULTY-ADVISOR	Faculty advisor.
GRADE	Grade received by the student for a course.
JOB-TITLE	Job title of alumnus.
MAJOR	Major discipline.
MAX-CREDITS	Maximum credits for which a student can register.
MINOR	Minor discipline.
NAME-EMPLOYER	Name of employer.
NAME-INSTR	Name of instructor.
NAME-STUDENT	Name of student.
NEXT-OF-KIN	Name and address of the next of kin of the student for emergency purposes.
NO-COURSE	Number of course.
NO-COURSE-FINISHED-SEMESTER	Number of course finished in the semester by the student.
NO-STUDENT	Number of student.
NO-TEL-BUS	Number of telephone at business of the student, if any.
NO-TEL-DIRECTOR	Number of telephone of the director.
NO-TEL-RES	Number of telephone at residence of the student.
PREREQ	Prerequisite courses that must be successfully finished before taking a specific course.
SEMESTER	Every semester starts on a specific day and ends on a specific day.
STATUS	Status of student.
STUDENTS'-COMMENTS	Students' comments about a course.
TOTAL-CREDITS	Total credits earned by the student.
TOTAL-STUDENTS-COURSE	Total number of students enrolled in a course.
TOTAL-STUDENTS-DEPT	Total number of students in a department.
TOTAL-STUDENTS-SCHOOL	Total number of students in the school.

Table 1. Cross-Reference Table between Data Elements and Reports

| | Reports | | | | | | | |
Data Elements	Student Schedule List/ Semester	Course Listing	Classroom Assignment/ Semester	Catalog	Alumni	Student Infor- mation	Instructor Record	School Report
SEMESTER	X	X	X				X	
DSTRTSEM	X	X	X					
DENDSEM	X	X	X					
NO-STUDENT	X	X			X	X		
NAME-STUDENT	X	X			X	X		
STATUS	X							
MAJOR	X							
MINOR	X							
FACULTY-ADVISOR	X					X		
NO-COURSE	X	X	X	X			X	
COURSE-TITLE	X	X	X	X				
NAME-INSTR	X	X	X				X	
CREDITS	X							

Reports

Data Elements	Student Schedule List/Semester	Course Listing	Classroom Assignment/Semester	Catalog	Alumni	Student Information	Instructor Record	School Report
CAMPUS	X	X	X					
DAY-TIME	X	X	X					
BLDG-NO-ROOM	X	X	X					
DEPT		X		X				X
PREREQ		X		X				
DEGREE-SOUGHT		X						
GRADE		X				X		
TOTAL-STUDENTS-COURSE		X						
MAX-CREDITS				X				
COURSE-DESCR				X				
ADDR-STUDENT-BUS					X	X		
ADDR-STUDENT-RES					X	X		
DEGREE-REC					X			
DEGREE-DATE					X			

Table 1 (*Continued*)

Data Elements	Student Schedule List/ Semester	Course Listing	Classroom Assignment/ Semester	Catalog	Alumni	Student Infor- mation	Instructor Record	School Report
					Reports			
NAME-EMPLOYER					X			
ADDR-EMPLOYER					X	X		
JOB-TITLE					X			
NO-TEL-BUS					X	X		
NO-TEL-RES					X	X		
NEXT-OF-KIN						X		
CREDITS-EARNED-HERE						X		

CREDITS-TRANSFERRED		X	X
TOTAL-CREDITS		X	
NO-COURSE-FINISHED-SEMESTER		X	
STUDENTS'-COMMENTS	X		
COURSE-CAN-TEACH	X		
COURSE-CAN-BACKUP	X		
DIRECTOR			X
NO-TEL-DIRECTOR			X
TOTAL-STUDENTS-DEPT			X
TOTAL-STUDENTS-SCHOOL			X

Suggestion to the reader: Use some names with fewer qualifiers (e.g., phone number, address, name) in the reports, and use this combined list to detect and resolve synonyms and homonyms. This is an important part of the real life design process.

STEPS I.3 and I.4 (refer to Chapters 4 and 5)

I.3 Determine the relationships between the data elements, such as identifying the primary key data elements and the nonkey data elements.

I.4 Develop third normal form relations for each set of data elements. Where this is not possible for individual reports, merge data from reports to establish third normal form relations.

Student Schedule List/Semester

The data elements representing the entities of this report are shown in Figure B.8*a*.

SEMESTER, DSTRTSEM, DENDSEM, NO-STUDENT,
NAME-STUDENT, STATUS, MAJOR, MINOR,
FACULTY-ADVISOR, NO-COURSE,
COURSE-TITLE, NAME-INSTR, CREDITS,
CAMPUS, DAY-TIME, BLDG-NO-ROOM

Figure B.8a

The relationships between the data elements from Figure B.8*a* are:

1. SEMESTER ◀──▶ DSTRTSEM, DENDSEM. For a given SE-MESTER there is only one DSTRTSEM (date of start of semester) and also only one DENDSEM (date of end of semester) and vice versa. This is a one-to-one mapping, represented as ◀──▶ or as $\xrightarrow[\text{one}]{\text{one}}$. The primary key picked is SEMESTER from the candidate keys SEMESTER, DSTRTSEM, and DENDSEM.

2. NO-STUDENT ◀◀──▶ NAME-STUDENT, STATUS, MAJOR, MINOR, FACULTY-ADVISOR. For a given NO-STUDENT (number of student) there is only one NAME-STUDENT, STATUS (of the student), MAJOR (major discipline of the

student), MINOR (minor discipline of the student), and FACULTY-ADVISOR. But for a given status there can be many students. There can be many students with the same major and minor disciplines. And a faculty advisor may be advising more than one student. This is a one-to-many mapping, represented as ◀◀───▶ or ⟶◀◀‾.

3. SEMESTER*NO-COURSE ◀◀───▶ COURSE-TITLE, NAME-INSTR, CAMPUS, DAY-TIME, BLDG-NO-ROOM. In a given SEMESTER and for a given NO-COURSE (number of course) there is only one COURSE-TITLE, one NAME-INSTR (instructor teaching the course; if more than one instructor is teaching the course, we consider it one team of instructors), one CAMPUS, one DAY-TIME and one BLDG-NO-ROOM where the course will be taught.

But there may be a number of courses with the same course title (e.g., Introduction to Computer Science, taught in different sections with course numbers CS601.1, CS601.2, etc.). The same instructor may be teaching a number of courses in a semester, and a number of courses may be taught on a specific campus in a specific semester at the same time on the same day and in the same room in the same building.

This is a one-to-many mapping with SEMESTER and NO-COURSE being the compound key, represented as ◀◀──▸ or ⟶◀◀‾.

3a. NO-STUDENT*SEMESTER ◀◀───▶▶ NO-COURSE, CREDITS. A given student (NO-STUDENT) may be taking in a given SEMESTER many courses (NO-COURSE) and also a set of CREDITS. A given course may also be taken by many students in a specific semester, and a given number of credits may be taken by many students as well. This is a many-to-many mapping, represented as ◀◀───▶▶ or ⟶▶▶‾.

Relations 1, 2, and 3 are in the third normal form, because the nonkey data elements from these relations require the full keys for their identification. There is no transitive dependency between the nonkey data elements as well. But relation 3a is not even in the first normal form, because the mapping is many-to-many. The first normal form requires the mapping between the primary key and the nonkey data elements to be one-to-many (◀◀──▶) or one-to-one (◀──▶). The second normal form requires that the nonkey data elements have the full primary key for their unique identification. And the third normal form requires that there be no transistive dependency between the nonkey data elements.

Relation 3a can be transferred into a third normal form relation if the primary key is further qualified, that is, if the primary key is further "compounded" with NO-COURSE.

3b. <u>NO-STUDENT*SEMESTER*NO-COURSE</u> ◀◀──▶ CREDITS. Relation 3b is now in the third normal form. A given student (NO-STUDENT), in a given SEMESTER, and for a given course (NO-COURSE) takes a specific number of CREDITS.

Figure B.8b shows the four third normal form relations for the end user's view from Figure B.1 regarding Student Schedule List/ Semester.

```
4  SEMESTER ◀──▶ DSTRTSEM, DENDSEM
5  NO-STUDENT ◀◀──▶ NAME-STUDENT, STATUS, MAJOR,
                       MINOR, FACULTY-ADVISOR
6  SEMESTER*NO-COURSE ◀◀──▶ COURSE-TITLE,
                              NAME-INSTR, CAMPUS,
                              DAY-TIME, BLDG-NO-ROOM
7  SEMESTER*NO-COURSE*NO-STUDENT ◀◀──▶ CREDITS
```

Figure B.8b Third normal form relations for the end user's view from Figure B.1.

***

Course Listing (Instructors's Copy)

The data elements representing the entities of this report are:

```
SEMESTER, DSTRTSEM, DENDSEM, DEPT,
NO-COURSE, COURSE-TITLE, NAME-INSTR,
CAMPUS, BLDG-NO-ROOM, DAY-TIME, PREREQ,
NO-STUDENT, NAME-STUDENT,
DEGREE-SOUGHT, GRADE,
TOTAL-STUDENTS-COURSE
```

The relationships between the data elements are:

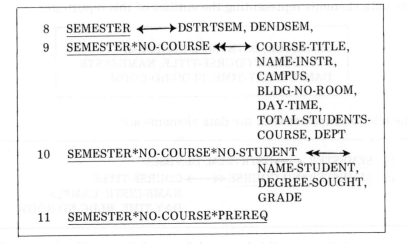

Relations 8 and 9 are in the third normal form; relation 10 is in the first normal form. Relation 11 is in the third normal form. The data elements NAME-STUDENT and DEGREE-SOUGHT depend only on the part NO-STUDENT of the full key. The resulting third normal form relations are:

```
12  SEMESTER ←——→DSTRTSEM, DENDSEM
13  SEMESTER*NO-COURSE ←←——→COURSE-TITLE,
                              NAME-INSTR, CAMPUS,
                              BLDG-NO-ROOM,
                              DAY-TIME, TOTAL-
                              STUDENTS-COURSE,
                              DEPT
14  NO-STUDENT ←←——→ NAME-STUDENT,
                      DEGREE-SOUGHT
15  SEMESTER*NO-COURSE*NO-STUDENT ←←——→GRADE
16  SEMESTER*NO-COURSE*PREREQ
```

The five relations 12, 13, 14, 15, and 16 are in the third normal form with the data element(s) underlined as primary keys.

Classroom Assignments/Semester

The data elements representing the entities of this report are:

> SEMESTER, DSTRTSEM, DENDSEM,
> NO-COURSE, COURSE-TITLE, NAME-INSTR,
> CAMPUS, DAY-TIME, BLDG-NO-ROOM

The relationships between the data elements are:

> 17   SEMESTER ←——→DSTRTSEM, DENDSEM
> 18   SEMESTER*NO-COURSE ◀◀——→ COURSE-TITLE,
>   NAME-INSTR, CAMPUS,
>   DAY-TIME, BLDG-NO-ROOM

The two relations are third normal form relations with the data element(s) underlined as primary keys.

Catalog

The data elements representing the entities of this report are.

> DEPT, NO-COURSE, COURSE-TITLE,
> MAX-CREDITS, COURSE-DESCR,
> PREREQ

SEMESTER is a hidden data element not printed in this report. The relationships between the data elements are:

> 19   SEMESTER*NO-COURSE ◀◀——→ COURSE-TITLE,
>   MAX-CREDITS,
>   COURSE-
>   DESCR, DEPT
> 20   SEMESTER*NO-COURSE*PREREQ

Relations 19 and 20 are third normal form relations with the data element(s) underlined as primary keys.

Alumni

The data elements representing the entities of this report are:

> NO-STUDENT, NAME-STUDENT,
> ADDR-STUDENT-BUS,
> ADDR-STUDENT-RES,
> NO-TEL-BUS, NO-TEL-RES,
> DEGREE-REC, DEGREE-DATE,
> NAME-EMPLOYER, ADDR-EMPLOYER,
> JOB-TITLE

The relationships between the data elements are.

> 21   NO-STUDENT ⬌ NAME-STUDENT,
> ADDR-STUDENT-BUS,
> ADDR-STUDENT-RES,
> NO-TEL-BUS, NO-TEL-RES,
> DEGREE-REC,
> DEGREE-DATE,
> NAME-EMPLOYER,
> ADDR-EMPLOYER,
> JOB-TITLE

The relation is a third normal form relation with the data element(s) underlined as a primary key.

Student Information (to be updated every semester)

The data elements representing the entities of this report are:

> NO-STUDENT, NAME-STUDENT, ADDR-EMPLOYER,
> ADDR-STUDENT-BUS, ADDR-STUDENT-RES,
> NO-TEL-BUS, NO-TEL-RES, NEXT-OF-KIN,
> FACULTY-ADVISOR, CREDITS-EARNED-HERE,
> CREDITS-TRANSFERRED, TOTAL-CREDITS,
> NO-COURSE-FINISHED-SEMESTER, GRADE

The relationships between the data elements are.

22 NO-STUDENT ◄◄───►NAME-STUDENT, ADDR-
       EMPLOYER, ADDR-
       STUDENT-BUS, ADDR-
       STUDENT-RES, NO-TEL-
       BUS, NO-TEL-RES, NEXT-
       OF-KIN, FACULTY-
       ADVISOR, CREDITS-
       EARNED-HERE, CREDITS-
       TRANSFERRED, TOTAL-
       CREDITS
23 NO-STUDENT*SEMESTER*NO-COURSE
       ◄◄───► GRADE

Relations 22 and 23 are in the third normal form.

Instructor Record

The data elements representing the entities of this report are:

NAME-INSTR, NO-COURSE,
STUDENTS'-COMMENTS, SEMESTER,
COURSE-CAN-TEACH,
COURSE-CAN-BACKUP

The relationships between the data elements are:

24 NAME-INSTR*SEMESTER*NO-COURSE ◄◄───►
       STUDENTS' COMMENTS
25 NAME-INSTR*NO-COURSE ◄◄───►
       COURSE-CAN-TEACH,
       COURSE-CAN-BACKUP

Relations 24 and 25 are in the third normal form.

School Report

The data elements representing the entities of this report are:

> DIRECTOR, NO-TEL-DIRECTOR,
> DEPT, TOTAL-STUDENTS-DEPT,
> TOTAL-STUDENTS-SCHOOL

The relationships between the data elements are:

> 26 SCHOOL ⟷ DIRECTOR, NO-TEL-DIRECTOR,
>   TOTAL-STUDENTS-SCHOOL
> 27 SCHOOL*DEPT ⟷ TOTAL-STUDENTS-DEPT

The resulting third normal form relations are:

   I. Relations 4, 12, and 17 are identical:
     SEMESTER ⟷ DSTRTSEM, DENDSEM

  II. Combining relations 5, 14, 21, and 22 results in:
     NO-STUDENT ⟷ NAME-STUDENT, STATUS, MAJOR,
                 MINOR, FACULTY-ADVISOR, DEGREE-
                 SOUGHT, ADDR-STUDENT-BUS,
                 ADDR-STUDENT-RES, NO-TEL-BUS,
                 NO-TEL-RES, DEGREE-REC,
                 DEGREE-DATE, NAME-EMPLOYER, JOB-
                 TITLE, ADDR-EMPLOYER, NEXT-OF-KIN,
                 CREDITS-EARNED-HERE,
                 CREDITS-TRANSFERRED,
                 TOTAL-CREDITS

 III. The composite keys of relations 6, 13, 18, and 19 are identical.
     The resulting relation is:
     SEMESTER*NO-COURSE ⟷ COURSE-TITLE, NAME-
                       INSTR, CAMPUS, DAY-TIME,
                       BLDG-NO-ROOM, TOTAL-
                       STUDENTS-COURSE, MAX-
                       CREDITS, COURSE-DESCR,
                       DEPT

IV. Relations 7, 15, and 23 have identical composite keys. The combination of these two relations results in:

NO-STUDENT*SEMESTER*NO-COURSE ◄◄───► CREDITS,
                                        GRADE

V. Relation 24 can be carried over:

NAME-INSTR*SEMESTER*NO-COURSE ◄◄───► STUDENTS'-
                                        COMMENTS

VI. Relation 25 can be carried over:

NAME-INSTR*NO-COURSE ◄◄───► COURSE-CAN-TEACH,
                              COURSE-CAN-BACKUP

VII. Relation 26 can be carried over:

SCHOOL ◄───► DIRECTOR, NO-TEL-DIRECTOR,
              TOTAL-STUDENTS-SCHOOL

VIII. Relation 27 can be carried over:

SCHOOL*DEPT ◄◄───► TOTAL-STUDENTS-DEPT

IX. Relations 11, 16, and 20 are identical:

SEMESTER*NO-COURSE*PREREQ

I. SEMESTER ◄───► DSTRTSEM, DENDSEM

II. NO-STUDENT ◄◄───► NAME-STUDENT, STATUS,
                        MAJOR, MINOR, . . .

         . . .

         TOTAL-CREDITS

III. SEMESTER*NO-COURSE ◄◄───► COURSE-TITLE, . . .

         . . .

         COURSE-DESCR

IV. NO-STUDENT*SEMESTER*NO-COURSE ◄◄───► CREDITS,
                                            GRADE

V. NAME-INSTR*SEMESTER*NO-COURSE ◄◄───► STUDENTS'-
                                            COMMENTS

VI. NAME-INSTR*NO-COURSE ◄◄───► COURSE-CAN-TEACH,
                                    COURSE-CAN-BACKUP

VII. SCHOOL ◄───► DIRECTOR, NO-TEL-DIRECTOR
               TOTAL-STUDENTS-SCHOOL

VIII. SCHOOL*DEPT ◄◄───► TOTAL-STUDENTS-DEPT

IX. SEMESTER*NO-COURSE*PREREQ

Figure B.9 The set of third normal form relations. (PREREQ are the courses that must be taken as prerequisites.)

STEP I.5   Draw a conceptual model on the basis of the third normal form relations from step I.4 (refer to Chapter 5).

Relations I to IX can be represented in a pictorial format as follows:

1. A relation for which the primary key consists of only one data element represents an entity. Relations I, II, and VII represent the entities SEMESTER, STUDENT, and SCHOOL, respectively. All entities of this type are placed on level 1. In Figure B.10 the boxes SEMESTER, STUDENT, and SCHOOL on level 1 represent the entities in relations I, II, and VII. The data elements are written inside the boxes. The primary keys of the entities are underlined. If a box cannot hold all the data elements representing an entity, they are shown by three dashes, — — —.

2. Relations with primary keys of two data elements are placed on the second level. In relations III, VI, and VIII, the primary keys consist of two data elements each. The boxes for relations III, VI, and VIII are drawn on level 2. The primary keys in boxes III, VI, and VIII are compound keys and are underlined. The compound key of relation III is SEMESTER*NO-COURSE. This key represents the relationship between the two entities SEMESTER and COURSE. There is a box for the entity SEMESTER on level 1, but no box for the entity COURSE on level 1. To establish the relationship between the entities SEMESTER and COURSE on level 2, a new entity relation for COURSE will be created on level 1, because no unique relationship in Figure B.9 is defined only by number of course (NO-COURSE). The box with relation III on level 2 interconnects the relation SEMESTER and the newly created relation COURSE on level 1. Relation VI on level 2 interconnects the entity COURSE and the newly created entity INSTRUCTOR on level 1. Relation VIII shows the relationship between the entity SCHOOL and the newly created entity DEPARTMENT on level 1.

The single-headed and double-headed arrows between relations I and III from Figure B.10 mean that in a given semester many courses can be taught, and a given course may be taught in many semesters.

3. The procedure for level 2 is repeated for level 3 and so on.

The resulting diagram for relations I to IX is shown in Figure B.10.

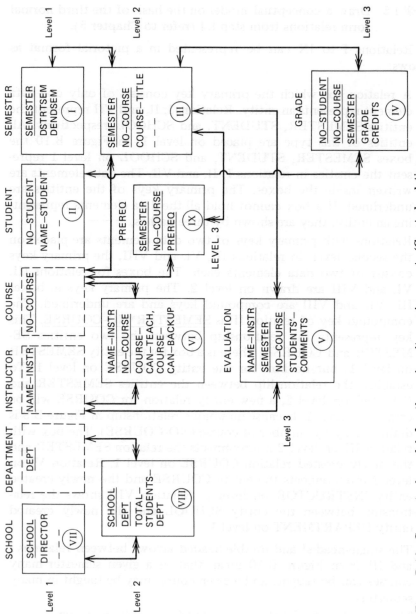

Figure B.10 Conceptual model for the university environment. (Created relations are shown in dashed boxes.)

The resulting third normal form relations are based on the assumptions made regarding the specific environment. Since the assumptions are subjective, there is a good chance that someone will challenge them. It is possible that some of the following questions have entered the reader's mind:

Q.1 If there is no student with a specific MAJOR or MINOR subject, how can any information on the MAJOR or MINOR exist?

A.1 The assumption we are making here is that MAJOR and/or MINOR subjects are the same as DEPARTMENTs. A student may take computer science as a major or a minor but may not take the subject "artificial intelligence," taught in the department, as a major or a minor. In other words, even if no student takes a specific major or minor, the information about the DEPARTMENTS, that is, about all possible MAJORS and MINORS is there.

Q.2 Why are COURSE-DESCR (course description) and COURSE-TITLE (course title) nonkey attributes of relation III with SEMESTER and NO-COURSE as the primary key? Why aren't COURSE-DESCR and COURSE-TITLE nonkey attributes of the relation COURSE with NO-COURSE as the primary key?

A.2 It is possible that the same course (i.e., the same NO-COURSE) is taught in two different semesters with different course descriptions and different course titles. Given a SEMESTER and given a NO-COURSE, however, the COURSE-DESCR and the COURSE-TITLE are uniquely determined.

Q.3 Why is NAME-INSTR a part of relation III with SEMESTER and NO-COURSE as the primary key?

A.3 It is possible that the same course (NO-COURSE) is taught by two different instructors in two different semesters. But in a specific semester the course is taught by a particular instructor. As a result of this assumption, given a specific semester and a specific NO-COURSE, the NAME-INSTR is uniquely identified.

Note that the assumption was made that a course is taught by only one instructor. If more than one instructor teaches a course, the team is considered as one instructor.

Q.4 Aren't COURSE-CAN-TEACH and COURSE-CAN-BACKUP the same as the course?

A.4   COURSE-CAN-TEACH and COURSE-CAN-BACKUP reflect the association between an instructor and a course. If an instructor can teach a course, the implication is that relatively little time will be required for preparation before actually teaching the course. If an instructor can "backup" a course, the implication is that relatively more time will be required for preparation before actually teaching the course.

Q.5   Is a faculty advisor the same as an instructor?

A.5   In some instances a faculty advisor is not necessarily an instructor. A program director or someone from the departmental staff may be a faculty advisor but not necessarily an instructor.

If these or the other assumptions are changed, the third normal form relations change. The moral is, then, that the data base design staff has to be competent with an excellent understanding of the way the environment runs.

STEP II   Design a logical model of a data base (refer to Chapters 4, 5, and 6).

STEP II.1   Draw a logical model based on the conceptual model from step I.5 above for a data base management system, using:

1.   A relational data model.
2.   A hierarchical data model.
3.   A network data model.

STEP II.1.1   Mapping to a relational data model

In Chapter 4 we saw that a relational data model is made up of a number of relations (tables). A table is a user's interface.

A logical model for a data base management system using a relational data model consists of the following relations and the corresponding attributes. All of the following tables from Figures B.11 to B.22 are related to one another, as shown in the conceptual model of Figure B.10.

Relations from Level 1

SCHOOL:

SCHOOL	DIRECTOR	NO–TEL–DIRECTOR	TOTAL–STUDENTS–SCHOOL
STATE UNIVER–SITY	A.B. BRIGHT	212–845 – 1243	11,523
⋮	⋮	⋮	⋮

Figure B.11

DEPARTMENT:

DEPT
BUSINESS ADMINISTRA–TION
CHEMISTRY
COMPUTER SCIENCE
MATHEMATICS
PSYCHOLOGY
⋮

Figure B.12

INSTRUCTOR:

NAME–INSTR
A.B. ADAMS
J.S. FINK
⋮ Etc.

Figure B.13

COURSE:

NO–COURSE
CS601
CS605
CS623
PH500
⋮

Figure B.14

STUDENT:

NO–STUDENT	NAME–STUDENT	STATUS	MAJOR	MINOR	FACULTY–ADVISOR	DEGREE–SOUGHT	ADDR–STUDENT BUS	ADDR–STUDEN RES
123456789	JOHN F. SMITH	UNDER–GRADUATE	COMPUTER SCIENCE	GYMNASTICS	JOSEPH A. CORRIGAN	B.S.	81 Blind Bank Stamford, Conn. 34562	52 Birch Boulevard Old Greenwic Conn. 36
897645123	FRANK H. FRAN	GRADUATE	ELECTRICAL ENGINEER–ING	PHYSICS	JOHN F. SLATTER	M.S.	55 Main Street New Rochelle, N.Y. 16481	83 Scho Street, Rye, N. 10580
967831201	JANE F. BUNDY	GRADUATE	BIO–CHEMISTRY	RADIOLOGY	ABRAHAM S. GOLDSTEIN	M.S.	44 East 86 Street New York, N.Y. 10028	5 Bosto Post Ro Rye, N. 10580
⁞	⁞	⁞	⁞	⁞	⁞	⁞	⁞	⁞

Figure B.15

SEMESTER:

SEMESTER	DSTRTSEM	DENDSEM
FALL 1979	SEPTEMBER 10, 1979	DECEMBER 22, 1979
⋮	⋮	⋮

Figure B.16

416

TEL-	NO-TEL-RES	DEGREE-REC	DEGREE-DATE	NAME-EMPLOYER	ADDR-EMPLOYER	NEXT-OF-KIN	CREDITS-EARNED-HERE	CREDITS-TRANS-FERRED	TOTAL CREDITS
-423-	203-513-6774	----	----	PROGRAM-MING CORP.	81 Blind Bank, Stamford, Conn. 34562	LAURA M. CORRIGAN	15	----	15
-462-	914-456-1489	B.S.	AUGUST 15, 1972	CHIP COMPANY	55 Main Street, New Rochelle, N.Y. 16481	BRIGITTE H. SLATTER	21	9	30
-345-	914-684-1242	B.S.	MAY 30, 1973	ABM Inc.	44 East 86th Street, New York, N.Y. 10028	JOHN J. BUNDY	24	9	33

Relations from Level 2

SCHOOL and DEPARTMENT:

OOL	DEPT	TOTAL-STUDENT-DEPT
ATE VERSITY	BUSINESS ADMINISTRATION	180
ATE IVERSITY	CHEMISTRY	35
ATE IVERSITY	COMPUTER SCIENCE	150
ATE IVERSITY	MATHEMATICS	53
ATE IVERSITY	PHYSICS	120

Figure B.17

INSTRUCTOR and COURSE:

NAME-INSTR	NO-COURSE	COURSE-CAN-TEACH	COURSE-CAN-BACKUP
A.B. ADAMS	CS601	YES	YES
A.B. ADAMS	CS622	YES	YES
A.B. ADAMS	CS625	YES	YES
A.B. ADAMS	PH500	YES	YES
A.B. ADAMS	CS777	NO	YES
A.B. ADAMS	CS897	NO	YES
J.S. FINK	CS605	YES	YES
⋮	⋮	⋮	⋮

Figure B.18 If an instructor can teach a course, he/she can also "back up" the same course. But an instructor who can "back up" a course may need preparatory time before teaching it.

SEMESTER and COURSE:

SEMESTER	NO–COURSE	COURSE–TITLE	NAME–INSTR	CAMPUS	DAY–TIME	BLDG–NO–ROOM	TOTAL–STUDENTS–COURSE	MAX–CREDITS	COURSE–DESCR
FALL 1979	CS601	INTRO TO COMP SCIENCE	A.B. ADAMS	WHITE PLAINS	W 6–8 P.M.	AL201	35	4	---
FALL 1979	CS605	INFO STRUCT & ALGORITHMS	J.S. FINK	BROOKLYN	THU 8–10 P.M.	MAIN605	22	4	---
FALL 1979	CS623	SWITCHING & DIGITAL SYSTEMS	A.M. JONES	LONG ISLAND	TU 6–8 P.M.	Main 238	15	3	---
FALL 1979	PH500	FIELDS & WAVES	A.B. ADAMS	BROOKLYN	THU 8–10 A.M.	ACCT 389	18	3	---
SPRING 1980	•••	•••	•••	•••	•••	•••	•••	•••	•••

Figure B.19

Relations from Level 3

INSTRUCTOR, SEMESTER, and COURSE:

NAME—INSTR	SEMESTER	NO—COURSE	STUDENTS'—COMMENTS
A.B. ADAMS	FALL 1979	CS601	EXCELLENT
J.S. FINK	FALL 1979	CS605	VERY GOOD
⋮	⋮	⋮	⋮

Figure B.20

SEMESTER, COURSE, and PREREQUISITES:

SEMESTER	NO—COURSE	PREREQ
FALL 1979	CS601	NONE
FALL 1979	CS605	CS601
FALL 1979	CS605	CS602
⋮	⋮	⋮

Figure B.21

419

STUDENT, COURSE, and SEMESTER:

NO–STUDENT	NO–COURSE	SEMESTER	GRADE	CREDITS
123456789	CS601	FALL 1979	A	3
123456789	CS605	FALL 1979	B	3
897654321	CS601	FALL 1979	A	3
⋮	⋮	⋮	⋮	⋮

Figure B.22

STEP II.1.2   Mapping to a hierarchical data model

A   Derive a hierarchical data model without regard for a particular DBMS.

A.1   Eliminate transitivity.

In the example of Figure B.10, the relationship between NO-COURSE and SEMESTER*NO-COURSE*PREREQ is transitive and is removed. (See Figure B.23.) (It may be reinserted later in performance considerations.)

A.2   Derive parent-child relationships.

In the conceptual model of Figure B.10, the boxes represent segments, and the arrows, ◄──►►, represent parent-child relationships between these segments. When substeps A.1 and A.2 are applied to the conceptual model of Figure B.10, the intermediate result of Figure B.23 is obtained.

A.3   Resolve multiple parentage.

When the rules for resolving multiple parentage are applied to the intermediate re-

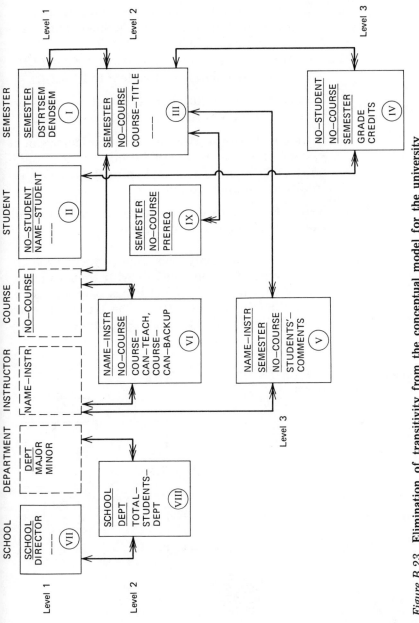

Figure B.23 Elimination of transitivity from the conceptual model for the university environment.

421

sult of Figure B.23, the second intermediate result in Figure B.24 is obtained. This is the hierarchical model.

We are now ready to apply the rules of the data base management system to be used.

B **Modify the hierarchical data model to eliminate conflicts with the rules of the DBMS to be used.**

If we decide to use IMS (Information Management System of IBM) as the DBMS, none of the conditions of IMS is violated in Figure B.24; hence no modifications are required.

C **Refine the modified data model according to "obvious" performance considerations.**

- Parents having only one child segment type are candidates for combination with their children. In Figure B.24, SEMESTER has only one child, SEMESTER*NO-COURSE. The trade-off is between redundancy and performance. The

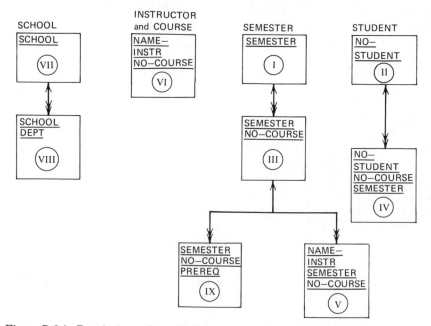

Figure B.24 Resolution of multiple parentage from Figure B.23 for the university environment.

SEMESTER has only two data elements, DSTRTSEM and DENDSEM. This suggests that very little redundancy is created, and since these data elements are permanent, no updating of redundant data is necessary. Thus combining SEMESTER with its child seems intuitively to be a good move.

- Redundancy can also be eliminated (or reduced) by combining certain segments. Consider the segment NAME-INSTR*NO-COURSE (currently a root-only data base in Figure B.24). We also have the segment NAME-INSTR*SEMESTER*NO-COURSE. Since the simple elements NAME-INSTR and NO-COURSE are common to both keys (both segments), these segments can be combined. In doing so, a root-only data base is eliminated.

Note that there were other alternatives for eliminating redundancy completely, such as keeping the NAME-INSTR*NO-COURSE segment and implementing a logical relationship, but eliminating a data base is normally a much stronger consideration.

These are the only obvious performance refinements until quantitative information becomes available. Our third intermediate result is shown in Figure B.25.

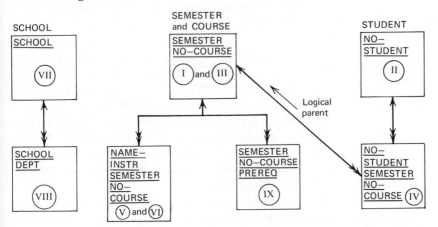

Figure B.25 Logical model after implying "obvious" performance refinements to the model in Figure B.24.

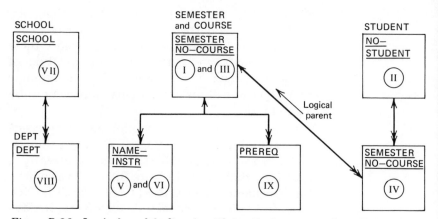

Figure B.26   Logical model after simplifying the key names from Figure B.25.

D   **Simplify key names.**

Compound keys that represent logical children, which relate parents in different paths, are retained. The result is shown in Figure B.26.

E   **Add relationships that exist between the data (i.e., add intrinsic requirements).**

The refined logical model in Figure B.26 satisfies the functional data requirements and possesses better performance characteristics than does the original model of Figure B.23. At this point the logical design could be considered complete.

However, the designers may want to strengthen the logical design by adding some intrinsic data relationships. In the design in Figure B.23, IN-STRUCTOR and DEPARTMENT are two unrelated segments. But the designers know that the instructors belong to departments, and they feel that this intrinsic relationship should be included in the design for the reasons mentioned above. This is an M : 1 (parent-child) relationship that will be implemented logically.

Applying this to the design of Figure B.26, we get the final form of the logical hierarchical data model in Figure B.27.

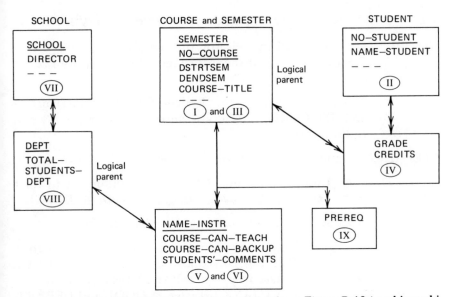

Figure B.27 Mapping of the conceptual model from Figure B.10 to a hierarchical data model, using IBM's Information Management System (IMS)—University Environment.

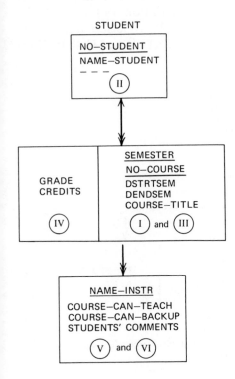

Figure B.28 External model for Student Schedule List/Semester, based on the logical model from Figure B.27 for IMS.

425

STEP II.2   Draw external models for the reports in Figures B.1 to B.8 on the basis of the logical model from Figure B.27 (a hierarchical data model).

The external models for Student Schedule List/Semester and for Course Listing are shown in Figures B.28 and B.29, respectively.

STEP II.1.3   Mapping to a network data model

A   Derive a network data model without regard for a particular data base management system (DBMS).

A.1   Derive owner-member relationships.

The record types that can be identified from Figure B.10 (conceptual model) are SCHOOL (relation VII), DEPARTMENT (created relation), LINK between SCHOOL and DEPARTMENT (relation VIII), INSTRUCTOR (created relation), COURSE (created relation), EVALUATION (relation V), PREREQ (relation IX), GRADE (relation IV), SEMESTER (relation I), STUDENT (relation II), and the LINK between SEMESTER and COURSE (re-

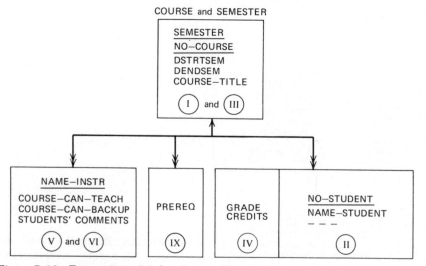

Figure B.29 External model for Course Listing (Instructor's Copy), based on the logical model from Figure B.27 for IMS.

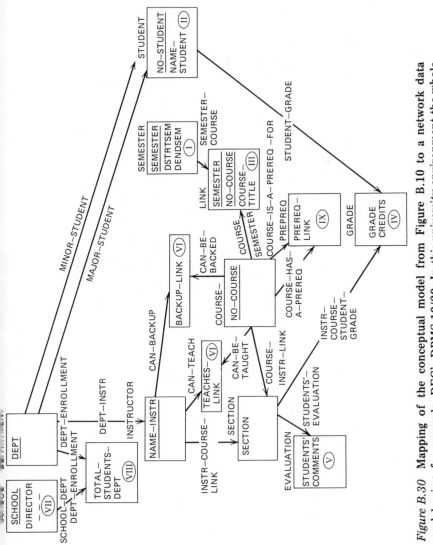

Figure B.30 Mapping of the conceptual model from Figure B.10 to a network data model using, for example, DEC's DBMS-10/20. In this university environment the whole department (e.g., COMPUTER SCIENCE) is considered as a MAJOR or a MINOR.

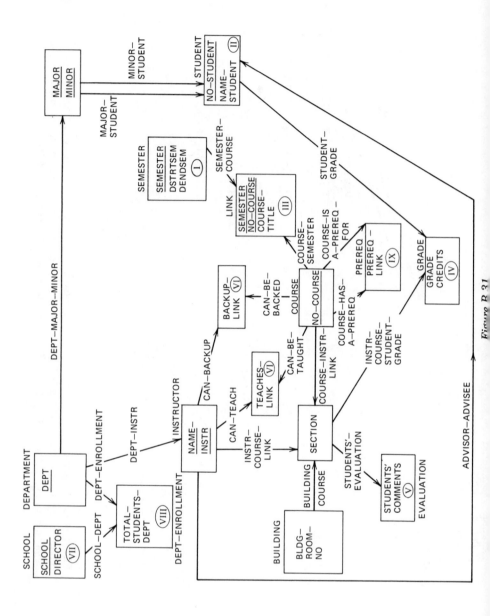

Figure B.31

lation III). The record type with relation VI is missing, because the relationship between INSTRUCTOR and COURSE regarding teaching or "backup" capability can be established with set types. However, because a many-to-many relationship exists between INSTRUCTOR and COURSE, the relationships between the two must be resolved with LINK records.

The owner-member relationships shown in Figure B.30 were derived from the conceptual model from Figure B.10. A few modifications to some assumptions from Figure B.30 are reflected in Figure B.31. Both versions (Figures B.30 and B.31) can be used for Digital Equipment Corporation's (DEC's) DBMS-10/20.

The following steps have already been taken care of in the versions from Figures B.30 and B.31.

A.2   Resolve any violations of unique ownership.

B   Modify the model to eliminate conflicts with the rules of the DBMS to be used.

C   Refine the modified model according to some "obvious" performance considerations.

D   Simplify key names.

STEP III   DESIGN A PHYSICAL MODEL OF A DATA BASE (refer to Chapters 7, 8, and 9). (Exercise for the reader.)

STEP III.1   Draw an internal model (also called a "physical" model) on the basis of the logical model from step II.1.

Figure B.31   There are three differences between this figure and Figure B.30:

1. A student can select as a MAJOR or a MINOR a specific area from a department in this model.
2. Here we assume that the faculty advisor is the same as the instructor.
3. A BUILDING record type associates with the information regarding courses and rooms.

STEP IV   EVALUATE THE PHYSICAL MODEL OF A DATA BASE (refer to Chapters 7, 8, and 9, and Appendix C on statistics). (Exercise for the reader.)

STEP IV.1   Develop space estimates for the internal model above (as in step III.1). Develop input/output probabilities for the internal model above (as in step III.1).

STEP IV.2   Draw external models for the reports in Figures B.1 to B.8 on the basis of the internal model as in step III.1.

STEP IV.3   Develop time estimates for the external models as in step IV.2.

Basic Concepts: Probability Theory and Mathematical Statistics

PROBABILITY

Suppose that an event E can happen in N ways out of M possible and equally likely ways. Then the probability of occurrence of the event is denoted by

$$p = \text{probability } (E) = \frac{N}{M}$$

The probability of nonoccurrence of the event is denoted by

$$q = \text{probability } (\text{not } E) = 1 - \frac{N}{M} = 1 - p$$

Thus p + q is 1 or

$$\text{Probability } (E) + \text{probability } (\text{not } E) = 1$$

that is, the probability of an event is a number between 0 and 1. Since the words "equally likely" basically mean "equally probable," the definition of probability is made up of probability itself. To avoid this pitfall, the estimated probability or empirical probability of an event is the relative frequency of occurrence of the event when the number of observations is very large. The probability itself is the limit of relative frequency with the number of observations approaching infinity.

A variable quantity, such as the length of a segment, is called a variate (or a variable), and the frequency distribution specifies how frequently the variate takes each of its possible values. If the variable does not take any intermediate value within its range of variation, it is called a discrete valued random variable.

Example (refer to Chapter 9). Suppose that the length of a segment type has the following distribution:

Length in Bytes	Probability of Occurrence
1	p_1
2	p_2
3	p_3
4	p_4
.	.
.	.
.	.
N	p_N

(with $L =$ bracing the Length in Bytes column)

The variable L does not take any values between 1 and 2, 2 and 3, 3 and 4, and so on. Therefore, L is a discrete valued random variable, and

$$\text{Probability } (L = i) = p_i \qquad \text{for } i = 1, 2, 3, 4, \ldots, N$$

MATHEMATICAL EXPECTATION

If X denotes a discrete random variable that can assume the values $x_1, x_2, x_3, x_4, \ldots, x_N$ with respective probabilities $p_1, p_2, p_3, p_4, \ldots, p_N$, where $p_1 + p_2 + p_3 + p_4 + \cdots + p_N = 1$, the mathematical expectation of X or simply the expectation of X, denoted by $E(X)$, is defined as

$$E(X) = x_1 \times p_1 + x_2 \times p_2 + x_3 \times p_3 + x_4 \times p_4 + \cdots + x_N \times p_N$$

$$= \sum_{i=1}^{N} x_i \times p_i$$

If the probabilities p_i in this expectation are replaced by the relative frequencies f_i/M, where $M = \sum_{i=1}^{N} f_i$, the expectation reduces to

$$\frac{\sum_{i=1}^{N} x_i \times f_i}{M}.$$

This is the arithmetic mean $\overline{X}$ of a sample of size M in which x_1, x_2, x_3, x_4, ..., x_N appear with the relative frequencies

$$\frac{f_1}{M}, \frac{f_2}{M}, \frac{f_3}{M}, \frac{f_4}{M}, \ldots, \frac{f_N}{M}$$

Example. For the distribution of the length of a segment type,

$$E(L) = 1 \times p_1 + 2 \times p_2 + 3 \times p_3 + 4 \times p_4 + \cdots + N \times p_N$$

is the average segment length.

Index

Access efficiency, 193-196, 199-
    200, 203-205, 207
Access method, 8, 303, 312
  basic, 221
  dependency, 210
  efficiency, 250
  external model, 191-192, 208,
    215, 218, 236
  generalized, 9
  implementation, 218
  internal model, 191-192, 208,
    215, 218, 222, 236
  inverted, 236
  near, 213
  parent or owner, 213-214
  random, 225, 236
ADABAS, 160, 218, 257-259,
    262, 264, 268, 270, 304
  see also Software, AG
Adaptable Data Base System, see
    ADABAS
Address converter, 262
Algorithm, 246, 261
  see also CALC; Hashing algorithm
ANSI (American National
    Standards Institute), 18
Archiving, 127
Area, 110, 239, 250
  see also CODASYL; Network
    Data Model
Associator, 263
Attribute, 3, 69, 78, 89-90, 93,
    98, 111, 131, 158-159
  key, 139-140, 144, 160

nonkey, 134-135, 139-140,
    144, 160, 164
  see also Data element; Data item
Auditor, 52, 54, 60, 68-69, 76

Bachman, C. W., 253
  arrow, 181, 253
Backup, 313
  copy of data base, 311
Basic direct access method, see BDAM
BDAM, 193, 262
Block 197-199
  size, 305, 313
Buffer, 305, 319-320
  size, 313
Burrough, 202

CALC, 238-241, 247-248, 250, 257,
    274
  see also Hashing algorithm
CALL, 316-317
  see also DL/1
Channel, 200, 306
Checkpoint, 309
Child, 222
  see also Child node; DL/1;
    IMS
Child node, 96-98, 104, 166-167,
    169, 175, 214
  see also Child; DL/1;
    IMS
Cincom, 90
  see also TOTAL
COBOL, 254

435